Psychoeducational Tutoring

Joseph M. Strayhorn, Jr., M.D.

Psychological Skills Press

Psychoeducational Tutoring

Wexford, PA: Psychological Skills Press

psychologicalskills.org

optskills.org

author's email: joestrayhorn@gmail.com

ISBN: 978-1-931773-22-5

Table of Contents

Chapter 1: The Crucial Task: Improving Psychological Skills......................11
 What is psychoeducational tutoring?..11
 Society's biggest problem..12
 From the global level to the personal level...14
 "Human nature" language..16
 "Disorder" and "disease" language..16
 The language of sin, crime, evil, and guilt..17
 Skills language...18
 Return to problems and their solutions, using skills language..................20
 How to live well? How does one learn to live well?.................................20
 Current state of the mental health art: Drugs and psychotherapy delivered
 by professionals..21
 What happens to people in need of mental health improvement: The "drop
 in the bucket" phenomenon...21
 What often happens to those in need of behavioral improvement: prison 26
 The call for rebooting of psychotherapy..27
Chapter 2: Psychoeducation Distinguished from Psychotherapy..................29
 Discovering for yourself versus using others' discoveries........................29
 "You have to talk" versus "You can read and do exercises".....................29
 Focus on your particular problems vs. focus on the problems all face.....30
 Focus on confidential situations versus hypothetical situations drawn from
 a list...31
 Emphasis on discoveries about oneself vs. emphasis on learning useful
 skills...31
 Need to admit the existence of a mental disorder in oneself.....................32
 Stigma...33
 Written curricula...34
 The purpose of chatting..34
 Time spent on assessment of ICD or DSM diagnosis................................34
 Assessment of dangerousness...35
 Emergency readiness...36
Chapter 3: Quick Examples Of Psychoeducational Modules.......................37

CO2 physiology instruction and breathing exercises for hyperventilation
....37
Instruction on non-withholding for encopresis.............................38
Teaching parents to regulate excitement level with stimulus seekers.......39
Rehearsal versus catharsis for anger control..............................39
Self-reward versus self-punishment for depression and work block........40
Phonemic and spatial awareness for children who can't read well..........41
Obsessions and the white bear problem....................................42
Chapter 4: The Psychological Skills People Need..........................43
Classifying psychological health skills...................................43
Diagnosis and specific treatment, or broad-spectrum curriculum?..........44
Two major aims...46
The skills axis..46
    Productivity..46
    Joyousness...47
    Kindness...47
    Honesty..47
    Fortitude..48
    Good decisions: individual...48
    Good joint decisions, or conflict-resolution.......................49
    Nonviolence..49
    Respectful talk..49
    Friendship-building..49
    Self-discipline..50
    Loyalty..50
    Conservation...51
    Self-care..51
    Compliance...51
    Positive fantasy rehearsal...51
    Courage..52
Some tests of the list...53
Chapter 5: Methods Of Influence..54
The methods of influence list..54
    Objective-formation, or goal-setting...............................54
    Hierarchy..55

Relationship...56
Attribution and prophecy...57
Modeling...58
Practice opportunities (including fantasy rehearsal)......58
Reinforcement and punishment contingencies................59
Instruction...60
Stimulus control..61
Monitoring...61
Mnemonic..61
Using them all at once...62
Chapter 6: Service Delivery Methods......................................63
By therapists...63
By parents at home..63
Via entertainment and literary media.................................64
Via religious education..66
By self-help books and videos and web sites......................67
By schoolteachers, with classroom groups.........................68
By students for other students, at school, one on one.........68
By telephone tutors...69
Chapter 7: Does Psychoeducation Work? The Evidence Base....72
Insomnia, anxiety, depression, obsessive-compulsive disorder..............73
Disruptive disorders, parent training..................................77
Social skills training..79
Marital satisfaction...80
Schizophrenia...80
Executive function and decision-making.............................80
Conclusion...81
Chapter 8: Academic Skills Training To Foster Psychological Growth........82
Competent individual tutoring is the most reliable way to increase
academic skill..82
The relation of academic skills to mental health outcomes.......................83
Causal arrows, all of which probably operate......................83
"Work therapy": how working on academic skills can grow mental health
skills...84
Big ideas in reading instruction...85

Some big ideas in teaching math..88
Some big ideas in teaching writing...91
Not just achievement, but pleasure in achievement..................93
Chapter 9: Programmed Instruction and "Alternate Reading"......95
Programmed instruction begins..95
Problems with programmed instruction....................................97
Alternate reading...98
Some experience with alternate reading..................................103
An unachieved goal: production and expression versus recognition......103
Chapter 10: Psychological Skills Exercises................................107
The "big idea" of psychological skills exercises.....................107
The celebrations exercise...107
Celebrating others' choices...108
Skills stories..108
The divergent thinking exercise...109
Brainstorming options..109
Listing choice points..110
The pros and cons exercise...110
The guess the feelings exercise..110
The twelve-thought exercise...111
The four thought exercise...112
The tones of approval exercise...113
The reflections exercise..114
Listening with four responses..114
The social conversation role-play...115
The joint-decision or conflict-resolution role play..................115
STEBC fantasy rehearsals..116
UCAC fantasy rehearsals...116
Hypothetical situations are sometimes even better than real life ones....117
Psychological skills exercises as performance measures.........118
Hypothesis: Much more of mental-health-promotion time should be
devoted to psychological skills exercises................................119
Chapter 11: The Content of a Psychoeducational Curriculum....120
The preschool years...120
Story reading..120

Modeling plays...121
Spontaneous dramatic play...121
Pre-reading activities for preschoolers..................................124
Musical activities with preschoolers.......................................124
Social conversation skills should be nurtured early................125
Adult-directed activity and rule-governed activity...............125
Psychoeducation in the school-aged years...................................127
Reading...127
Good "hierarchy-ology" makes reading instruction fun..............127
The skills concepts: vocabulary guides thinking.........................128
Self-discipline as a central skill..130
Self-reinforcement, a.k.a. celebrating your own choices.............130
The celebrations exercise...131
Thoughts greatly influence feelings and behaviors, and we can choose our
thoughts...131
Ways of reducing unrealistic fears..132
The twelve thoughts...133
The four ways of listening...134
Ethical dilemmas...134
Assertion...134
Joint decision-making and conflict resolution..............................135
Decisions about compliance..136
62 skills...137
Friendship-building...137
Conflict resolution and anger control..139
The skill of self-discipline...143
Skills of anxiety-reduction and courage..147
Becoming a successful student...159
Task-switching...163
Chapter 12: Skills and Guidelines for Tutors.................................164
1: Commitment...164
2: Consistency, and communication about any lapses....................166
3: Quitting a job proficiently..167
4: Communicating with supervisors...167
5: Appointment-keeping..168

6: Promoting a positive emotional climate.................................172
7: Maintaining authority.................................173
8: Alternate reading.................................176
9: Chatting with the student.................................180
9a: Listening skills.................................182
9b: Avoiding the role of the advice-giver.................................184
10: Taking the role of an enthusiastic fellow learner.................................185
11: Competence in the psychological skills exercises.................................186
12: Fostering The effort-payoff connection.................................188
13: Hierarchy-ology: picking the right level of difficulty.................................191
14: Using and promoting self-care.................................194
15: Confidentiality.................................195
16: Dealing with lost books.................................196
17: Reinforcing goal attainment rather than expression of fatigue.........196
18: Constant awareness of differential reinforcement.................................196
19: Dealing with fear of failure and conditioned aversions to academic work and conversation.................................197
20: Calling things by their right names.................................200
21: Speaking clearly.................................201
22: Knowing when to leave personal matters private.................................202
23: Keeping the parents informed.................................202
24: Handling criticism from a parent.................................203
25: Dealing with it if the student doesn't like the tutoring.................................204
26: Record keeping and monitoring.................................207
27: Being aware of outcomes.................................208
28: Helping students tell what they have learned.................................209
29: Being a positive example collector.................................211
30: Promoting morale among tutors.................................213
Chapter 13: Psychoeducation for Parenting.................................213
On the goals of parenting.................................213
A generic skill-promotion program for use by parents.................................214
The need to be a "reasonable" authority.................................216
Understanding differential reinforcement.................................217
Dependability and honesty.................................218

Tones of voice, the approval to disapproval ratio, and positive emotional climate..218

 CCCT versus REFFF..219

Mutually gratifying activities...220

Avoiding negative models in entertainment media..............................220

Punishment..221

Parent as Psychoeducator..223

Chapter 14: Telephone Tutoring for Psychoeducation............................224

Why the telephone?..224

Spaced rather than massed practice...224

Time on task...225

The two reasons school programs are hard...225

Telephone tutoring as incremental change..225

Chapter 15: College Students as Tutors...227

The extent of college students' mental health problems........................227

Problems with the college environment..227

Psychoeducational tutoring to enhance students' mental health?...........229

Chapter 16: Psychoeducation and the Economy.....................................230

The argument of this chapter...230

The goals of the economic system...230

Agriculture and manufacturing require less human effort.....................231

People's buying choices don't always promote the greatest good...........232

Psychoeducational tutoring as a source of jobs and societal good.........238

Chapter 17: A Vision of a Psychoeducating Society..............................244

The story of "Each one teach one"...244

Vision for the nonprofessional model for psychological skills...............244

Research on the best ways of responding to situations.........................245

Being tutored, and being a tutor, is close to a universal experience.......245

The internalization of tones of approval is a result of both tutoring and being tutored...246

The content of psychoeducation is learned in tutoring and reviewed as a tutor..246

Psychological skills exercises are a routine part of life, as is physical exercise...246

Families incorporate tutoring into their agendas.................................246

The culture systematically produces and collects positive models of psychological skills...247
Psychological skills training as the frontier for humanity.......................247
Appendix 1: Example List for Psychological Skills...................................250
Appendix 2: The More Complete List of Psychological Skills...................259
References...264
Index..285

Chapter 1: The Crucial Task: Improving Psychological Skills

What is psychoeducational tutoring?

By psychoeducation, I mean teaching psychological skills, such as fortitude, conflict-resolution, relaxation, anger control, decision-making, social conversation, self-discipline, and others. Psychological skills, by definition, help people to be mentally healthy. Psychoeducational tutoring means teaching such skills in a one-to-one relationship. These are vastly underutilized methods with great potential to make the world a better place. Most of this book will explore what these methods consist of.

Psychoeducational methods may be used with great advantage by psychotherapists. However, this book draws upon experience with these methods not only in psychotherapy, but also in a method of service delivery that uses:

- half-hour sessions, delivered almost every day
- for one to three years or more
- by nonprofessionals (i.e. people other than licensed mental health clinicians)
- using manuals written in a "programmed" format
- most of which are read aloud in "alternate reading" by student and tutor
- covering a broad spectrum of psychological skills
- also covering academic skills, including reading and math
- with frequent use of "psychological skills exercises"
- with tutors trained in the art of relationship-building with students
- with psychoeducation that can hopefully be delivered to parents along with the child-centered training.
- delivered via telephone appointments, if the tutor is not the parent

An underlying assumption is that mental health, happiness, and an ethical culture are all promoted by people's learning a set of competences referred to as psychological skills. Emotional regulation, kindness, courage, friendship-building, self-reinforcement, assertion, awareness of one's own emotions, and many others make up this set of skills. Appendix 2 provides a list of 62 such skills, divided into 16 groups. The word *skill* implies that these may be taught and learned. This book argues for a much more vast and widespread effort to teach these skills than humanity has carried out so far.

In *psychoeducation,* ordinary educational methods may be used: instruction through verbal explanations or textbooks; modeling of competences through in-person, written, or otherwise recorded examples; practice exercises; monitoring and reinforcement of positive performance; and others. Although these methods have come to be used more and more often in psychotherapy, particularly with the advent of behavior therapy and cognitive therapy, most people appear to think of psychotherapy as something very different from psychoeducation.

Psychoeducation can be carried out with large groups or small groups. But particularly with children in their early years, and particularly with children who need psychoeducation the most, there is something magic about one-to-one instruction, or tutoring. Many people dismiss individual tutoring as too expensive. But part of the thesis of this book is that becoming an excellent psychoeducational tutor prepares people exquisitely for other important life roles, and is a major way to learn psychological skills oneself; the more excellent psychoeducational tutors there are in the world, the better world we will have. The gains to both tutor and student help justify the expenditure of energy and effort.

Society's biggest problem

A few years ago, the prime minister of the U.K. offered a million-pound prize for the person who could a) identify the biggest problem facing humanity, and b) solve that problem (BBC news, 2013). For such a feat, a billion or trillion pounds would be a bargain, and no one could do it single-handedly. Nonetheless, the central questions posed at the announcement of this prize – what are humanity's biggest problems, and how can we solve them – deserve all the attention and effort we can muster.

Suppose we search the news media to get an inkling of the biggest problem facing humanity. We see no shortage of problems! We read that:

Chapter 1: The Crucial Task: Improving Psychological Skills

- Weapons of mass destruction, and wars provoked by the threat of such weapons, threaten humanity.
- Global climate change, pollution, environmental destruction, extinction of species, threaten the ecosystem.
- Mass killings, serial murder, gang warfare, domestic violence, road rage, child abuse, execution of hostages, homicides, destroy lives as well as making trust in fellow human beings difficult, and raising anxiety.
- Major causes of premature death in adolescents and young adults – accidents, suicides, homicides, drug overdoses – are all "behavioral."
- Lifetime prevalence of "mental disorders" in the U.S. is about 50% of the population.
- Drug and alcohol abuse help create a culture of sexual assault.
- Drug and alcohol abuse throughout society continues to result in deaths, illness, robberies to support the habit, family dysfunction, inadequate work performance, and violence.
- Obesity affects a high fraction of the U.S. population, posing major health risks.
- Anorexia and bulimia result in tragic premature deaths in some and lasting illness in others.
- About 3% of U.S. population is in prison, probation, or parole.
- Poverty, and the behavioral problems attending poor neighborhoods, persist.
- Racism persists.
- Sexual trafficking remains a large problem.
- Verbal abuse, bullying, sexual abuse, and exploitation remain prevalent.
- When infectious disease epidemics threaten, bad decisions appear to worsen the problem.
- Many of the wealthy exploit and blame the less wealthy classes.
- Some people waste resources while others live with almost no resources.

- When people need to follow a certain regimen (for example, taking a medicine) to cure or prevent an illness, a large fraction of them fail to do so.
- Gambling addiction is prevalent.
- Addiction to "electronic screen" entertainment is a prevalent problem.
- Unwarranted police killings show up on videos taken by bystanders. Yet police complain that they put their lives on the line often, and are put in the position of trying to assess instantly the dangerousness of people they do not know.
- Animals are treated with cruelty.

What do these problems have in common? They are all **behavioral** problems. They all result from human beings' not being able to act wisely, kindly, or rationally enough. If every human being were capable of consistently wise and good behavior, these problems would be markedly diminished or nonexistent.

From the global level to the personal level

Suppose we aren't interested in solving the "world's" problems, but are more interested in our own lives and the lives of those we know personally. What sorts of problems come up? What issues do people complain about to advice columnists, to therapists, and to each other? Let's list some common ones.

- Someone in my family, my work, or my school makes life unpleasant by being too bossy, greedy, insulting, argumentative, or threatening.
- There is conflict with someone over scarce resources.
- There is conflict over who should do a certain piece of work.
- I, or someone who affects me, acts badly because of a drug or alcohol problem.
- Someone appeared to be a loyal friend, but turns out to be rejecting.
- There is too little challenge, and I am bored.

Chapter 1: The Crucial Task: Improving Psychological Skills

- There is too much challenge, and I am frustrated and overly stressed.
- There are things I should do, but I don't have the self-discipline to do them.
- There is conflict between other people and it affects me.
- I am in the habit of worrying or putting myself down and making myself feel bad even when things are not so bad.
- I can't find suitable friends.
- I can't find a suitable mate.
- I would like to do something worthwhile, but the available jobs are for doing hardly-worthwhile activities.
- Someone around me is so often angry, scared, uncooperative, or depressed that it makes my life unpleasant.
- I would like to be trained to do something worthwhile, but the training program is too competitive and unpleasant.
- I am afraid of others' violence.
- People make promises to me and do not keep them.
- Someone is injured because of someone's carelessness.
- Someone suffers illness because of bad health habits.
- People don't know how to have fun in safe, nondestructive ways.
- Someone wastes money.

Again, these are behavioral problems. Either I, or someone who affects me, is behaving with insufficient "psychological skill." There are problems that are sheer bad luck – I get a certain unpreventable illness, bad weather causes injury or destruction, a tree limb happens to fall on me. But it appears that the vast majority of causes of human unhappiness in everyday life, as well as for the world at large, involve regrettable human behavior. If only I, and the people I interact with, consistently acted with great kindness, wisdom, and rationality, life would be a lot more fun and/or less miserable. ***Humanity's biggest problem is that people act with insufficient psychological skills***.

"Human nature" language

How do we speak (and thus think) about the changes that human beings need to make in order to bring about a better world, a better life?

We can use the language of "human nature," most frequently employed to say, "You can't change human nature." But history shows that the way human being act can change dramatically as civilization progresses. For example, it formerly was "human nature" for people to enslave other people, for husbands to have authority to beat their wives, for people to be executed for being witches, and for people to be made criminals because of their sexual orientation. And while all of these things still go on, the prevalence of them has become dramatically lower.

"Disorder" and "disease" language

At the time of this writing, the language of disease or disorder takes center stage in thinking about mental health. The most common classification system internationally for mental health problems is the International Classification of *Diseases* (World Health Organization, 1992); in the USA the most influential is the Diagnostic and Statistical Manual of Mental *Disorders* (American Psychiatric Association, 2013.) People who lose their temper in destructive ways may be diagnosed with intermittent explosive disorder. People who gamble too much may be diagnosed with gambling disorder. Children who are angry, argumentative, defiant, and vindictive may be diagnosed with oppositional defiant disorder. The "diagnosis" of "mental disorders" language tends to have several effects on our thinking, as follows.

1. The "medical model" tends to be applied: for this disorder, we should see a doctor, get "treatment" by a professional, and have medical insurance pay for such treatment – but only when such treatment can be justified as "medically necessary."

2. Just as lay people shouldn't do surgery, the knowledge and skill needed to improve "disorders" or "diseases" appears too complex and specialized for lay people to grasp without years of training.

3. We tend to look for pharmacological treatments, as for other illnesses or disorders.

4. We tend to look toward neuroscience, rather than toward improved educational techniques and better societal conditions, for research breakthroughs that may solve society's behavior-related problems.

5. Responsibility for such disorders tends to be delegated to professionals rather than to the individual or to the people in his or her environment. For example, if college students are suicidal, we tend to think about treatment for depression rather than improving the emotional climate of the institution or teaching students how to be happier.

6. Research tends to focus on questions such as: "What's the cause of this disorder?" "How can this disorder be best treated?" "What are the subtypes of this disorder?" "Which treatments work best for which subtypes?" These questions tend to displace research on the question, "How can we teach a set of skills that have a chance to reduce mental health symptoms of all sorts, and to help people to be happier and to make others happier?"

Medical model thinking has proved quite useful for many individuals. In no way am I suggesting that such a model be abandoned. However, for best results, other systems of examining the human condition are also necessary. It appears to me that "disorder language" at this point in history is dominant, and "skills language" is highly underrated. This may be because medical insurance companies are in charge of disbursing most of the finances that go toward psychotherapy.

The language of sin, crime, evil, and guilt

Someone carries out a seemingly irrational shooting. Is that person mentally ill, or just a bad person? Judges and juries deliberate this question often. Are there cases where it is impossible to answer this question? What if being a bad person is a type of mental disorder?

For most of the behavioral influence that governments seek to carry out, the method is the same: make unwanted behavior a crime, and devise suitable punishments for criminal behavior. If we wish fewer drug problems in society, we imprison drug dealers. If we wish for more humane workplaces, we make a wide variety of employers' behaviors criminal. If we want fewer sexual assaults on college campuses, we crack down with criminal penalties for those convicted of such. Just as using the language of mental disorder seems to dispose us to thinking of psychoactive drugs as solutions, using the language of illegal behavior tends to dispose us to punishment-oriented solutions. And indeed, punishment is sometimes the only effective means of behavior control, and by no means am I suggesting that society can afford to dispense with all punishment.

Nonetheless: how sensible, and how humane, is a society that incarcerates huge numbers of people for violent offenses, without ever having systematically taught those people the skills of nonviolent conflict-resolution, anger control, and nonviolent sources of power? How sensible and humane is it to punish people for impulsive bad decisions, when we have never even attempted to train those people in decision-making skill? This is not to say that lack of training should excuse people from punishment. It is to say that given a choice between psychoeducation and punishment as methods of behavior change, psychoeducation is vastly kinder and more just, and more effective – provided that it starts early enough and delivered with enough quality and quantity.

Skills language

We can think of anxiety "disorders," but we can also think of "courage skills" – the mental or physical acts people can learn how to do, that will reduce unwanted fear. We can think of conduct disorders, but we can also think of "skills" of kindness, empathy, honesty, nonviolence, respectful talk – the habits people can learn that are the opposite of a conduct disorder.

Some people, even some mental health professionals, resist the notion that kindness and courage and other such traits are "skills." But a central thesis of this book is that the word "skill" does apply perfectly to a large part of what makes people have better "mental health."

Chapter 1: The Crucial Task: Improving Psychological Skills

Let's think of skills such as typing, playing a musical instrument, solving math problems, dancing, performing a surgical operation. What are the essential features that lead us to call these skills?

1. They can be taught and learned. People tend to get better at them when they get good instruction, expert models, lots of practice, and expertly delivered feedback or reinforcement on practice trials.

2. Although some people are naturally more talented than others in all these competences, differences in aptitude (genetically determined, or otherwise) do not change the fact that almost all people need the right type of learning experiences in order to get very competent at these. And almost all people can get at least a little better at them with the right type of learning experiences. People who become true experts tend to have accumulated many hours of such learning experiences.

3. The sorts of learning experiences we are speaking about tend to be the same as with other skills. For almost all skills, instruction, modeling, practice, and reinforcement are very important ingredients. (Later in this book we will enlarge this list of ways to teach or influence.) We are not starting from scratch, from zero knowledge, when we undertake to teach each new skill. We know how to teach competences, in general, if we know exactly what constitutes the competent patterns. (And this is a very big "if.") If disorders of anxiety, depression, conduct, or social relations are all separate illnesses, we may not be able to generalize much from one to the other. But if courage, joyousness, kindness, and friendship-building are skills, we may apply the same skill-teaching techniques to each. The curricula differ, but the teaching methods may be similar or identical.

Although I have conducted several randomized controlled trials of interventions in my life, I would challenge the established wisdom that such trials are the only way to decide what is useful for people. The mental health community does not seem particularly incensed that courses taught to undergraduates have not been shown efficacious by randomized controlled trials. And although the notion of randomized trials of ways of teaching typing, dancing, golf, tennis, or chess skills is interesting, progress in teaching these skills seems to take place without such trials. In teaching such skills, we seem to save time by skipping the randomized placebo-controlled trials. Instead coaches and teachers assume that instruction, modeling, practice, performance monitoring, feedback and reinforcement, and others are effective methods of education; they focus their efforts on refining the content of the curriculum. In today's psychological research world, you can read of many clinical trials where the details of research design are meticulously reported, but the curriculum is condensed into the phrase "cognitive behavior therapy" or the letters CBT. The manuals that constitute the curriculum are often difficult to come by. Only through a detailed examination of the training manuals can we determine exactly what skills are being taught and how they are taught.

Return to problems and their solutions, using skills language

Now let's return to the original questions: What are society's, and individual people's, biggest problems? And what is the solution to these problems? If we are ready to use skills language, the answers are succinct: *The biggest problems result from insufficient psychological skills in people. A solution is to devote much time and effort into teaching psychological skills, systematically.*

How to live well? How does one learn to live well?

If we accept the notion that psychological skills may be taught and learned, the following two questions loom large for research and practice.

1. How do you live well? What choices are better than others? What works the best in dealing with people, with the demands of the world, and in dealing with ourselves? What is a body of expert "how to" knowledge on dealing with conflict, unrealistic fear, provocations, social conversation, self-discipline challenges, unpleasant behaviors of others, and other classes of life situations? To make the pursuit of knowledge on this even more complicated, there may be quite different answers for different subcultures of humanity.

2. Presuming that we have some idea that some ways of behaving (and thinking and feeling) work better than others, how do people learn to do those things, rather than the very maladaptive things they quite often do instead? How can people improve their psychological skills? How does one person influence another, or how does one person rig the influences upon himself or herself, so as to yield higher psychological functioning?

What thoughts, feelings, and behaviors, in which situations, constitute higher psychological functioning? How can these patterns be promoted? These should be central research questions of mental health and education – of psychoeducation.

Current state of the mental health art: Drugs and psychotherapy delivered by professionals

How do mental health professionals get people better? People think of two main interventions: drugs and psychotherapy. These are of course not the only two. There are the locked doors of hospital walls for the provision of safety, electroconvulsive treatments, bright light for seasonal affective disorder, and others. But in our society, when people are very unhappy, are failing, or are making other people unhappy, the first reflex of the health system is to apply one of the big two: drugs or psychotherapy.

What happens to people in need of mental health improvement: The "drop in the bucket" phenomenon

A very significant fraction of children have diagnosable mental disorders. According to the National Comorbidity Study, a substantial fraction of chronic mental disorders begin in childhood. About 22% of a representative U.S. sample of youth met criteria at some time by age 18 for a disorder with *severe* impairment or distress (Merikangas et al., 2010). Of surveyed children and youth with disorders, a minority (about one third) had ever received any services for their mental health problem (Merikangas et al., 2011). Of those who received services, only about 16% were seen for more than 20 visits; about 68% were seen for 5 visits or fewer (Merikangas et al., 2011).

These results for children are consistent with other results reported for adults. Wang et al., 2005, report that for adults, "Of 12-month cases, 41.1% received some treatment in the past 12 months." Less than a third were treated by mental health specialists. "Of the treated patients with disorders, only 32.7% were classified as receiving at least minimally adequate treatment." Minimally adequate treatment was defined, for this study, as receiving either "pharmacotherapy (at least 2 months of an appropriate medication for the focal disorder plus at least 5 visits to any type of physician) or psychotherapy (at least 8 visits with a professional lasting an average of at least 30 minutes). The median number of visits over 12 months for those treated in the mental health sector was 7.4; for those treated in the general medical sector it was 1.7. Thus according to the standards for this study, a total of four hours of psychotherapy was defined as "adequate" treatment, and the vast majority didn't even receive this! Wang et al. conclude: "Most people with mental disorders in the United States remain either untreated or poorly treated." (p. 629)

The Wang et al. (2005) study revealed a very skewed distribution among adults, with respect to the number of mental health visits they received. A few patients made a disproportionate share of visits. "For example, although nearly 60% of patients seen by psychiatrists made fewer than 5 visits in the year, they accounted for only one sixth of all visits to psychiatrists. Those making 50 or more visits to psychiatrists in the year, while representing only 1.6% of all patients seen by psychiatrists, accounted for 20.2% of all psychiatrist visits." This skewed distribution raises the question: what would happen if all people in need of mental health services, or even if all those with "severe" disorders, could somehow be prevailed upon to show up weekly? The answer is that insurance premiums would shoot up to impossible levels, or the insurance system would go bankrupt, and there would not be room in therapists' offices to treat them all. The current financial structure of the mental health system depends, for its sustainability, upon the premise that most people will receive inadequate treatment!

One more noteworthy point comes from the Wang et al. (2005) study: violent and angry people underutilize the mental health system. Episodes of violence, such as mass shootings, stimulate calls for increasing the mental health service force. "Intermittent explosive disorder" is the label applied to some people's patterns of episodic acts of violence. Those with this disorder had the lowest rate of service utilization among all the diagnostic categories studied, with only 14% seeing any mental health provider. Among those seeing a provider, the median number of visits in the year was 3.5, a completely inadequate number for this disorder. Again, the "drop in the bucket" conclusion faces us.

Other studies on the mental health treatment of children confirm that by even minimal estimates of the time necessary for successful treatment, the current system is woefully failing. Gopalan et al. (2010) confirm that the majority of children with mental disorders have no contact with mental health treatment. Of those referred for psychosocial treatment, it is estimated that at least a third never keep the first appointment (Gopalan et al., 2010). And of those who start treatment, the median hours of therapy is in the single digits (Gopalan et al., 2010; McKay et al., 2002; Harpaz-Rotem & Rosenheck, 2004). Of children receiving treatment, many receive antipsychotic drugs (with serious side effect potential) without first having received any psychosocial treatment (Finnerty et al., 2016).

If a child seems disposed to poor functioning in a variety of psychological skills, how much "time on task" is necessary to teach that child to have much higher functioning? From clinical observation, by analogy to other skills, and from years of anecdotal observations from the telephone tutoring intervention, and from rather rare research studies employing large times on task, (such as those reported by Lovaas, 1993, 1987), I hypothesize that for many children, several hundred hours may be effective, whereas under 30 hours may be a "drop in the bucket." Lovaas (1993) wrote, about the autistic children he worked with, "The treatment may have to start early in life and continue for most or all of the clients' waking hours, for a long period of time. There are not enough professionals to deliver the necessary treatment. This means that we will have to give away our professional skills to lay persons, and the sooner the better." (p. 628)

Another fact that leads us to the "time on task" hypothesis is the chronicity of mental health impairment (Copeland et al., 2015). To expect a few weeks of training, one hour a week, to remedy impairment that typically persists for years, or even lifetimes, appears unrealistic. (Despite this, obtaining measurable positive results in such a short time does give us a very valuable hunch that continuing training long "enough," however long that turns out to be, may alter long-term trajectories.)

A survey of instructors cited by de Bono and de Saint-Arnaud (1982) reported the following numbers of hours to obtain "not virtuoso ability, but a good operating or performing ability or skill" (p. 192): violin, 1200 hours; kung fu, 600 hours; piano, 450 hours, harmonica, 50 hours. Mathematics is a skill that society values; if a high school graduate has put in one hour per school day on mathematics from grades k through 12, for a 180 day school year, the total time invested in this activity comes to 2,340 hours. Conscientious math students may invest several times this many hours.

To remodel a small bathroom (according to conversations on the Internet, and recent personal experience) takes in the neighborhood of 200 person-hours. Can people remodel their interpersonal skills, or anger control skills, in a tenth of that time?

Benjamin Bloom (1985) and colleagues published the results of interviews with highly talented people in various fields – concert pianists, research neurologists, mathematicians, tennis players, sculptors, swimmers. A common denominator for talent development seemed to be much practice over many years. The following is a quotation about the concert pianists. "In the interviews the pianists tended to make little of the time they spent practicing as youngsters. A typical comment when asked about practice time was, 'Oh, very little. Not much at all. Maybe four or five times a week for an hour each time.' The average of five hours a week plus one hour of instruction time seems like a lot to this researcher. Perhaps it seems insignificant to the pianists because they now tend to practice more than four hours a day." (p. 35) The tennis players, throughout the "middle years" from age twelve or thirteen through the end of high school, practiced tennis an average of about 21 hours a week in the summer and 14 hours a week in the winter. (p. 247) Regarding the swimmers: "Two years into AAU [Amateur Athletic Union] swimming all but one or two of our subjects were swimming four hours (or more) a day, six and sometimes seven days a week. During the summer even more time was spent in practice." (p. 166)

Chapter 1: The Crucial Task: Improving Psychological Skills

Ericsson et al. (1993) studied talent development as a function of "deliberate practice" time. Among violinists, "the best players at age 18 had accumulated an average of 7,410 hr of practice, which is reliably different from 5,301 hr, the average number of hours accumulated by the good violinists.... The average of the best two groups was reliably different from that of the music teachers, who had accumulated 3,420 hr of practice by age 18.... Hence, there is complete correspondence between the skill level of the groups and their average accumulation of practice time alone with the violin." (p. 379)

I discuss musical instruments, sports, mathematics, and so forth because they are skills, just as mental health is a set of skills. Why do I present data on these skills, rather than presenting, for example, the average number of hours that it takes a group of children with intermittent explosive disorder to gain good anger control skills, or the number of hours for children with social anxiety disorder to be comfortable with almost all social interactions, or for perpetrators of bullying to become very kind people? It's because the numbers are not known. Working with a number of children to the criterion of success, and recording the number of hours necessary to achieve those successes, is a research strategy that, as far as I can tell, has not been used in the mental health field. Our predictions about the numbers of hours necessary to acquire a certain degree of mental health skill, from various starting points, are at present sheer guesswork.

Our mentality in research so far has been: define a course of "cognitive behavior therapy" as lasting a certain number of hours, usually well under 30. Deliver that fixed number of training hours to a group of research participants. Measure the effects. The answer is called the efficacy of CBT for that problem. Here's a different mentality: Keep delivering training until the desired results are achieved, or until a certain very high upper limit is reached. Note the distribution of the number of hours of training required for the various research participants.

Let's consider a hypothesis. Let's imagine common psychological problems: anger control, depression, anxiety, work aversion, interpersonal difficulties. The hypothesis is that there are learnable skills that would solve these problems, but for certain individuals, the amount of "time on task" required to learn these skills is several hundred hours. How useful, for these individuals, is a system where the median number of visits is a single digit number? It would probably be much the same as teaching people math for an average of under 10 sessions, and abandoning math education after that point. To be blunt: the system would be a failure.

There are surely some people for whom a small amount of work can yield benefits; otherwise the effect sizes of brief interventions would be zero. As I will discuss in a later chapter, there are many studies of fairly brief interventions that yield positive effects. But I believe that there are many people for whom the requisite time on task required for really substantial gain is at least a few hundred hours. If this should be true, our highly professionalized system for improving psychological skills is delivering a "drop in the bucket" to most of the people it attempts to help.

To summarize: too many people have disorders for professionals to treat them all. Most people with disorders don't get treatment. And a very large fraction of those who get treatment get so little of it that it is almost inconceivable that much lasting learning would take place.

What often happens to those in need of behavioral improvement: prison

Torrey et al. reported in 2010 (using 2004-2005 data) that "in the United States there are now more than three times more seriously mentally ill persons in jails and prisons than in hospitals." Glaze and Herberman (2013) report that "In 2012, about 1 in every 35 adults in the United States, or 2.9% of adult residents, was on probation or parole or incarcerated in prison or jail.... An estimated 1 in every 50 adult residents was supervised in the community on probation or parole at year end 2012, compared to 1 in every 108 adults incarcerated in prison or jail." The same authors reported that about 7 million U.S. residents were under the supervision of the correctional system, and about 3 million were incarcerated.

If the experience of being in prison were truly a "correctional" experience for the prisoners, our huge expenditure of resources on incarceration would perhaps be worthwhile. But according to the evidence we have, prison appears more often to worsen psychological skills than to better them; the experience renders people more inclined to criminal behavior upon release (Aizer & Doyle, 2013). Why might this be the case? First: criminal behaviors can be learned from fellow prisoners. Second: the experience of being punished creates anger and mistrust which increase the probability of antisocial acts. Third, having been a prisoner creates a stigma that makes it less possible to obtain gainful employment in legal areas (e.g. areas other than the drug trade). Fourth, experiencing verbal and physical abuse from fellow prisoners or prison staff tends to make people more abusive themselves.

Regarding learning criminal behaviors from fellow prisoners, a man posted this on the Internet as a comment on a National Public Radio piece by Vedantam (2013):

"When I was 22 years old, I was arrested for drunk driving. Guilty, I might add. Not being able to post the required bail bond, I was remanded to a county jail (Cook County, Illinois) to await a court date. While there, I learned in the first three days how to: field test a diamond with a wet piece of toilet paper to check for flaws; tell if an oriental rug is worth rolling up and stealing (and if it is, to call the fence and negotiate a price before taking it from the home); hot wire a home or business alarm system; "slim jim" and hot wire a car and find a fence late at night. I bailed out on my fifth day in jail."

The call for rebooting of psychotherapy

The realization that the current mental health care system, without supplementation, stands little chance of lightening the total burden of psychological skill deficiencies was the message of an article by Kazdin and Blase (2011) that was widely read and discussed (but, to my knowledge, not widely acted upon so far). These authors proposed a "rebooting" of mental health research and practice to reduce the burden of mental illness in the population, arguing that the traditional psychotherapeutic service delivery model fails to bring about sufficient accessibility of evidence-based procedures to have a large enough impact on the mental health of populations. These authors called for a more diversified portfolio of methods for improving mental health, making much greater use of, among other things, nonprofessionals and electronic connections between people.

Regarding nonprofessionals, they wrote, "It is heresy within psychology to mention that one does not need to have a PhD to deliver effective or evidence-based individually tailored treatments. Indeed, it would be difficult to support empirically that PhD trained individuals are more effective than those with less training." (p. 30) Regarding the use of the telephone, these authors write, "Interestingly, telephone-administered psychotherapies have lower rates of attrition than traditional individual psychotherapy (Mohr et al., 2008). Thus, phone-based treatment may not only broaden the population with access to therapeutic intervention, but also potentially increase the likelihood that clients will remain in treatment. Such a model has low cost and may even reach population segments to which Internet-delivered models may not have access." (p. 25)

Psychoeducational tutoring, I hypothesize, is a potential way to reboot mental health service delivery, or at least to add to its options.

Chapter 2: Psychoeducation Distinguished from Psychotherapy

The word *psychotherapy* can mean many different things. There are many brands of psychotherapy, perhaps the most common of which is "eclectic," or drawing upon whatever styles seem appropriate for the client at hand. Some psychotherapists may do pure psychoeducation. But by way of explaining further what is meant by psychoeducation, let's contrast its characteristics to those that are often conventionally associated with psychotherapy.

Discovering for yourself versus using others' discoveries

Some branches of psychotherapy teach that the therapist should not try to inform or teach the patient, but should let him or her discover for him or herself the important insights.

Psychoeducation, on the other hand, fully utilizes learning from the collective experiences of others. For example: if you want to get over an unrealistic fear, here are tips that people have used to accomplish this successfully. If you want to control your temper, maintain a healthy body weight, have good social conversations, be a successful student or employee... here's how people have done it successfully. In addition, here are some reasons you may want to accomplish those goals.

"You have to talk" versus "You can read and do exercises"

As a child psychiatrist, I sometimes hear parents say to their children, before they start a session with me, "You have to talk!" The assumption probably is that good things are going to happen by the child's opening up about problems in life, conflicted feelings, goals and obstacles to those goals, and so forth. Unfortunately for this model, many children have very little ability to talk meaningfully about these things and even less enjoyment of attempting to do so. Many children, when asked about problems or goals, will not be able to come up with any, or do not want to disclose them. Some of them view as torture the unspoken expectations that they will have to confess all the bad or unwise things that they have done and that they will have to come up with the reasons why they did these things.

In psychoeducation, by contrast, if a child doesn't want to talk about problems or goals, that is no problem! The tutor and the student may launch into taking turns reading the sections of a manual that teaches about psychological skills. (If the child can't read well enough, they launch into learning to read well enough!) Or the tutor teaches the student how they can do a "psychological skills exercise" together, one that requires no particular self-disclosure by the student. (We'll go into these exercises in much more detail later.)

Focus on your particular problems vs. focus on the problems all face

Psychotherapists are expected to help people solve particular problems in their lives – I feel depressed, I have trouble getting along with these people, I keep doing this behavior even though it's bad for me, and so forth. For that reason, people often spend a large amount of time in psychotherapy attempting to communicate to the therapist all sorts of relevant facts about the problem; the assumption is that the therapist must understand it before helping to solve it. Some patients complain bitterly, "Since these things haven't happened to you, you can't possibly understand how I feel." To which an accurate response may be, "Fortunately, being understood is not necessary for your life to get better. Learning to handle certain situations more skillfully can make your life better even if you're not completely understood."

The psychoeducational tutor, by contrast, does not necessarily focus on and seek to understand particular life problems that the student has, unless the student happens to want to bring these up in the course of social conversation. The tutor's job is to teach a body of knowledge, some of which will surely be relevant to various life problems that come up. If a wide enough body of psychoeducational knowledge is mastered, the person is better equipped to deal with a wide variety of life situations.

Focus on confidential situations versus hypothetical situations drawn from a list

Psychotherapy is traditionally shrouded in secrecy; it is often viewed as a place where people go to reveal their innermost secrets. Indeed, sometimes the sharing with the therapist of information the client thinks is too shameful for the person to talk about with anyone else is seen as an important healing ingredient. Psychotherapists may get into trouble by inadvertently leaking even the information that a certain individual is in treatment.

In psychoeducation, confession of secrets may be bypassed. The student of anger control may practice with a long list of standard conflicts and provocations, without needing to recount all the times when he lost control of his temper. The student of decision-making may practice with a long list of standard choice points, without recounting the bad decisions she has made. Very frequently people spontaneously observe that situations from a standard list directly apply to their own lives. But a crucial assumption is that you can practice skills using situations that are not exactly the same ones that are facing, and still become more competent at facing your own life situations. "Stimulus generalization" can allow the positive skills practiced with some situations to be used for other similar ones.

Emphasis on discoveries about oneself vs. emphasis on learning useful skills

Psychotherapy is sometimes seen as a journey to discover the hidden inner reaches of oneself. It is sometimes seen as a way of allowing clients to achieve crucial insights about the unique workings of their minds.

A portion of psychoeducation does have to do with self-knowledge: skills such as awareness of one's own emotions, putting one's feelings into words, being aware of one's own automatic thoughts, and so forth. Many other skills focus primarily upon analyzing situations and opportunities that the external world provides to us, and coming up with insight about the best possible response to these situations. Thus various skills have to do with arriving at insights. But improvement in the quality of life is seen to come usually from improving these skills and others, and applying those skills in life, rather than through a flash of insight in and of itself.

Need to admit the existence of a mental disorder in oneself

Often people refuse to get psychotherapy because they will not "admit that they have a problem." Child psychotherapists are sometimes stymied by children who honestly can't think of any problems to solve or work on, when it is obvious to others that such problems exist.

The financing of psychotherapy services is now largely controlled by medical insurance companies. Insurance companies do not want to pay for services to people without a "mental disorder." Thus it is not advisable for someone to walk into a therapist's office and simply to say, "I have no disorder, but like most other people, I could improve in skills of anger control, self-discipline, organization, and friendship building; unlike most other people, I'm willing to work at these; that's why I'm here." In order for the person to have the insurance company pay for the sessions, he or she must list symptoms, be assigned a diagnosis, and join the set of people with a "diagnosed mental disorder." Insurance company guidelines for "medical necessity" have explicitly excluded "self-improvement" as a reimbursable goal; having a DSM or ICD disorder and functional impairment are among the criteria for medical necessity (Anthem Blue Cross Blue Shield, 2015).

In a medical insurance model, it makes sense to restrict costly services to those who really need them. But for the good of the individual and for society, we shouldn't restrict psychological skills training to people with diagnosable disorders and functional impairment. One problem with this "medical model" procedure is that for most people with a severe disorder, there was once a time when there was not a disorder yet, but there were opportunities for psychological skill training. Perhaps if those opportunities had been taken, the learnings might have made the disorder emerge in a milder form or perhaps might have prevented it altogether. In a system that won't pay for psychological skills training until the skills deficiencies have created a "disorder," it could be that for many people, the most advantageous time for skill learning is being bypassed.

Another problem with the medical insurance-centered system is that many people who meet criteria for one or more disorders simply will never get psychotherapy if it necessitates their admitting to having a mental disorder. Being willing to admit having a "mental disorder" to oneself and to strangers just isn't considered an option for many people.

And a third problem with this system is that many people who may not ever meet criteria for a disorder, but who could have the quality of their lives greatly improved by psychological skills education, will be unserved by a medical model system.

In practice, almost any person who wants psychotherapy can be fitted, without fraud, into some mental disorder category, by employing a liberal enough interpretation of the diagnostic criteria, especially for the "not otherwise specified" categories. The therapist agrees to assign a diagnosis, and the client agrees to accept one. They both have an interest in coming up with the labels that will result in insurance payment. But this routine seems often not to serve the truth well. It would feel more honest to assign many people the label of "improvement-seeker." Many of these improvement-seekers may be as psychologically healthy as, or more so than, the average person who doesn't seek treatment, but are different mainly by their deciding to work on getting psychologically healthier.

The psychoeducational model could bypass the problems created by medical model thinking entrenched by the insurance industry. Manuals on psychological skill-building can truthfully state that no one is perfect in psychological skills, and the vast majority of human beings can benefit from improvement in them. Even if you are already perfect in these areas, other people that affect you will not be! People still may not want to learn about these topics. But all one has to "admit" is that the topic may be worth studying.

Society may eventually come to see an interest in funding psychological skill training outside the medical insurance model, as well as within it. My guess is that not discarding the medical model, but supplementing it greatly with an educational model, will allow us to arrive at the best system.

Stigma

There have been great efforts to reduce the stigma associated with getting mental health treatment. And indeed, in some limited subcultures having a therapist is more a badge of status than something to be ashamed of. But among vast segments of humanity, having people know about your mental health treatment would be a source of embarrassment. And many people use the faulty reasoning that goes like this: "Treatment is for crazy (or otherwise undesirable) people; I refuse treatment; therefore I am not crazy (or otherwise undesirable)."

So far my experience with psychoeducational tutoring by phone is that the stigma is less than with mental health patient status. It remains true, though, that children and adolescents sometimes seek any opportunity they can find to tease and taunt another, including noticing that someone has a tutoring session.

Written curricula

Although "manualization" is becoming more and more common in psychotherapy research, the manuals tend to be directed to the therapists and not directly to the clients.

In what I see as best practice of psychoeducation, students receive textbooks in psychological skills just as they would in history or science, and a major learning method is to read these books in entirety. (As I will discuss more later, the manuals are usually read aloud, with student taking turns with the tutor.)

The purpose of chatting

In psychotherapy, the assumption is that the conversation between therapist and client is carried out in order to understand and solve problems.

In psychoeducation as we practice it, there is social conversation between tutor and student, which is carried out for the primary purposes of having fun, making the sessions pleasant, and practicing the enjoyment of social conversation. Social conversation is a major psychological skill and a fine art. Sometimes parents of tutored students worry that social conversation is a waste of time. But the person who has learned to take great pleasure in social conversation has a source of pleasure that protects against depression, anxiety, loneliness, and a wide variety of other problems.

Time spent on assessment of ICD or DSM diagnosis

As I mentioned before, mental health practitioners usually must submit to insurance companies the diagnosis of each patient. Incorrect diagnosis can be an issue in lawsuits. Much time is spent in asking about symptoms in order to establish a defensible diagnosis. If that diagnosis dictates a specific efficacious treatment, the time is well spent. But people who have one diagnosis tend to have others. People who have skill deficiencies in one area tend to have them in others also. Rather than only one clear-cut diagnosis, people tend to have "some of this and some of that." (Merikangas, 2010)

Psychoeducational tutoring can proceed without establishing a diagnosis, or even with a diagnosis of "normal." Medical insurance payment is not sought (and would not be given if it were sought). The "diagnostic" activity for psychoeducation would primarily involve listening to specific examples of the person's behavior, to decide which subset of psychological skills education is of highest priority at any given time. Another approach is simply to teach a broad curriculum of psychological skills, hypothesizing that people need competence in all of them. Funneling effort into skills training rather than into assessment and classification may be the most efficient way to do good.

Assessment of dangerousness

One of the most frequent causes of lawsuits against mental health practitioners is suicidal behavior on the part of the client. Mental health practitioners may also be liable for harmful acts their clients carry out toward others. For this reason in many mental health clinics there is incessant questioning of clients as to whether they have homicidal or suicidal wishes, or psychotic features. In brief encounters between therapist and client, a fair fraction of the session time may be spent with the therapist attempting to carry out due diligence to assess danger.

Are the methods mental health professionals employ to assess dangerousness accurate enough to justify the diversion of time and energy from skill-building? To try to answer this question would be a formidable undertaking; I will not undertake it here.

However, providers of psychoeducational tutoring may disclaim explicitly the duty of assessing dangerousness. College students or other nonprofessional tutors are not licensed or trained to assess dangerousness.

Being delivered of the responsibility to predict future behavior relieves a major stress and a major time sink for practitioners.

When the necessity to understand particular problems, the necessity to establish a correct diagnosis, and the necessity to assess dangerousness are removed, psychoeducators can devote nearly 100% of their time to skill-building.

Emergency readiness

When a clinician signs a contract to be a mental health provider with an insurance company, a clause usually holds that the provider or someone sharing call with him or her should be available in case of emergencies 24 hours a day, 7 days a week.

I certainly do not deny the existence of mental health emergencies, nor do I regret the existence of crisis services. Some people use such availability to regress to a state of childlike dependency. For others, the services may be life-saving.

But a very large number of people who could use improvement in psychological skills will never need emergency mental health intervention. The costs entailed in emergency readiness are considerable. A system that saves such services for those who really need them conserves lots of money. For many people, the role of student who is presumed able to take care of oneself fits well with the person's dignity and with the person's skills of self-care.

Chapter 3: Quick Examples Of Psychoeducational Modules

I've heard of psychotherapy described as "talking to a therapist." It can be very useful to bring up the information that resides in one's own memory, reshuffle it, rearrange it, think about it, have new insights about it, and so forth. But often it's most efficient, and necessary, to simply get information from someone else, either by reading it or hearing it. Sometimes simply getting educated is the answer to one or more of life's problems.

The entire corpus of ideas that can reasonably be included in psychoeducation is very large. In this chapter I've picked just a few of them, selected to illustrate circumstances where psychoeducation works much better than, say, nondirective counseling. In these examples, there's a crucial piece of knowledge that people have come up with, a pearl of wisdom, the sharing of which can make all the difference in the client's progress. My purpose is to illustrate the point that straightforward education can improve mental health.

CO2 physiology instruction and breathing exercises for hyperventilation

Panic attacks are very unpleasant. A good fraction of them are made more unpleasant because of the "vicious cycle of hyperventilation." This cycle may start when in an automatic response to fear, someone breathes faster than usual. Breathing fast is an automatic response to fear, which probably evolved in order to "blow off" carbon dioxide in preparation for the large amount of carbon dioxide produced in the muscles during flight or fight. But fast breathing not followed by high exertion eliminates too much carbon dioxide. When there is a "carbon dioxide deficit" (or respiratory alkalosis), the result is an unpleasant feeling.

"Normally" the unpleasant feeling of CO_2 deficit gets automatically interpreted by the brain as a signal, "I should breathe more slowly." The person automatically adjusts the breathing rate to allow more CO_2 to build up, and the deficit is cured. But sometimes, for some people, the unpleasant feeling of CO_2 deficit gets interpreted by the brain as, "I'm not getting enough air." Then the person breathes faster, which only increases the unpleasant feeling. The faster the person breathes, the greater is the feeling of not getting enough air, when really the problem is that the lungs are exchanging too much air.

Thus the cure for hyperventilation is breathing more slowly. The problem doesn't have anything to do with how much oxygen the person is getting. It doesn't require "deep breathing." It simply requires a lower rate of air going into and out from the lungs.

Just understanding this physiology can be of great help. But in the heat of the moment, it's hard to remember this. Thus one needs to practice in calm moments. There are two exercises that get people into good habits of regulating the breathing rate. In the first, one holds the breath for a bit, notices the feeling of "too much carbon dioxide," and cures that slightly unpleasant feeling by taking a couple of fast breaths. In the second, one purposely hyperventilates for anywhere from five to twenty breaths, feels the unpleasant feeling of carbon dioxide deficit, notices how different it feels from carbon dioxide excess, and cures it by breathing very slowly for a while.

I have worked with a fair number of people who have been able to eliminate totally their hyperventilation episodes by learning these ideas and practicing the exercises. By receiving this purely educational intervention, people have been able to accomplish great improvement much faster than they would have by nondirective therapy. The breathing exercises and their rationale are described in Strayhorn (2012).

Instruction on non-withholding for encopresis

A child past the age of toilet training who defecates into his pants or into other non-toilet places is said to have "encopresis," and this has been classified as a "mental disorder." What could be more natural than to encourage such a child to learn to hold back feces more effectively, so that he or she can wait until the right moment? It turns out that such a message is not just incorrect, but the diametric opposite of what children with encopresis need to do. Most of them have their problem because they have already held back feces excessively and are greatly constipated. The constant state of stretch of the rectal wall causes the normal reflex that stimulates defecation to be weakened or lost. Feces leak out at unpredictable times and places.

Thus the message to children with encopresis, and to their parents, should be that defecating as often as possible, and as soon as possible after any urge, is the solution to the problem, not more holding back of feces. Often laxatives or bulking agents are given to help break the cycle of withholding and constipation.

To expect parents and children to reinvent this solution by talking about the problem would be very unreasonable – what helps is straightforward education about the problem and how it is solved.

Teaching parents to regulate excitement level with stimulus seekers

When a child misbehaves, for many parents the most natural response is to get excited and yell a reprimand to the child. But the excitement that parents generate can reinforce the misbehavior rather than punish it, particularly if the child is a "stimulus-seeker" who finds excitement very reinforcing (and boredom very punishing). Straightforward education of parents about this fact – including a suggestion to try elevating the excitement level in response to positive child behaviors, and lowering it by speaking in a monotone in response to misbehaviors – is often very helpful.

Rehearsal versus catharsis for anger control

What should we do about anger? For many people, it seems to be only common sense that when we have anger "inside us," the way to get rid of it is to "let it out." Hitting a pillow, screaming in an enclosed place, or pounding on modeling clay, boxing, or playing violent video games seem to be great ways of "releasing pent-up hostility."

The problem with this idea, which has been referred to as the "catharsis hypothesis," is that it's wrong. A good number of carefully done research studies contradict the idea that we get anger out of ourselves by expressing it or acting it out (Geen et al., 1972; Bandura, 1973; Bushman et al., 1999; Bushman, 2002; Tavris, 1989). Rather, it appears that the more we act in angry ways, the more we rehearse angry behaviors. Angry behavior toward a pillow or toward imagined characters appears to be in the same "response class" as aggression against a person – that is, practicing one behavior tends to make more likely the other behaviors in the same class.

Thus people wishing to improve their anger control skills should be taught that the goal is not "getting anger out," but rather learning to select the wisest possible response to any provocations that come along. The process of rationally deciding how to respond to the situation often helps greatly in turning down maladaptive degrees of anger.

Self-reward versus self-punishment for depression and work block

When faced with an important but unpleasant task, such as writing a thesis, many people find themselves in the condition of "work block": they just can't get themselves moving on the project. They find themselves procrastinating over and over.

One of the most natural behavior change techniques for people appears to be to punish unwanted behavior. Thus it comes naturally for many people who find themselves procrastinating to use verbal self-punishment: "Why are you being so lazy? This is stupid. Just get it done! What's the matter with you? You've got to have something wrong with you," goes the internal diatribe.

Such self-punishment tends to be demoralizing and depressing. It also sets up a conditioned association between the thought of doing the project and emotions of shame and guilt and frustration. It further sets up the person to self-punish his fledgling efforts at work on the project: "That will never do. That was really bad writing." Thus the more the person self-punishes, the worse the work block tends to get.

The solution is to turn off the self-punishment as much as possible, and to use self-reinforcement instead. "Hooray, I sat down and got started! I actually wrote something. Even if it's not perfect, it's progress. I can change it later!"

Again, it is much more efficient simply to teach the person what other people have found about overcoming work block than to simply encourage the person to talk for a long time in hopes that the person will discover it for himself.

Phonemic and spatial awareness for children who can't read well

There's a DSM 5 term for reading problems: "Specific Learning Disorder with Impairment in Reading." It's good that reading problems are classified as mental disorders, because reading is a very important psychological skill. The psychological sequelae of poor reading are large and serious – one can imagine how frustrating and mortifying it would be to try to carry out school tasks when one can't read the worksheets, especially if one's classmates can. Techniques for reading remediation fall into the class where something other than the obvious or common sense thing to do often turns out to be the best technique. When someone has trouble reading, it comes naturally to many people to try to get the person to read, tell the person the words she does not know, teach new words, and so forth. But a good deal of research substantiates the idea that we should often go further "down the hierarchy" to more foundation level skills.

One such skill is phonemic awareness, the ability to put sounds together to make words, and to take words apart into their component sounds. "I'm thinking of an animal. It's a kuh aah tuh. Can you guess it?" This is an example of practice in "blending." When the student gives the same sort of question to the tutor, and has to take a word apart into its component sounds, this is called "segmenting." Lots of blending and segmenting practice can prepare the brain for realizing how letters make sounds that are blended together to form words. Phonemic awareness predicts later reading achievement, and phonemic awareness skills may be taught (Snider, 1993).

Another such skill I have called *spatial awareness*. This is the ability to distinguish right from left, and images from their mirror images. (The term *spatial awareness* is sometimes used in other ways.) Without this, it's difficult to tell the difference between lower case b and lower case d, and the difference between *was* and *saw*. At the bottom of the hierarchy for this skill is looking at pairs of arrows and deciding whether they are pointing in the same direction or in different directions. A fun point on the hierarchy is looking at three pictures, two of which are identical and the third of which is a mirror image of the other two. The learner's task is to pick which thing is not like the others. At the top of the hierarchy is successfully identifying a series of b's, d's, p's, and q's.

   With exercises such as these, the foundation skills for reading can be taught in ways that assure nearly every learner success at every stage of the process. Sometimes helping a student to be a successful reader does more for her psychological well-being than any amount of psychotherapy could do.

Obsessions and the white bear problem

   What should people with obsessive-compulsive disorder do if images of immoral and forbidden actions intrude into their minds and horrify them – for example, the image of stabbing a family member, wrecking a car, undressing in public, etc.? The automatic goal of most people with these intrusive thoughts is to suppress them, to get them out of consciousness, to make them go away. But trying not to think a certain thought tends to make it return. This has been called the "white bear problem," after a mention in a memoir by Leo Tolstoy (Birukov & Tolstoy, 1911) of childhood experiments with futile attempts not to think about a white bear. Researchers have gradually realized that the engine driving the persistence of such obsessions is the horror they trigger, and the ensuing efforts not to think them, which tend to bring them back to mind. (This is a different situation from one in which the person takes pleasure in antisocial fantasies.) Through experience people with obsessions have found that a better goal is to celebrate the barrier between imagery and action, to let the intrusive thoughts run their course, and to engage in whatever behaviors are most appropriate while they do so. Wegner (2011) refers to these strategies as "thinking about and accepting unwanted thoughts rather than suppressing them--and so, setting free the bears." Again, through nondirective talking and getting to know oneself better, one could participate in therapy for years without landing on the best strategy, whereas capitalizing on what others have learned can dramatically accelerate progress.

Chapter 4: The Psychological Skills People Need

Classifying psychological health skills

The ICD and the DSM are aimed at classifying what goes wrong with mental and psychological functioning. But there is also a need for a classification of what can go right: an answer to the question, what do psychologically healthy persons do? What can those persons do well, that less well-functioning people can't do as well?

A famous answer to this question was apparently contributed by Sigmund Freud: "To love and to work." (People have searched in vain for this quotation among Freud's published works; the statement was attributed to him by another famous theorist, Erik Erikson (Fleming, 2004; the Freud Museum, 2016). Freud (1930) wrote something less succinct: "The communal life of human beings had, therefore, a two-fold foundation: the compulsion to work, which was created by external necessity, and the power of love.... ")

Here's a different answer to the question, "What are the goals that mental health is meant to achieve?" The goals are: 1) to be happy and 2) to make other people happy. To care for oneself and be caring toward others; to be good to oneself and good to others; to love one's neighbor as oneself; these are restatements of these very important goals.

The goals of happiness for oneself and others, if widely adopted, would tend to define life as a "cooperative game" – one in which people are trying to help each other rather than defeat each other. On the other hand, many people, perhaps without explicitly stating it, define the major aim of existence as a series of competitive games: to defeat one's enemies, to surpass one's competitors, to come out on top in the struggle. This is the world view of the Darwinian struggle for survival and dominance. But in this world view, there is still a need for cultivating friends, or at least allies, and making these other people happy, because one needs helpers in defeating the opponents.

It is useful to make a longer list of the psychological health skills that enable people to be happy and to make others happy. The more we understand the various skills that allow people to be psychologically healthy, the more equipped we are to help people gain these skills. A longer version of the "psychological skills axis" is presented in Appendix 2 of this book.

Diagnosis and specific treatment, or broad-spectrum curriculum?

When I began to write about the various skills that constitute mental health, (e.g. Strayhorn, 1983, 1988) my idea was to have a "diagnostic axis" comparable to the various axes of the DSM. When a person comes for mental health related help, the clinician could determine which of the psychological skills were most in need of improvement. Having made this "skills axis diagnosis," psychological skills training could be specifically directed toward the highest priority skills. This method of thinking still remains useful. There are some people who are very good at many skills, who just need help with certain selected ones and not others.

But the more I have seen of people, and children in particular, the more I come to two conclusions:
1. Most children can benefit from education in the entire list of psychological skills.
2. The children who are especially in need of help in a certain skill area tend to also need special help in most other skill areas.

In other words, it looks as though the broad-spectrum approach rather than the narrowly targeted approach is useful most of the time. We should use the list that answers the question, "What skills is a mentally healthy person good at," as the outline of a psychological skills curriculum, and not just as a diagnostic axis.

Two studies of rating scales wherein parents, classroom observers, or teachers rate students on their psychological skills demonstrate a fairly high intercorrelation among children's ratings for various psychological skills, resulting in a high coefficient alpha for the scales. That is, when for example, a child with a high score in friendship-building also tends to have a high score in self-discipline, and so forth. (Strayhorn et al., 1990; Strayhorn, 2014) On the average (with some notable exceptions) the children who are good at some psychological skills also tend to be good at others, and those who are deficient in some, also tend to be deficient in others. If children who strongly need help in some skills also tend to need lots of help with others, it makes sense to give them broad-spectrum skills training rather than spending too much time figuring out which skills they need the most.

A major research study reported by Merikangas et al. (2010) presents findings that also seem to imply the usefulness of broad-spectrum intervention. This study collapsed the many types of psychiatric diagnoses that adolescents can receive into four broad categories: problems of anxiety, mood, behavior (i.e. conduct), and substance abuse problems. Even with these broad categories, there was lots of overlap. Of the adolescents with a diagnosis in one category, 39% of those had a diagnosis in at least one other category. Thus these disorders are not isolated – they very often occur together.

Why might having certain psychological skill deficiencies, or diagnoses, tend to make other ones more likely? It's easy to see how this might be the case. Let's make up an all-too-often-true story. Suppose someone for some reason has a great deal of social anxiety – great shyness, fear of disapproval of others. This interferes greatly with the person's ability to make friends, and the person feels sad and depressed about this. In adolescence, the person finds acceptance in a group of drug-using peers. But the drug culture leads to lots of lying and ultimately to stealing to support a drug habit. Thus in terms of Merikangas's categories, we started with an anxiety disorder and added a mood disorder, then a substance use problem, and finally a conduct problem. In skill categories, we started with a courage skill deficiency, which affected joyousness skills, then skills of self-care and good decisions, and in turn, skills of honesty and compliance.

Or imagine someone who has great deficiency in the ability to concentrate and stay on task. This interferes with compliance skills in school, and the child starts getting into more and more trouble. The child develops a major fear of failure and covers it up with bravado and defiance. Other children start to reject him, and this plus his repeated failures in school lead him to get depressed. He starts self-medicating with substances. Again, we have a chain of events that lead to diagnoses in all four areas, and to multiple skill deficiencies.

There is another reason for treating the list of psychological skills primarily as a curriculum outline rather than a diagnostic axis: it doesn't hurt people's feelings or stir up so resistance and defensiveness so much. Which feels better to hear: "You need to work on this, because you have a disorder making you much worse than others in this," or, "You need to work on this for the same reason that everyone else should work on this: it's an important skill for living, and everyone needs to get good at it." The second statement has an advantage of being totally true.

Two major aims

Factor analyses of ratings of behavior yield two major factors: internalizing problems and externalizing problems (Achenbach, 1978). Internalizing disorders such as anxiety and depression represent difficulties in maximizing one's own happiness; externalizing disorders such as aggression and conduct problems are shortcomings in making others happy. Thus factor analysis brings us to the two major aims of mental health, i.e. to be happy and to help others to be happy. It tends to affirm the commandment recorded over a thousand years b.c.e. (in the book of Leviticus): "Love thy neighbor as thyself."

But how do we go about making ourselves and others happy? There are numerous separable, teachable skills that equip one for these goals. The list that follows describes sixteen groups, each of which may have subskills.

The skills axis

The following list of psychological skills was gleaned from study of treatment manuals, recorded cases, and my own experience with people. It is an attempt at an answer to the question, "If we want people to be mentally healthy, what should we teach them to do?"

Productivity

To work, to expend effort, to exert action to achieve some purpose is the first group on our list. Subskills include purposefulness – having a reason for working toward a certain goal; persistence and concentration, or sustaining attention to trying to achieve a goal; and organization, the ability to keep objects, papers, tasks, and computer files in order. In addition, there are specific competences for the type of work undertaken; the more competent one is in these, the easier it is to be productive. Thus academic skills are an important subskill for school productivity, as are work skills for career productivity.

Joyousness

The pleasure-producing part of the brain is a major motivator for activity. The ability to take pleasure in lots of things is the opposite of depression. The psychologically healthy person can take pleasure from being with other people, but also from being alone. She can enjoy the approval of others, but also has an internal beacon that produces good feelings about her accomplishments or kind acts or discoveries, even without other people's acknowledgment. She can feel grateful for the favorable acts of other people and of fate. She can enjoy relaxation, gleefulness, humor, and affection.

Kindness

I have written of various subcategories of kind acts: consoling, listening, helping, working to someone's benefit, teaching, complimenting, entertaining, giving, and "not spoiling." Empathy, the ability to recognize others' feelings and viewpoints, is central to kindness. The other side of the ability to take pleasure from one's kind acts is the skill of feeling appropriate guilt when one harms others – the possession of a well-functioning conscience.

Honesty

Honesty, along with other skills, illustrates that the skills constituting psychological health also constitute ethical behavior. This skill includes not lying, cheating, or stealing, being dependable, and keeping promises. It also includes honesty to oneself, including courageously assessing one's own strengths and weaknesses.

Fortitude

The fortitude group of skills has to do with responding to the adversity of life – unwanted events, from minor frustrations to full blown trauma. Separation, rejection, criticism, one's own mistakes and failures, someone else's getting what one wants for oneself, painful emotions, and unwanted mental images and events are some of the categories of events that deserve specific sets of instructions. Fortitude is easiest when bad things make us feel bad enough to mobilize corrective efforts, but not so bad as to paralyze or demoralize or cause us to give up. The main key to fortitude is attempting to choose the best possible response to unwanted events, not worrying too much about what to do about the unpleasant feelings they engender.

Good decisions: individual

Life presents us all with a series of "choice points": situations where we get to choose how to respond. The quality of our choices largely determines the quality, and in many cases the length, of our lives. We can divide this skill into various parts. One subskill is that of noticing, observing, and recognizing the important aspects of the situation that one is in. Another is forming worthwhile and wise objectives for responding to that situation – deciding what variables to maximize when making the decision. Another is information-gathering: being a good reference librarian for oneself, or real-life experimenter or observer in getting the knowledge necessary for informed choice. A widely studied subskill is that of option-generating: listing a variety of possible responses to the situation. The best decision-makers tend to be able to generate multiple options, and the worst ones tend to get stuck at a low number. Once the options have been generated, accurate prediction of consequences and weighing the positive and negative consequences (which we can call advantages and disadvantages) is a separate teachable maneuver. Carrying out the choice that was decided upon, and learning from the results of that choice, constitute more subskills. Throughout the entire process, good general verbal skills are of great help, because much of the thinking is in words. Being aware of, in touch with, one's own emotions and those of others is crucial, because often the goal of a given choice is to maximize the happiness and minimize the emotional pain of all concerned.

Good joint decisions, or conflict-resolution

Many of the decisions of life are made jointly with other people. Some joint decisions start out as conflicts, where the two person's wishes appear to be incompatible. Others start at a more exploratory stage, where the two or more people have not taken opposing positions.

The skills of appraising situations, determining objectives, listing options, predicting and weighing consequences, implementing a decision, and learning from the experience are similar to those of individual decision-making. In addition, great demands are often placed on the ability to remain rational and calculating, especially when the partner to the joint decision speaks irrationally, and to avoid getting into a power struggle if possible. When power is something of an issue, as it often is, the ability to rely on nonviolent sources of power is central.

Nonviolence

Nonviolence could be considered a logical outgrowth of kindness, fortitude, and good decisions. But it is important enough to deserve a class by itself. The achievement of nonviolence in human relations is one of the major frontiers for humanity. Avoiding unwarranted violence is perhaps the most crucial criterion for individual mental health.

Respectful talk

Speaking respectfully to others, even in the face of great disagreement, is a skill that not only predisposes to nonviolence, but that also greatly improves the quality of life. A world where people neither physically nor verbally abuse one another is a paramount goal for humanity.

Friendship-building

Forming, building, and keeping good relationships with other people is central to psychological health. This skill is greatly assisted by subskills of "social initiations" -- being able to start interacting with others in ways comfortable for both. Social conversation skills, including the skills of both disclosing to others and being a good listener, are a crucial part of the friendship-building category. Discernment and trusting constitute another crucial part of relationship-building. The person with discernment and trusting skills can size up other people accurately enough so as not to expect too much and be too gullible, but neither have too negative views of others, or too crippling fears of being treated badly.

Self-discipline

Self-discipline is needed when the best choice is not the most pleasurable one. Self-discipline is the ability to hold oneself back, at times, from choosing short-term gratifications of food, drink, drugs, sex, laziness, electronic "screen" entertainment, gambling, and many others, in the service of worthy long-term goals.

Loyalty

Loyalty is the skill of tolerating and enjoying long-term closeness, commitment, and attachment to another person. It entails deciding how to weight our responsibilities to the different people on the planet. The decision not to force my family members to live in poverty for the sake of donating almost all our assets to the poor of the world is a decision about my relative loyalty. Loyalty is involved in not discounting old relationships in favor of the novelty and excitement of new ones. A government official who breaks laws in order to get advantages for family members is of course not using good loyalty skills. Nor is the woman who stubbornly stands by a man who abuses her – sometimes people make commitments that are mistakes, and part of loyalty skills involves when and how to correct those mistakes. Feeling obligated to "enable" substance abusers by protecting them from the punishing consequences of their abuse is usually a loyalty mistake rather than a loyalty triumph. Loyalty skills involve good decisions about which relationships are most important, and how much of what type of support is owed to which people.

Conservation

This skill group involves two related areas. One is the more globally oriented ethical principle of not wasting the Earth's resources and spoiling the environment, but preserving a sustainable habitat for future generations, both of human beings and nonhuman animals. The second is thrift and frugality in one's personal life – avoiding wasting money and things, resisting the temptation toward needless spending and consumption.

Self-care

A subskill in this group is of carefulness and safety-consciousness – avoiding unnecessary risks (for others, as well as oneself). Other subskills include following health guidelines with respect to exercise, diet, sleep, drug use, smoking, noise exposure, ultra-violet light exposure, and others. Another aspect of self-care is being able to use self-nurturing thoughts: to be one's own friend, not to be too hard on oneself, to have a caretaking and nurturing relationship with oneself.

Compliance

The skill of compliance does not mean blind obedience to authority – in fact part of this skill includes rational decisions about whom and when to disobey. But the listing of this skill acknowledges that the "rule of law" is a very favorable human invention. The rule of law is the alternative to the "law of club and fang" -- the most powerful person wins in any given conflict. The rule of law stipulates, for example, that assaulting a homeless and destitute person is just as illegal as assaulting a rich and powerful person. The rule of law depends upon people's being willing to obey. People who have a strong urge to disobey any rules or commands handed down from authority figures can have a very difficult time in life.

Positive fantasy rehearsal

Many studies have corroborated the hypothesis that rehearsing actions in imagination can make them easier to perform in real life (Suinn, 1972; Cautela, 1974; Kazdin, 1974 a-d, 1976; Lazarus, 1977; Singer, 1974). Neuroimaging studies have revealed that the neural activity involved in imagining certain behaviors is very similar to that of actually carrying out those behaviors (Rodriguez, 2014; Sharma and Baron, 2013). The principle of fantasy rehearsal is grasped by almost all elite athletes (Clarey, 2014; Ungerleider & Golding, 1991). It has been the subject of many popular books on how to be successful and happy, e.g Maltz (1960). It appears to be nonetheless greatly underutilized. The principle appears to be denied by the apologists for violent entertainment.

Courage

Anxiety symptoms are among the most prevalent complaints; courage skills are the learnable maneuvers that overcome unrealistic or unwanted fears and aversions. One such maneuver is doing the rational calculation to decide, in the first place, whether a certain fear is a realistic signal of danger (such as the fear of excessive speed on the highway) or whether the fear greatly exceeds the actual danger (such as with a phobia of butterflies). Making such a decision clearly helps to make it clear to oneself which way to go in the "avoidance versus mastery choice point": for certain (usually realistic) fears, I want to simply avoid the dangerous situation; for others, (usually unrealistic ones) I want to master the fear. An important anti-fear skill is the use of positive fantasy rehearsal, as well as real-life rehearsal, to practice being in the scary situation, responding well to it, trusting in the knowledge that prolonged exposure and practice handling the situation will eventually result in fear reduction. "Responding well" to the feared situation entails choosing thoughts that most facilitate rational responses rather than avoidance and escape. Figuring out and moving along a series of gradual steps, or a hierarchy, of feared situations, starting with the easiest and working up to the more difficult ones, greatly improves the chance of success. Another specialized subskill is that of regulating the rate of one's breathing, so as to avoid the hyperventilation that accompanies lots of unpleasant anxiety states, particularly panic attacks. Relaxation skills, mentioned earlier in the joyousness category, are also a major aid to the task of fear-reduction. The ability to think independently and resist social pressure, standing by good decisions while tolerating the resulting disapproval or rejection of those pressing for a worse decision, represents a special type of courage skill.

Some tests of the list

The skill categories listed above, and many of the subskills I mentioned, are reproduced in a more complete list in Appendix 2 of this book.

I have tested this list, and others can test it, in several ways. Foremost, in years of listening to people tell me about mental health problems, I asked myself the question, "What could this person learn to do better, that would relieve this problem?" If the answer to that question was not on the list, I added it. Also, in examining both treatment manuals and self-help books addressing mental health problems, I've searched for teachable skills. Beyond the realm of mental health pathology, we can observe high-functioning, happy, productive, successful people, and look for the components of what they do well. We can also do thought experiments – we can imagine people who are quite expert at each of these skills, and then try to imagine how the person can fail to be happy and successful, other than by bad luck or the oppression of others. We can imagine a society filled with people and groups expert at each of the above skills, and try to imagine what could go wrong with such a society, other than natural disasters.

If you test the list in these ways, you may find that while there are always other candidates to be added to the list, the skills axis (particularly the longer version) covers the bases reasonably well. An individual, or a society, with expertise in all of these is in very good shape indeed.

A further test of the list is whether these attributes are indeed teachable. The next chapter will go over another list, designed to answer the question, how may these skills (or any others) be taught and learned?

Chapter 5: Methods Of Influence

How do we teach someone psychological skills? Or how do people teach themselves? The answer to these is the same as the answer to the question, how do people learn unfortunate patterns of thinking, feeling, and behaving, that cause unhappiness and failure?

The combination of a list of skills and a list of teaching methods constitutes an overall agenda for psychoeducation. Any combination of a worthwhile skill plus an effective method of influence represents a chance for good to be done. I have divided methods of influence into ten sets, as follows.

The methods of influence list

Objective-formation, or goal-setting

By the phrase *objective-formation* I refer to the process whereby someone forms the conviction that a certain skill is worth having, that certain positive behaviors are desirable. A well-known riddle goes, How many psychotherapists does it take to change a light bulb? Answer: One, but the light bulb has to want to change.

There are at least two ways of measuring motivation toward a certain goal. One is simply to ask, on a scale of 0 to 10, how much do you want this? A second is to find out how much time the person is willing to devote, daily, to the pursuit of the goal. Often these metrics yield different results.

The field of advertising devotes itself to convincing people to buy goods or services. It's interesting to imagine what the world would be like if a similar quantity of persuasive energy focused on selling productivity, joyousness, kindness, honesty, fortitude, and the rest to the population. Short of this improbable scenario, various of the same methods used in advertising may be useful: the sheer repetition of statements that the skills are useful and desirable, the association of the skills with people whom the child already admires and wishes to emulate; letting the child listen to others speak admiringly of people who exemplify the skills. Also useful are rituals such as repetition of the Scout Oath "I will do my best... to help other people at all times" or the Scout Law "A Scout is trustworthy, loyal, helpful, friendly..."

Many of the other influence methods, such as modeling and reinforcement, to be discussed later, in addition to teaching how to do the skills, also provide motivation for them.

A goal-setting influence that we use in psychoeducational tutoring is simply to expose the child to many stories embodying the skills, and to ask the child to carry out the intellectual exercise of deciding which skill the story illustrates. The underlying assumption that these skills are desirable is communicated indirectly, rather than through a direct sales pitch.

Hierarchy

I use the word "hierarchy" to refer to a series of steps, each of which involves greater proficiency than the previous. When working on courage skills, someone with a fear of butterflies, for example, might construct a hierarchy where simply picturing a dictionary with the word "butterfly" in it may be at the bottom of the hierarchy, and letting a live butterfly walk around on her forearm may be at the top of the hierarchy; looking at photographs of butterflies may be in the middle. In the hierarchy of reading skills, guessing games like, "I'm thinking of a type of furry pet, and it's a kuh-aah-tuh. Can you guess it?" may be at the bottom of the hierarchy, and understanding and enjoying college-level textbooks may be near the top. For compliance skills, following very easy commands with an immediate reward thereafter, given when one is bored, may be at the bottom of the hierarchy. Obeying commands to stop doing a very pleasurable and enthralling activity (such as video games), even though no reward is offered, may be closer to the top. For the skill of productivity, correct choices about hierarchy positions are crucial: if a child is asked to do much more work than the child can tolerate, rebellion and work aversion often result; if the work expectations are too little, the productivity skills do not develop fast enough. Robert Eisenberger (1992) has written about the development of "learned industriousness" by moving along a hierarchy for work expectations. Pierce et al. (2003) among others, provide more empirical evidence for the idea that by working for reinforcers, performing tasks that require successively greater effort, people can learn to increase their persistence and work capacity; the sensation of exerting effort can become a "secondary reinforcer."

For any skill, there is a hierarchy, and a major task of education is to find challenges that are neither too hard nor too easy. Too easy tends to result in boredom; too hard tends to result in frustration and demoralization; just right tends to result in enjoyment and maximally efficient learning.

In academic learning, the opposite of "hierarchy-ology" is the "standards" approach: "All children should be able to do X competently by Y grade." Among children of any given age, there is a wide range of skill levels, and any standard that some committee adopts will be too easy for some children and too hard for others. The goal of finding the best point on the hierarchy and working right at that level is quite difficult with a classroom full of children; it is much easier in one-to-one tutoring.

Relationship

Learning takes place best under conditions of a positive relationship between teacher and learner. What makes a positive relationship? One aspect is dependability – for example, when the two people promise to get together at a certain time, they actually show up. When the possibility of abandonment or ending of the relationship does not distract, the learning task can proceed more effectively. Another aspect of a positive relationship is that the two people are what the behaviorists call "generalized reinforcers" for each other – that is, they like each other and like interacting with each other. In most teacher-learner relationships, it greatly helps if the learner desires the positive feedback from the teacher, and is willing to comply with the teacher's directives. It greatly helps if the teacher lives and works under conditions allowing the teacher energy to put into optimizing the learning experience. It is very helpful if the teacher has the autonomy to make decisions about how to optimize learning, rather than being coerced by authorities who are not familiar with the particular learners.

A positive relationship does not exist independently of the activities that the two people do together. If those activities are "right" for the learner, a positive relationship is much more possible. For example: if the activity the teacher insists upon is that the learner talk about the problems in his behavior and what he needs to improve on, and the learner has a very strong aversion to doing that, a positive relationship is difficult. If a different teacher promotes activities the learner can enjoy, a positive relationship is much more attainable.

Much research has documented that for children, positive relationships with adults, or at least one such relationship, is key to psychological health. According to Masten and Reed (2002), "The best-documented aspect of resilient children is a strong bond to a competent and caring adult, who need not be a parent. For children who do not have such an adult involved in their lives, this is the first order of business." (p. 83). According to Luthar and Zigler (1991), "The presence of social supports was among the significant factors differentiating parents who repeated an intergenerational cycle of child abuse from parents who did not. Finally, there is an abundance of literature indicating that intervention programs that offer support services to high-risk children and their families can be of great benefit in terms of providing protective functions and promoting positive outcomes." (p. 12-13).

Attribution and prophecy

By these words I refer to statements about what potentials are attributed to the person, and what the possible future of the person is. A deleterious way to use attribution is to attribute negative traits and make negative prophecies, such as "You're lazy. You'll never be able to succeed." or "You're just like that crazy Uncle Lunk. Some day you're going to do something that you're really going to regret." A better way to use attribution and prophecy for the child with low work capacity is to say, "You have the capability to do a lot of work, even if you haven't developed it much yet. When you do get lots better at working, we'll really have reason to celebrate!" For the aggressive child, better attribution is, "I think you can learn really good anger control and kindness skills. If you do get to be a master of anger control and kindness, that will be a huge achievement!"

These methods of influence are based on the fact that people's beliefs about their own capabilities and their "anticipated life histories" (or predicted life courses) often become self-fulfilling prophecies.

Modeling

The study of imitation learning, the tendency of human beings to learn from models they observe, was pioneered by psychologist Albert Bandura, who did many studies of and constructed theories about the effects of observing models (Bandura, 1971). Not only real-life models, but also those of fictional or historical characters, can be greatly influential. Models tend to be more influential the more the observer admires the model. When models receive positive consequences for their actions, and when the models are perceived as similar to the observer, these too add to the effects, but these may be overridden if the observer somehow sees the model as attractive or emulation-worthy.

Practice opportunities (including fantasy rehearsal)

If we compare the ability levels of a concert pianist or violinist with a novice in these instruments, the differences are mind-boggling. The complexity, speed, and precision of the expert's performance would be thought impossible if we didn't actually see it done. Likewise, the performance of expert dancers, gymnasts, pole-vaulters, mathematicians, divers, chess players, surgeons, and others, are orders of magnitude above the performances of novices in these areas. The act of reading, also, is amazing – so many little symbols can be processed so quickly, with such rich understanding resulting – who would have thought it possible? If someone announced a set of drugs that could instantly produce expertise in these skills, the scientific world would be incredulous. But we already have something that reliably can produce great skill in these areas, although admittedly innate talent also plays a role. And that something is thousands and thousands of practices, (with good models, and moving along a hierarchy of difficulty, and constant monitoring of performance). Daily, or at least very frequent, practice in a skill brings about the amazing neural changes (whatever they are) that result in competence.

Humanity has known for centuries the types of practice it takes to produce an expert pianist. But the study of what sorts of practice it takes to produce a "kindness expert" or "decision-making expert" or "joyousness expert" is in its infancy. One of the major promises of psychoeducation is to discover and enact the type of practices that will eventually result in expertise in psychological skills.

I have written two books about "psychological skills exercises" (Strayhorn, 2001, 2013). These exercises are meant to be ways of practicing the psychological skills listed in the previous chapter. We will go into more detail about these exercises later on.

Many of these exercises simply ask the learner to use some mental maneuver that is useful in real life, only with hypothetical situations. For example, in the "brainstorming options" exercise, the student and the tutor take turns coming up with reasonable options for hypothetical choice points. They can compare their list to a list that others have compiled.

The fact that fantasy rehearsals, as well as real-life rehearsals, are effective in improving skills is well established by research cited elsewhere in this book. This literature makes it scary that the amount of time spent on "shooter" videogames alone is probably several orders of magnitude greater than all the time spent in purposive fantasy rehearsal of psychological skills.

If society can somehow engineer the volume of rehearsals in positive psychological patterns that some people carry out for sports, music, or video games, the results could present a revolutionary improvement in the human condition.

Reinforcement and punishment contingencies

We tend to choose behaviors so as to get something pleasant or to avoid something unpleasant. The field of applied behavior analysis, a.k.a. behavior modification, relies greatly on discovering how consequences strengthen or weaken behaviors, i.e. make them more or less likely to recur.

In psychoeducation, how can we possibly induce someone to do thousands of practices of positive patterns? We must provide consequences that lead the learner to want to do another practice – such consequences are called positive reinforcement.

In one-to-one tutoring, the most important reinforcer the tutor possesses is enthusiastic approval, including tones of voice that communicate not only "You did well!" but also "This activity is worthwhile!" and even, "It's great to be alive!" In addition to pure social reinforcers, secondary reinforcers such as points and tangible reinforcers such as certificates of achievement and prizes can be quite helpful.

Tying reinforcers to work produces an outcome other than simply the performance of more work. The knowledge that one can get what one wants by work of some kind produces a different feeling about life – a sense of being in control, a sense of being empowered. I refer to this feeling, or this conviction, as the "effort-payoff connection." Having a strong sense of effort-payoff connection is the opposite of being depressed.

Children get a large fraction of what they want from their parents. If a child finds that a certain behavior leads a parent to give him what he wants, that behavior will be reinforced and more likely to occur again. Upon studying reinforcement and punishment, many parents find that they have been inadvertently rewarding negative behavior and/or punishing admirable behavior. One of the most important parts of psychoeducation is teaching parents to be acutely aware of which of their behaviors are reinforcing, nonreinforcing, and punishing for their children, and to reinforce the positive and avoid reinforcing the negative – to be experts in differential reinforcement.

Instruction

One of the major differences between psychoeducation and what most people think of as psychotherapy is the quantity and structured nature of instructional materials. For the psychoeducational tutoring program which I help direct, around 18 instruction books have been produced so far. Topics include self-discipline, anger control and conflict-resolution, friendship-building, anxiety reduction, and others. It's not unusual for an elementary school student in our program to read three or four books, on the order of 100,000 words each. It *is* unusual for an adult psychotherapy client to read this much. One of the differences is that in psychotherapy, reading instructions is often assigned as homework; in psychoeducational tutoring, the reading takes place in the sessions themselves.

Instructional materials will become more and more crucial as the world accumulates more and more empirical information about how to be psychologically healthy. It will be less and less efficient for each learner to try to reinvent conclusions about how to be psychologically healthy, and more efficient to take advantage of the accumulated body of wisdom.

It is crucial that instructional materials be subject to revision as more knowledge accumulates. Various writings in the 1960's advocated therapy by screaming and other means of "letting hostility out," spending lots of time analyzing what dreams mean, and searching through one's past to find the origin of symptoms. The current best writings in psychoeducation emphasize more effective techniques.

Stimulus control

Certain stimulus situations make certain behaviors much more likely. Having a plate of cookies within easy reach makes it more likely that people will eat cookies. Being in a group of rowdy kids makes it less likely that a child will focus intensely on a school book. Being in a one-to-one situation with a friendly adult makes it much more likely that a child will practice appropriate social conversation, and less likely that the child will use loud or disruptive ways to attract attention. Stimulus control as a positive method of influence means arranging the stimulus situations so as to bring out the desirable patterns in the learner.

Monitoring

A great deal of piano practice does little good if the learner is practicing incorrect patterns – such as for example by largely disregarding the time values of the notes. Similarly, when one practices psychological skills, at least three types of monitoring are necessary: first, is the learner practicing positive patterns well? Second, is the practice generalizing to real life? Third, is the learner's quality of life improving as a result of the learning?

Mnemonic

I have remembered these ten methods of influence by the mnemonic OH RAM PRISM: Objective-formation, Hierarchy, Relationship, Attribution, Modeling, Practice, Reinforcement and punishment, Instruction, Stimulus Control, and Monitoring.

Using them all at once

A "psychoeducational tutoring" session can sometimes use all nine of these methods. The tutor and the student take turns reading **instructional** materials to each other, most of which contain positive **models** of psychological skills. The tutor is very **reinforcing** of the student's attentiveness, and **models** an upbeat and caring demeanor. The complexity of the reading material, plus the length of time to persist at it, are chosen so as to be at the correct level on the **hierarchy** of difficulty for that student at that time. The alternate reading gives **practice** in the skill of reading, after which they do skills exercises that allow **practice** of other psychological skills. As they do these, the tutor **monitors** progress and gives feedback to the student. The **stimulus situation** of one-on-one work tends to bring out the student's best behavior. They have unstructured social conversation, and sometimes in the midst of this the tutor has the chance to assist in **objective-formation** by continuing to communicate admiration for skillful behavior. Perhaps the tutor directly **attributes** to the student the capacity to keep improving in these skills; at other times the **attribution** is simply inferred by the fact that they continue working enthusiastically. The process of getting together regularly and dependably, doing activities that are enjoyable enough, and exchanging approval results in a positive **relationship** between tutor and student, that in turn disposes toward future successes.

Chapter 6: Service Delivery Methods

How is psychoeducation to be delivered – by whom, and where?

By therapists

Psychoeducation will certainly remain a very important part of the practice of psychotherapy. Cognitive behavior therapists, dialectical behavior therapists, and others already do a great deal of psychoeducation. But as we've discussed in an earlier chapter, this method of delivery presents the problem that there will never be enough therapists to produce a mentally healthy population, that many people who can benefit from psychoeducation do not want psychotherapy. Psychoeducation, while demanding of interpersonal skill, can be done very well by people who have not received the specialized training and licensure of psychotherapists.

By parents at home

It would appear that teaching parents to do psychoeducation with their own children would be an ideal method. The sessions provide a wonderful opportunity for parent and child to connect with each other. The parent has the opportunity to learn the psychological skill concepts along with the child – and the ideas are identical for children and adults. They gain a common vocabulary with which to communicate about life events. Twenty to thirty minutes a day is more than sufficient to get the job done.

What's the problem with this seemingly perfect solution? Unfortunately, it appears to me so far that most parents, for one reason or another, can't provide such psychoeducation daily. The U.S. Department of Labor, Bureau of Labor Statistics, reports bafflingly low amounts of time devoted by parents to activities with their children (Bureau of Labor Statistics, 2010). According to this report, the average parent spends only 6.6 minutes per day with a child in "education related activities, 2.4 minutes per day in "reading to/with children," 3 minutes a day in "talking to/with children," and 18 minutes in "playing/doing hobbies with children."

Parenting is a very demanding job, even if the parent doesn't also become a home educator in psychological skills. In our culture, those parents who have the time and energy to do home education in the evening after school often devote all this energy to a sometimes herculean-seeming task: homework.

This said, the difficulties I have had in getting parents organized for psychoeducation may be because I have not yet mobilized their efforts expertly enough. Many parents engage in large sacrifices of time and energy to foster their children's sports participation – see for example the phrase "soccer mom." The fact that there are around 1.8 million homeschooling families in the USA, about 3.4% of the school-aged population (Smith, 2013), attests to the fact that many parents are willing to invest large amounts of time into home education. Surely with adequate organization and motivational tactics, groups of parents can be enlisted successfully to carry out psychoeducation with their children.

We can fantasy a culture that expects all parents to carry out psychoeducation with their children. In this vision, psychoeducation by parents is at the center of the daily to do list; parents communicate with and support each other in these efforts; much attention in the media is given to parental psychoeducation; people grow up imagining that structured psychoeducation will be part of what parenting means. This would be a very different culture from our current one; I believe it would be vastly superior.

Via entertainment and literary media

What about embedding lessons about psychological skills within entertaining stories – television shows, movies, novels?

I spent years campaigning against violence in the entertainment media. Countless research studies have supported the notion that modeling and fantasy rehearsal through television shows, movies, video games, and written fiction affect our behavior in the expected way – that is, that experiencing violent behaviors tends to increase the likelihood that behaviors in the same "response class" will be enacted. But the competitive marketplace for entertainment creates a huge market for violent or otherwise bad models, and always has. From *Beowulf* to *Hamlet* to *Candide*, to *The Stranger*, *In Cold Blood*, and *Lord of the Flies*, the literature we consider great as well as that which we consider second-rate or worse, very often centers around actions that are violent or otherwise misguided – models of what not to do. The advent of television and video games has made the rate of exposure to negative models much greater. Models and instruction in psychological skills can be made fun, but they may never be as entertaining as media constructed purely to maximize entertainment value, and probably will rarely be able to compete successfully in the entertainment marketplace.

I have come to acknowledge that the stories human beings find most entertaining are fairly reliable sources of models of bad behavior. Stories where all the characters present imitation-worthy models don't often sell. We can not look to the entertainment industry or the communications media in general to provide psychoeducation. In fact, the negative psychoeducation of violent models in the media does great harm to humanity (regarding the media in general, see Bushman and Anderson, (2001); regarding videogames, see Anderson and Bushman, (2001)).

That said: within the vast store of fiction, biography, history, and other narratives that humanity has created so far, there are embedded countless positive models, many of which are more moving or interesting than those constructed purely for didactic purposes. If a wise and discriminating editor searches for them conscientiously and selects examples for attention, they are quite useful for psychological skill-building. An example of such an anthology is Greer and Kohl (1995); an example of a guidebook describing sources of positive models in literature is Kilpatrick et al. (1994).

Joseph Strayhorn and Jillian Strayhorn have ventured into the "skillization" of novels, i.e. asking questions about a novel that directs the learner's attention to the skills concepts that the characters illustrate. *Psychological Skill Questions on Novels* (Strayhorn and Strayhorn, 2014) is used in our psychoeducational tutoring along with novels that are rich in positive models. There is one question for each page of the novel, linking some thought or behavior or emotion to a psychological skills concept, i.e. the sixteen skills, the twelve thoughts, four ways of listening, and so forth.

I feel very confident that we cannot simply sit back and count on the entertainment and literary products of our culture to provide positive psychoeducation; I feel fairly confident that the net effect of the entertainment media as a whole is negative. But I am also confident that embedded in the media is a vast repository of psychological skill examples which can be very useful, if the additional labor is available to select them and examine them.

Via religious education

Anyone (such as myself) who promotes psychoeducation is tempted to think of it with terms such as new, modern, and innovative. But religious education has been going on for millenia, and at its best, it embodies many of the characteristics I list as important for psychoeducation:

1. participation of nonprofessionals as educators
2. use of written curricula
3. long-term and frequent participation without a discrete stop date, rather than a small dose delivered once
4. focus on skills and principles that make human society better, such as loving kindness, forgiveness, and self-discipline.
5. positive models and positive rehearsals
6. rituals for reminder of certain principles, that are akin to psychological skills exercises
7. promotion of socialization and social networking

This list sounds like perfect conditions for psychoeducation. But religion is carried out by human beings, and human beings have the capacity to misuse any set of ideas. People can harness their religious fervor to deny or suppress scientific findings, commit tribalistic atrocities against an outgroup of infidels, and in many other harmful ways.

It can be argued (and I would agree) that progress in applied ethics and psychoeducation is most likely to occur when the way to resolve disagreements is careful scientific observation rather than interpretation of ancient scriptures or having personal revelations of God's will. This is not to say that scientific methods can not also be misapplied in harmful ways. To mention a couple of misuses, there have been pain and suffering needlessly inflicted upon animals, and the withholding of useful treatment from people in the interest of comparison with treatment. The "Tuskegee Study" in which antibiotics were withheld from men with syphilis in a misguided attempt to establish the natural history of untreated syphilis is a famous example of the latter (CDC, 2016).

In the best of worlds, scientific study of psychoeducation and the practice of religion would both borrow liberally from one another's insights, using the criterion: "What teachings and practices result in the greatest happiness and welfare for humanity (and other sentient beings)?"

By self-help books and videos and web sites

Psychological self-help books are central to the psychoeducation enterprise. They can bring about positive outcomes, without any intervention by a trained therapist. Several studies (e.g. Scogin et al., 1989; Floyd et al., 2004; Naylor et al., 2010) have reported positive effects on depression, simply by prescribing that people read the book *Feeling Good* by David Burns (1980), a popular exposition of cognitive therapy. Internet sites that educate people about cognitive behavior therapy principles have also been found effective in alleviating depression (Christensen et al., 2004).

If simply handing people psychoeducational books and giving a verbal sales pitch for them were sufficient to induce many people to actually read them, the world would be a very different place. Just as there is a need for colleges and not just college bookstores, there is a need for a social structure that successfully encourages people to read and be influenced by psychoeducational material. This need spurred the development of psychoeducational tutoring by telephone.

While some self-help books are excellent, others contain questionable advice. For example, Lee (1993, cited by Bushman, 2002), in defiance of the empirical work on the catharsis hypothesis, wrote, "Punch a pillow or a punching bag. Punch with all the frenzy you can. If you are angry at a particular person, imagine his or her face on the pillow or punching bag, and vent your rage physically and verbally. You will be doing violence to a pillow or punching bag so that you can stop doing violence to yourself by holding in poisonous anger." (p. 96) Our best evidence tells us that this advice is wrong and harmful. (Please see the discussion of the catharsis hypothesis in Chapter 3 of this book.) Two of the roles of wise, highly trained, and deeply experienced professionals are both the writing and the selection of psychological self-help literature.

With the advent of the Internet, it's tempting to become dreamy about making high quality psychoeducation available for free for everyone, and thus changing the world. But access to the information is not the rate-limiting step toward a healthy society; taking the time and energy to read it and practice it, after careful selection, is that crucial step.

By schoolteachers, with classroom groups

I have seen some teachers do a beautiful job of teaching psychological skills in classrooms; some of them have used curricula I have developed. The psychological skills curriculum can be thoroughly interwoven with instruction in reading and writing. With thoroughly trained teachers who are very enthusiastic about taking on this mission, classroom instruction can be a big success.

Indeed, "character education" and "social and emotional learning" are already allotted at least a little time in the curricula of many schools. Health courses usually discuss psychological skills.

But there are problems with trying to introduce these methods into classrooms. Many teachers have little interest or aptitude for psychological skills instruction, and requiring them to take on this mission would often induce resentment. At the time of this writing, there appears to be a great deal of anxiety in the U.S. over other countries' scoring higher than ours on standardized tests, and there is a widespread belief that standardized test scores are good predictors of the future economic competitiveness of a country. Thus lobbying for psychological skills in school curricula, when the accepted tests do not measure these skills, appears to be an uphill battle.

Another problem with carrying out psychoeducation in classrooms is that the "Magic of One-to-One" is usually not employed.

By students for other students, at school, one on one

Many studies have established the effectiveness of arrangements where students teach other students – either same-age peers, or older students teaching younger ones (Strain, 1981; Kalkowski, 1995). I have experimented with this method of psychoeducation – teaching high school students to work with first grades, teaching fifth graders to work with kindergartners and first graders, and so forth. Such methods have the advantage of providing the Magic of One-to-One. The training of tutors provides a great service to the tutors as well as to the students they will work with.

I believe that this method has huge potential (Strayhorn et al., 1993). If it becomes fully exploited, it could take its place beside telephone tutoring and parental psychoeducation as a major transformer of the human condition. But in the current climate, it's hard for schools to find time (and space) for such. diverting time from test preparation to psychological skills training appears politically very difficult. The training of the older tutors and the monitoring of their performance is quite labor-intensive. Not all older students have interest in or aptitude for tutoring. Close supervision of tutors is also needed to prevent such things as verbal abuse of tutees, or worse, or lawsuits over minor problems. The delegation of certain teaching tasks to peers or older students may be seen as a threat to the idea that teaching can only be done by trained and licensed professionals, even though the job of training and supervising tutors requires professionals of the highest order. Despite all these problems, both cross-age and same-age peer tutoring has been demonstrated to work well, for both tutors and tutees (Greenwood et al., 1984; Strain, 1981). But pulling off a transformation of school culture such that excellent peer tutoring takes place routinely is no easy feat.

It may be easier to transform preschool culture. Enlisting psychoeducational tutors to work one-to-one with preschool children would be a major undertaking, but it may not meet with such strong inertial resistance. And it could be that the preschool years are even more important than subsequent ones in getting psychological skill learning started on the right track.

By telephone tutors

This is the method of psychoeducation our organization (the Organization for Psychoeducational Tutoring) now uses. Tutors call their students often, ideally six days a week. They hold half-hour sessions by phone. They engage in alternate reading of instructional materials, psychological skills exercises, and social conversation. If the student needs training in reading, they employ a specialized curriculum to teach the child to read. The "text reading" practice, even with the students in the reading track, is with stories meant to model psychological skills.

This type of service delivery has many advantages. Geographical distance between the tutors is no barrier. With the proliferation of inexpensive phone service, our organization has (temporarily) delivered psychoeducation across international boundaries, with half a planet separating tutor and student. No one has to travel anywhere for the sessions to take place, relieving much of the burden on parents that stands in the way of psychotherapy. There is little or no time wasted outside the minutes of the actual tutoring. Tutors and students can develop strong interpersonal bonds with voice communication alone. Some students actually seem to be able to pay attention better when there is only audio communication rather than audio plus visual. One of the main advantages is that permission and consent are required only from the student and the parent, and there is no need to convince a whole school bureaucracy, or a community of possibly polarized parents, that the program is worthwhile. Continuity of relationships is much easier to ensure than with face to face tutoring – when the tutor or the student moves to a different location, usually even the phone numbers don't change.

This method is not without disadvantages. Children are usually only available in the afternoons and evenings after school, when they are tired from the school day, burdened by homework, and often still more burdened by extracurricular activities. For many of them, the idea of doing any more work than already demanded by school is very difficult to sell. For the tutor, the sessions interrupt evening social activities or homework; we refer to being a telephone tutor as "wearing the ball and chain." Medical insurance tends to induce a mindset in consumers that after paying large premiums, they do not want to pay any more for mental-health related educational services, even if the rates are so low that the organization runs at a loss. Perhaps the largest disadvantage of telephone tutoring is that it becomes most feasible only when children are about 5 or 6 years old. The years from 0 to 5 may turn out to be even more crucial than the later years in teaching psychological skills.

Chapter 6: Service Delivery Methods

There are formidable problems with each of these methods of service delivery. This is not surprising; if there were a method with no problems, it probably would have already blossomed into a widely used and effective way of improving the mental health of society. However, the goal is too important not to take advantage of any of these delivery methods. With a critical mass of positive results accumulated, perhaps people will find ways to build more psychoeducation into all of the above possible arenas.

Chapter 7: Does Psychoeducation Work? The Evidence Base

There are thousands of studies in which investigators have taught psychological skills and measured the outcomes, often in comparison to a randomly selected comparison group. To review all the research on this would require a very large volume, or perhaps a large set of volumes. Upon reading a great deal of this research, my conclusion is as follows:

A. When you teach people skills, they tend to learn them, especially if you teach them well.
B. When people learn those skills that wise people think will be very useful to them, the learners' lives tend to be improved.
C. Most studies have used small doses of training; probably lots more good could be done by lots more training.

In the world of "therapy" and "the health professions," it is usual to insist upon the same sorts of research designs that are appropriate for drug trials, and to have the same sort of "ineffective or harmful until proven otherwise" mentality that is very appropriate for a drug. We appear not to have that attitude toward academic education. Why do we not require a randomized, placebo-controlled trial of every mathematics textbook that is published? Why don't we assume that that particular text is not "evidence-based" until such trials are done? What mathematics teachers do seems reasonable: they examine the contents of the book, asking the questions, "Is this what I want my students to learn?" and "Is it explained clearly?" They examine the problems, asking the question, "Do these exercises represent the skill set that I want students to have as a result of this course?" They assume that we do not have to reinvent the wheel by proving that the ordinary methods of education work: i.e. reading instructions and models of problem-solving and doing exercises, under conditions where students are motivated, where the course material is a logical next step in the hierarchy given their current skill set, where students are reinforced and not punished for learning the skills, where the relationship between students and the teacher is decently positive – etc. And yet, without many randomized, placebo-controlled trials, our ability to teach mathematics, at least with some learners, seems to have reached a high level. Similarly, we seem to be able to turn out excellent sports performers and musical performers, singers, dancers, etc. without meta-analyses of many randomized controlled studies of how to educate such performers.

I'm suggesting that some day our methods for evaluating psychoeducation may be altered so as to take into account that we already have discovered a few things about how to do "education" in general, that don't need to be demonstrated over again for every area of content.

But the purpose of this chapter is to arrange a "convenience sample" of studies, using the traditional methodology, for the purpose of demonstrating that psychoeducation "works." In this chapter I'm leaving out studies of academic tutoring; I'm focusing on psychological skills other than academic competence. I have looked for the newer articles, which reference older ones. But the older studies are still very relevant. One recommended source for them is the book, *Teaching Psychological Skills: Models for Giving Psychology Away*, by Larson (1984). This book, in keeping with the generosity implied in its title, has been placed in full text on the Internet and is accessible at no cost. It references hundreds of studies on psychoeducation.

Insomnia, anxiety, depression, obsessive-compulsive disorder

Some of the literature on tests of psychoeducation go under the label of CBT, or cognitive behavior therapy. My book on anxiety-reduction (Strayhorn, 2012) includes a chapter on suggestions for overcoming insomnia. These suggestions were gleaned from a number of studies of CBT for insomnia over several decades. To mention a recent one: Manber et al. (2011) report the effectiveness of CBT for insomnia. The intervention was conducted in 7 group meetings over 9 weeks, in which the agendas were such topics as stimulus control treatment (e.g. not watching TV in bed, getting out of bed when one can't sleep) sleep restriction treatment (e.g. staying in bed few enough hours that some sleep deprivation is on your side in getting to sleep), relaxation training, scheduled worry time, and cognitive restructuring (e.g. realizing that it is not horrible if you don't get to sleep when desired). Obviously educational methods are at the heart of this intervention. From pre to post, the participants significantly reduced not only insomnia, but also depressive symptoms and suicidal ideation. The majority of participants reported that the intervention made symptoms somewhat or a lot better, with 91% reporting such improvement for insomnia. Because this was an observational study of the results of clinical intervention, and thus did not include a no-treatment or placebo control group, it would be thrown out of many meta-analyses. But these results, taken with lots of other studies done with similar sorts of recommendations, I believe should reduce to a comfortably low level our subjective probabilities that the recommendations are meaningless or worthless or placebo only. Other studies (e.g. Watanabe et al., 2011) have demonstrated the effectiveness of similar instruction, using random assignment to "treatment as usual" versus "treatment as usual plus behavioral therapy." (According to my definitions, the "behavioral therapy" was equal to psychoeducation.) de Bruin et al. (2015) report a similar intervention for adolescents, tested with a randomized design: participants were randomly assigned to an in-person group intervention, education through "guided internet therapy," or a wait-list control group. Both the in-person intervention and the internet intervention were significantly more effective than the wait-list condition, and the two active groups were not much different from each other.

We have not even come close to a complete review of the effectiveness of psychoeducation on "sleep hygiene" for relief of insomnia. Many more studies could be cited (some of which are found in the reference lists of those I have cited). The recommendations for insomnia are contained in one of 23 chapters in one of some 20 psychoeducational books used in our program. There is often a very large evidence base behind the suggestions made in our psychoeducational texts.

Another chapter in my book on anxiety reduction summarizes the technique of imagery rehearsal for nightmares. This method involves altering the plots of recalled nightmares, so as to change a horrifying story into a positive one, writing out such stories, and rehearsing them often (during waking moments). The technique is an evidence-based application of positive fantasy rehearsal. Seda et al. (2015) carried out a meta-analysis of nightmare treatment using both imagery rehearsal training and prazosin, an alpha-1 adrenergic receptor antagonist. Both treatments appeared effective to a comparable degree, with a little over 0.5 standard deviation effect size.

One of the oldest forms of psychological skill training is training in meditation and relaxation. By "old" I do not just refer to writings on "progressive muscular relaxation" by Edmund Jacobson dating from the 1920s (Jacobson, 1924, 1976), but also to more ancient techniques taught by practitioners of Buddhism, Yoga, and others. Studies of relaxation as a treatment for anxiety have been reviewed by Manzoni et al. (2008) and Pagnini et al. (2009). The former of these reviews included a meta-analysis yielding an effect size of Cohen's $d = 0.57$, which the authors referred to as medium-large.

Seligman and Ollendick (2012) review CBT for anxiety in youth. "Effect sizes from randomized controlled trials are generally large, and posttreatment assessments suggest that approximately two out of three children treated with CBT can expect to be free of their primary diagnosis with a course of treatment that usually lasts between 12 and 16 weeks. Maintenance of treatment gains, and in some cases, further improvement, can seen in studies that follow treated youth up to nine years post treatment." (p. 3) These authors attest to the psychoeducational nature of CBT for anxiety: "CBT is a skills building approach. This means that clinicians are directive and sessions may appear very didactic. However, sessions are seen only as an initial step in the learning process. Meetings with the child and/or parents are used to introduce skills, provide initial practice and problem-solve; however, homework assignments outside of session provide the repeated practice required for complete skill acquisition and refinement. Moreover, given the importance of the context in which the anxious behavior occurs in behavioral theory, it necessarily follows that CBT for child anxiety often introduces new skills for parents, teachers, and sometimes even siblings or peers." (p. 3)

Because CBT therapists are sometimes in scarce supply, "computerized CBT" interventions have been formed. The phrase "computerized CBT" gives a clue that something akin to programmed instruction is usually taking place. Kaltenthaler (2006) has reviewed computerized CBT for depression, anxiety, phobias, panic, and obsessive-compulsive disorder. The results are mixed, but the overall conclusion is that computerized CBT usually is better than no treatment at all. Dettore et al. (2015) report a meta-analysis of randomized clinical trials of education for obsessive compulsive disorder, delivered by technology such as the Internet. Techology-delivered CBT was superior to control conditions; the difference between therapist-delivered and technology delivered CBT failed to reach statistical significance, although the therapists' outcomes were numerically better. (This analysis is consistent with my hypothesis that self-directed education is good, and education in the context of a positive relationship is usually better.) Donker et al. (2009) report a meta-analysis of "passive psychoeducation" for depression and anxiety – the giving out of leaflets or sending of emails or having very brief educational exposure. The effect size was small, but positive and statistically significant. This analysis is consistent with the idea that giving "drop in the bucket" interventions can yield small positive effects, enough to be statistically significant, although probably seldom life-changing. Tursi et al. (2013) review 15 studies of psychoeducation for depression, and report that the studies "suggest" that "Psychoeducation is effective in improving the clinical course, treatment adherence, and psychosocial functioning of depressive patients."

On the subject of depression, the term "bibliotherapy" is another index word that leads us to studies of psychoeducation. I have previously mentioned studies (Scogin et al., 1989; Floyd et al., 2004; Naylor et al., 2010) in which the intervention for depression was to assign adult patients to read David Burns' book, *Feeling Good* (1980); results appear to demonstrate that this psychoeducational intervention is effective.

A different psychoeducational intervention for depression involves teaching family members of a depressed individual how to prevent relapse. Shimodera et al. (2012) report an intervention for family members involving 4 two-hour group sessions. "A video tape and a textbook explaining depression and its treatment were prepared for this study and were used as teaching materials. The next 60–90 minutes were devoted to group discussion and problem solving for emotionally difficult situations experienced by participating families." (p 2). The intervention group ("treatment as usual plus family psychoeducation) enjoyed an average of 272 relapse-free days, whereas the control group ("treatment as usual" only) enjoyed an average of 214 such days; this difference was statistically different at the 0.002 level.

Stallard et al. (2015) report on a psychoeducational anxiety-preventive intervention delivered in 45 schools to whole classrooms of 9 and 10 year olds. There were three groups: training delivered by outside health professionals, training delivered by school personnel, and usual school activities, i.e. no training. Training consisted of nine one hour sessions, one session per week. After 12 months, there was a significant difference in anxiety scores among the health-professional trained children and the children who were not trained; after 24 months there were no longer any between-group significant differences, although all groups were less anxious than at the beginning. The authors conclude from this that "We found little evidence to justify the widespread use of universal anxiety prevention programmes in schools." (p. xv). This conclusion is interesting in view of our previous discussion of time on task, and the tendency for psychoeducational and psychotherapeutic intervention studies to base their conclusions on "drops in the bucket."Is it reasonable to expect 9 hours of training to continue to show effects 2 years later? Would we expect that 9 hours of foreign language training, or piano instruction, or math lessons, with no further education, would result in increased competence as measured 2 years later? If we found significant differences after one year but not two, which would we conclude: that the training was not worth the effort, or that it needed to be done for a longer time? The time on task variable is very important in these outcome studies.

Disruptive disorders, parent training

Forehand et al. (2014) state, "The goal of BPT [behavioral parent training] is to decrease coercive interchanges and, as a consequence, youth externalizing problems by teaching parents how to use their attention and other positive contingencies they control, provide structure, and, when inappropriate child behavior is emitted, apply effective discipline." Often parents are unaware of how they reinforce aggressive or hostile behavior in their children. Properly done psychoeducation helps parents to use the reinforcers they control in the service of strengthening positive behavior, to give commands in a way most likely to be followed by compliance, to give positive models, and other techniques that spring from straightforward learning theory. Forehand et al. (2014) state, "Behavioral parent training (BPT) has been identified repeatedly as an evidence-based treatment for the prevention and treatment of both disruptive behaviors and ADHD;" following this statement are references for 14 review articles in support. Kato et al. (2015) in another review article, argue that "population-level parenting interventions can lower the prevalence of mental health problems among children in the community."

Behavioral parent training has a long history of using technology such as video-recorded models for didactic purposes and video recordings of behavior by participants for monitoring and feedback. The state of technological aids to parent training is reviewed by Jones et al. (2013). An example of an outcome study of technology-assisted parent training is a study by Sourander et al. (2016) targeting disruptive behavior problems in 4 year olds. These researchers used an Internet-assisted training program, with weekly telephone coaching. Positive results were reported with respect to the Child Behavior Checklist total score and almost all the subscales (including both internalizing and externalizing).

Another method of delivering support and psychoeducation to parents is home visiting, usually by nurses, often with the desired outcome being the reduction of child maltreatment. According to Constantino (2016) "The list of child and adolescent psychiatric conditions that are caused or exacerbated by child maltreatment is long, and it can be argued that of all of the influences on child mental disorders, most which are genetic, child maltreatment is the single preventable cause with the highest associated disease burden, approaching 20% or more of the population-attributable risk for all psychiatric conditions of childhood." HomVEE, or Home Visiting Evidence of Effectiveness, a group supported by several U.S. agencies, "identified 17 home visiting models that meet the DHHS [Department of Health and Human Services] criteria for an evidence-based early childhood home visiting service delivery model." (Avellar et al., 2014). According to Constantino (2016), "The Nurse Family Partnership model advanced by David Olds and colleagues [Donelan-McCall et al., 2009] has achieved the strongest evidence base with 1 order of magnitude reductions in the incidence of child maltreatment among at-risk groups."

The National Collaborative Centre for Mental Health (2013) reviewed 202 randomized clinical trials aimed at treating or preventing antisocial and conduct disorders in youth. These include many parenting interventions, but also classroom, family, and individual-based interventions, most of which appear to be highly psychoeducational. According to this massive review, "As the following chapters show, there are scores of randomised controlled trials (RCTs) suggesting that [parent training] is effective for children up to about 10 years old." (p. 31).

Arnold Goldstein and his colleagues devoted many years to refining and testing psychoeducational approaches to antisocial behavior and aggression. Training methods emphasized direct teaching of prosocial behaviors, through modeling, role-playing, performance feedback, and generalization training. Goldstein and Glick (1994) reviewed some of the outcome studies completed to that date. One study of a successful intervention was carried out with intact gang groups. Findings included that that "Five of the 38 ART [Aggression Replacement Training] participants (13%) and 14 of the 27 control group members (52%) were rearrested during the 8-month tracking period (chi square = 6.08, p < .01)."

Hodgins and Peden (2008) review cognitive behavior therapy for impulse control problems: compulsive buying, compulsive gambling, and kleptomania. Although the research in these areas are not as developed as in some others, "There is a general consensus in the literature that cognitive-behavioral therapies offer an effective model for intervention for all these disorders." (p. S31).

Social skills training

Tse et al. (2007) report on social skills training for 13 to 18 year olds with Asperger Syndrome and high functioning autism, in a study without a control group. Participants met in a group, for 12 weeks, with one 1.5 hour session per week. Emphasis was on role-played practice of social skills. There was a significant improvement pre to post, both in measures of social competence and in problem behaviors. Reichow et al. (2013) review randomized controlled studies of social skills groups for autistic youth.

There is evidence that such training increases social competence and friendship quality, and decreases loneliness, with effect sizes in the region of half a standard deviation.

Marital satisfaction

Harmony between members of a couple is a protective factor against mental disorder in both children and the members of the couple themselves, just as discord and conflict are risk factors. Halford and Bodenmann (2013) review the effects of "relationship education" on couple satisfaction. These authors reviewed 17 studies evaluating relationship education that had follow-ups of at least one year; 14 of those studies found that relationship education helped maintain satisfaction with the relationship.

Schizophrenia

Xia et al. (2014) report a large review of psychoeducation for schizophrenia, examining 44 trials with 5142 participants. For the psychoeducation groups, noncompliance with treatment was lower, relapse and readmissions were lower, social and global functioning was higher, satisfaction with mental health services was higher, and quality of life was higher.

Executive function and decision-making

Kray et al. (2012) report that four sessions of task-switching training with children with ADHD improved executive functioning in those children, as measured by neuropsychological tasks. Whether task-switching training can generalize to better decisions and better organization in real life remains to be seen.

One of the major aspects of executive functioning is decision-making and problem-solving. Chang et al. (2004) give book length treatment to research on training in social problem-solving skills. Such research began in earnest in the 1970s; Spivack et al. (1976) is an example of this work. Many children who have psychological difficulties, when presented with real-life or hypothetical problem situations, can think of no more than one option. And when presented with an option, they can think of very few pros or cons for that option. The data strongly suggest that option-generating and generating of pros and cons are teachable skills, and that teaching them results in better decisions in real life.

Conclusion

The books and articles I have cited in this chapter are an inadequate representation of the total data base on the outcomes of teaching people psychological skills. But even the studies I cite here, and much more so the studies cited in those works, do begin to convey that many, many people have taught psychological skills and have demonstrated positive outcomes.

As I review these studies, I continue to note the altogether unsurprising finding that the time on tasks for the average intervention is of much shorter duration than what would be necessary to teach a foreign language, a musical instrument, mathematics, or other skills that are much less crucial to humanity than psychological skills. I take the evidence we have accumulated so far to suggest (and not to prove) that if we really made a serious investment of time into a broad-based psychoeducational intervention lasting years, the outcomes could be much more dramatic.

Chapter 8: Academic Skills Training To Foster Psychological Growth

Competent individual tutoring is the most reliable way to increase academic skill

Common sense observations would suggest that when a teacher can: customize the degree of difficulty of challenges to the individual student, give immediate feedback on the student's performance, intersperse relationship-building activities without worrying about getting a whole group off track, and permit the learner to ask questions and make comments without needing to ration the time among other students – then learning is maximally effective. These things can happen in individual tutoring. A classic article by Benjamin Bloom (1984) speaks of the "two sigma problem," or "the search for group instruction methods as effective as one-to-one tutoring. Bloom cites findings comparing learning with different instructional methods, one of which was individual tutoring. "Using the standard deviation (sigma) of the control (conventional) class, it was typically found that the average student under tutoring was about two standard deviations above the average of the control class (the average tutored student was above 98% of the students in the control class)."(p. 4)

Academic gains from tutoring have been found to exceed those from group instruction even when the tutors are not expert – in fact even in a version of peer tutoring in which elementary school students are randomly divided into pairs and one student tutors the other, and then they switch roles (Greenwood et al., 1984).

From many studies of individual tutoring, and from many experiences with children, I have come to refer to the "magic of one-to-one" interaction. One of those experiences was a study a colleague and I did in which both classroom teachers and individual tutors rated the behaviors of the same children. The improvement of behavior upon going from the classroom to the one-to-one situation was about as large with respect to

ADHD symptoms as is the typical improvement resulting from anti-ADHD medication (Strayhorn & Bickel, 2002).

The relation of academic skills to mental health outcomes

It has long been known that lower IQ scores predict delinquency in youth (Moffitt et al., 1981; Lynam and Henry, 2001). Because reading ability is more subject to change than is IQ, a study by Stanton et al. (1990) gave reason for optimism in preventing delinquency by reading instruction. This study found that both reading ability and IQ were correlated with behavior problem ratings. However, "Reading scores accounted for a larger proportion of the variance in the later behavior problem scores than did school-age IQ scores, and when reading ability was entered in the regression equation before IQ, then reading but not IQ significantly predicted change in problem behavior during the primary school years."

Another study (Coie and Krehbiel, 1984) actually randomly assigned low-achieving, socially-rejected children to groups for academic skills training, social skills training, combination, and control groups. The academic skills training group seemed to improve dramatically in behavior, and also in social skills! The authors stated, "Findings... support ... strategies of intervention that leave less opportunity for disruptive behavior by refocusing children on the successful performance of classroom tasks, ... reading and mathematics." (p. 1476)

Causal arrows, all of which probably operate

Why would academic skills and psychological skills be correlated? First, children who cannot read or do math well tend not to enjoy school. They tend to be less reinforced by teachers, and they find academic tasks unpleasant to do. All of these factors tend to dispose them to what I have called the "frustrate the authority game" and away from the "meet the challenge game."

Causality in the other direction also is likely to be prominent. The child who has deficiencies in productivity, concentration, and persistence will be handicapped for academic learning. Children with social skill deficiencies often tend to get involved in negative interactions that distract them from schoolwork, or to experience loneliness that also interferes with productivity.

"Work therapy": how working on academic skills can grow mental health skills

If we could magically turn children into proficient readers by the wave of a wand, we would expect greater happiness and cooperation in school by the mechanisms we just mentioned. However, there are also benefits in the arduous process of becoming a better reader. The student practices compliance skills each day in doing reading exercises. If the exercises are at the correct level on the hierarchy of difficulty, the student gets the chance to make the life-changing discovery that work at the correct level can be reasonably fun. As the student repeatedly hears the tutor's approving voice while doing the exercises, the student may internalize that voice, and become more expert at the crucial skill of self-reinforcement. If the student gradually expands the amount of work that can be done each day, the student grows in work capacity. If the tutor does the more tedious exercises first and follows them with more pleasant activities, the student may learn to use the "Premack Principle" in other tasks, letting the more pleasant activities reinforce the less pleasant ones by arranging the order of tasks from least pleasant to more pleasant. If the student discovers that by doing some hard work for many days on reading exercises, the skills develop so that a whole new world of very pleasant reading experiences open up for the student, very important pieces of learning have taken place: delay of gratification really can be a good strategy, and the effort-payoff connection can be real. The student, who has been implicitly or explicitly asked by the tutor to keep working and trust that the work will eventually pay off, learns that trusting another human being does not always lead to getting burned. If the student perceives that the tutor takes genuine pleasure in the student's achievement, the student gets a powerful model of kindness and caring.

For all these reasons, the experience of being taught to read by a caring and patient and enthusiastic tutor can do wonders for a student's mental health.

In a spirit of paranoia evoked by legal regulations regarding licensure, I hasten to point out that such mental-health enhancing intervention is not psychotherapy, counseling, or psychological services, and that tutors are not psychologists or counselors. If from time to time, for certain individuals, educational interventions happen to bring about as much or more improvement in global mental health than psychotherapeutic interventions can, perhaps tutoring organizations will not be prosecuted for that.

Big ideas in reading instruction

How do we teach reading well? The following are some principles, some "big ideas," mainly discovered by others, that we have found useful over several thousand hours of reading instruction.

1. A positive relationship is crucial. It is much easier for students to learn from people they like, admire, and/or respect.

2. The tutor's tone of voice is crucial. If the tutor sounds enthusiastic, approving, and alive, the tutor is much more likely to succeed than otherwise.

3. Work at points on the hierarchy of difficulty where the student can get at least 80% correct, if not 100% correct. "Errorless" learning, or something close to it, gives the learner the fewest memory traces that need to be crossed out in the mind. Plus, success feels good.

4. Phonemic awareness is a crucial foundation skill. This is the ability to hear buh-aah-tuh and guess that the word is bat, or to take the word bat and break it down into buh-aah-tuh. Some children seem to have this skill from an early age; with others, structured exercises will teach them the skill.

5. Spatial awareness, or the ability to distinguish images from their reversed images, such as lower case b and d, and to distinguish was from saw, is another skill that can be systematically taught if need be, starting with very easy exercises and working the way up. Examples of easy exercises are

saying whether pairs of arrows are pointing in the same or different directions; saying whether pictures are identical or mirror images of one another; and saying whether pairs of letters such as bb and bd are the same or different.

6. It's useful for the learner to memorize the most common sounds of the 26 letters of the English alphabet. "Letter stories" and "letter sound songs" make this task less tedious.

7. The exercise of "sounding and blending" is extremely useful in teaching reading. The student says aloud the sounds of the individual letters, or letter combinations that make one sound (these one-sound symbols are called phonemes), going from left to right. Then the learner blends the sounds together to say the word.

8. It's very useful to separate commonly used words into groups, or lists, where the phonetic principle is the same, so as to minimize "interference" with memory. For example, we can't help the fact that in English, ea makes the long e sound in team, leap, neat, each, and so forth, and that ea makes the long a sound in great, break, steak, and so forth. But at least we can have the learner practice with word lists such that in any given list, the ea makes the same sound.

9. In order to move down the hierarchy with sounding and blending, "sound and blend after me" is a very useful step. The tutor sounds and blends a word, and the student does the same thing with the same word immediately afterward. Later the student will "sound and blend on your own."

10. For sounding and blending, and other tasks that are hard work, it's important for the tutor to pick a length of time for the activity that is close to "just right" for the student's work capacity. If the tutor only stops the activity when the student starts to whine, the tutor is reinforcing whining and protest about work. Often 10 minutes a day of sounding and blending per day, every day, is enough for rather miraculous-seeming changes.

11. Meaningful text with interesting stories should be available close to the beginning of the enterprise, with the words in the easiest stories being the same as those in the easiest word lists.

12. When the student makes mistakes, the tutor should simply tell the student the answer and let the student give it again, rather than trying to pull the correct answer out of the student. Asking the same question repeatedly when the student doesn't know the answer makes tutoring very unpleasant for the learner, and is a very frequent behavior of untrained tutors.

13. Using a tally counter to keep track of the sounding and blending points and the text reading points for each session, and the cumulative points for the whole enterprise, and using certificates and prizes to celebrate milestones of points, increases the student's effort-payoff connection.

14. From the beginning, the stories the student is asked to read should model positive mental health skills. The reading venture and the behavioral health skills venture are done together, not as two separate activities.

15. Tests of reading recognition are usually best given fairly often (once every three or four months), as a further means of shoring up the effort-payoff connection. We have found the Slosson Oral Reading Test to be very useful. In addition, public domain tests, including the Burt and the Schonell, can be used to monitor progress. If these are used correctly, the learner will look forward to them, because their results will be cause for great celebration of progress.

16. Reading aloud, in large quantity, seems to be an almost magical way to increase reading skill. The feedback that the student gets from hearing the words on the page seems to do something for many students that silent reading may not do. In addition, reading aloud seems to have benefits for speaking ability.

17. The skill of reading comprehension benefits greatly from a) having materials interesting enough that the reader actually wants to understand

them, b) letting the reader practice answering comprehension questions over reading, and c) letting the reader practice paraphrasing or reflecting what was read.

Some big ideas in teaching math

1. As with most other subjects, math can be lots of fun if the learner is working at the correct point on the hierarchy of difficulty. If it's not fun, adjustments should be made. Individually administered tests are a good way of finding out where the learner is on the hierarchy; some of them do a very good job of presenting hierarchically arranged challenges. The KeyMath Test (Connolly, 2007) is a detailed test for elementary and middle school ages. A quicker test is the math subscale of the Peabody Individual Achievement Test (Markwardt, 1997).

2. It's very useful for the learner to use things that give visual representations of numbers: measuring sticks, weighing scales, dice, dominoes, playing cards, stop watches, other watches, number lines, Cuisenaire rods, etc.

3. There are lots of fun games that can increase math skills through play. Peggy Kaye's book *Games for Math* (Kaye,1987) is excellent in teaching tutors to use games to teach math.

      Math games can be arranged on a hierarchy of complexity and difficulty. For example: students can start with the game "high card wins," (a.k.a. "War") where two people draw randomly from their decks and the one with the higher card wins both. They can progress to "high sum wins," where they play two cards, and the one with the higher sum for both wins all four cards. More complex is "high sum wins, and one person gets to pick." Both people are dealt a bunch of cards, that they can look at. The tutor puts out a pair of cards, and the student gets to pick which pair of cards to play against them. Figuring out the strategy of picking cards so as to just barely beat the other sum, rather than wasting your higher cards when you don't need them, is an important mathematical "light bulb" experience.

      "Mystery number" is an example of a cooperative math game. One person picks a number, say between 0 and 100, and the other tries to guess it in as few guesses as possible, with the feedback after each guess being whether the right answer is lower or higher than the guess. After a while, and with modeling, the learner may come to the insight that the best strategy is to guess in the middle of the permissible number range, so as to eliminate the largest number of possibilities with each guess.

"Dice and chips" gives practice in addition and in place value. The players take turns rolling one, two, or three dice; they get points based on the sum of the numbers showing. The points are given in the form of chips, where whites represent ones, reds tens, and blues hundreds. When players get ten or more whites or reds, they can exchange for the correct number of reds or blues.

The game of blackjack, played with the ordinary rules, with betting of chips at the ordinary choice points, is another math game that involves addition as well as estimation of probabilities.

4. Many math learners never read the explanations or sample problems in their textbooks, if they even have textbooks. They go straight to problem sets, with the goal of finishing homework as quickly as possible. Taking the time to read, even to read aloud, explanations of mathematical ideas can have a large payoff. This is the premise of my book, *Reading about Math*, (Strayhorn, 2012) which is all explanation. It has reading comprehension questions after each section instead of math problems. Math problems are crucial for skill growth, but it is sometimes good to be able to sit back and think about what's going on, independent of doing problems.

5. Many math students lack fluency with the basic math facts: 7×8, 15-9, 42/7, 9+8, and so forth. Despite the advent of calculators, it is a tremendous advantage for a math student to be able to do elementary mental calculations far more quickly than they can be entered into a calculator.

It appears to me that many schools put lots of pressure on for speed in math facts for a short time, after which the curriculum moves on to other subjects and knowledge of math facts is assumed. The time pressure sometimes induces anxiety in students, without the student ever becoming fully competent in this rather prodigious act of memory.

The "standards" type of thinking tends to make many students nervous about time trials in math facts: there is a certain standard, and I am flunking it. A switch to "hierarchy" type thinking casts time trials in a different light. I started at this speed, I increased to this, I got even faster, hooray, each of these is a major cause for celebration. This is the idea behind one of the major activities of "precision teaching": the learner does lots of time trials, but primarily compares performance to the learner's own baseline performance, not to a passing or failing level. "Mastery learning" means that the time the learner takes to achieve a certain standard is variable, and the eventual mastery is specified, rather than dealing with a subject for a fixed length of time and letting the degree of competence be what varies, as reported by grades.

Math facts drill is tedious enough that it should not last for a long time each day. But it is important enough that it should be spread over a long enough time that the student masters it. Three to five minutes each day for a long time may provide great benefit to the student's ultimate mathematical achievement.

When doing math facts drill, a key idea is not to bite off too large a chunk of different facts to practice with in any one practice session. Practicing with too many at once produces too much "interference" with memory. To get faster progress, practice with a small enough number of facts at any given time that this limited set can be done with automaticity by the end of the practice session.

A strategy for learning math facts is the "broken number line method," described in a book I wrote (Strayhorn, 2016). Broken number lines provide visual aids that enable the math facts to be inferred while drilling; they also enable the learner to gain in "number sense" by having a visual representation of the numbers that one is dealing with. Here's an example of a number line broken after the number 5:

```
1   2   3   4   5
6   7   8   9   10
```

If you want to add 5 + 2, for example, you can start at 5 and make 2 jumps in the direction of greater numbers. You land on 7. But it's no coincidence that the answer is under the 2, the number you added to 5. For 5+3, the answer is under the 3; for 5+1 it's under the 1, and so forth. Thus you can look at this number line and say the "5 pluses" with ease. When you look at a page of broken number lines, drill with all the addition and subtraction facts is made much easier. Similar setups can be made for multiplication and division facts. These broken number lines provide a way station between not knowing the facts and knowing them with enough automaticity so that no visual aid is needed.

6. Math is a very cumulative activity: many bits of progress rely on mastery of prior concepts and skills. It's hard to simplify algebraic fractions involving literal numbers, for example, if one has never really understood simplifying numerical fractions such as 4/6. Thus it makes sense to keep working on skills until mastery is not only achieved, but also maintained, and not moving on prematurely to new concepts when the more foundation-level ones still need work. This is called the "mastery learning" approach. This is very different from the more common school strategy of having a set curriculum which is covered at a set speed. Obviously the mastery learning strategy is easier in individual tutoring than in classroom instruction. But a great deal of individual math tutoring squanders this advantage by trying to help the learner with homework from school, often disregarding the fact that the learner should be spending time on the prerequisite knowledge for that homework.

Some big ideas in teaching writing

1. Writing involves harnessing several skills at once. If you ask the learner to do all these well at once, before the learner is ready, you can provide a very frustrating and unpleasant experience for the learner.

What are these several skills? There's the physical act of putting letters on a page, either through typing or handwriting. There's spelling the words correctly. There's using correct grammar, capitalization, and punctuation. There's coming up with something reasonable to say, not only in your own mind, but to the mind of the teacher judging your work. There's figuring out how to organize and order the bits of information in the composition. And in many schools there's avoiding the crime of plagiarism while still telling about something you have no first hand knowledge of, while simultaneously avoiding quoting too much! There's figuring out how to follow the conventions of citations and references, according to an arbitrary rule book. And there may be a bunch of arbitrary rules enforced by a teacher, about the location of a thesis sentence, rules against posing questions to the reader, and so forth.

Almost all beginning writers go through a stage where it is impossible to do all these things well. Trying to do them all well at once tends to result in uncontrollable punishment, which leads to demoralization, "learned helplessness," and writer's block.

The antidote to such unfortunate teaching is to focus on one thing at a time. Each of the skills I listed above can take lots of time to develop. If the learner can move along a hierarchy for each one of them, then some day the learner is ready to put them all together. But that day should not be rushed. And each of those separate skills should be practiced enough that it becomes automatic.

2. Until the learner has achieved mastery of typing or handwriting, spelling, and grammar, capitalization, and punctuation, the learner can get great practice at various of the other skills by dictating to someone who quickly and efficiently makes the words and sentences appear.

3. As soon as the student is learning to read and spell, the student can start learning how to type, using the correct fingers on each of the keys. When the finger placement is standard from the beginning, the learner can get automaticity in typing. Six years old is not too early to start teaching this skill.

4. The psychological skills exercises, which we will discuss later, can almost all be done in writing as well as orally. These make excellent writing exercises. The student who has learned to do them orally can make a natural progression from that to dictating them, to writing them out.

5. It's nice if written work actually is useful for other people to read, not just for a teacher to slap a grade onto. This is what writing is for: to communicate

to others, not just to jump through a hoop and get approval, after which the written work is thrown away.

One of the psychological skills exercises is the "celebrations exercise," where one narrates something one is glad to have done, and decides which psychological skills that behavior is an example of. Another is "skills stories," where the student makes up positive examples of the various psychological skills. Another is the "social conversation role play," where the student makes up either half or all of a dialogue between two people who are getting to know each other better. Another is the "conflict resolution role play," where two people are both rational and cooperative while negotiating in a conflict situation. All these exercises, if written, could be compiled into archives which then serve as examples for the next class of students. It is very conceivable to develop a growing bank of positive examples, from the written versions of the psychological skills exercises. If the learner feels that she is contributing to a useful volume rather than just doing an assignment, the task takes on much greater meaning.

6. In the context of telephone tutoring, it is now easy to use the internet to put both tutor and student on one written page. Google Docs is one way to do this at no expense. Dictation, typing exercises, and other writing exercises can be done as a social activity rather than as a solitary one, and for many learners this difference is crucial.

Not just achievement, but pleasure in achievement

What's the goal of academic training? In the current climate in the U.S., among many the answer seems to be "high test scores." Or even, "high test scores relative to other nations we fear as economic competitors."

But the goals of academic teaching (as well as mental health skills teaching) should include not just a high performance by the learner. They should also include the emotional associations the learner has to the entire learning enterprise, and to the specific subject matter being worked on. Does a given course increase, or decrease the student's appetite for future learning in that area? If the student learns to take pleasure from the subject matter, the student will be much more likely to study the subject later on, and the skill level is likely to improve further. On the other hand, if the student has been pushed to the point of revulsion, a high achievement level will not make up for the harm done if the student is motivated to avoid the learning activities from then on.

Reading, writing, and math can be extremely pleasant activities, if the instructors make the right decisions. And the conditioned associations that develop under these circumstances may be even more important than the skill acquisition itself.

Chapter 9: Programmed Instruction and "Alternate Reading"

Programmed instruction begins

In 1958, B.F. Skinner wrote an article for Science magazine entitled "Teaching Machines." Skinner argued for the importance of the "productive interchange between teacher and student in the small classroom or tutorial situation." He decried the student's role as a "mere passive receiver of instruction," and looked for technology that would "encourage the student to take an active role in the instructional process."

The result was the use of teaching machines to deliver programmed instruction. A body of information was broken down into a series of small sections called frames. Each frame typically both presented information and required the learner to answer a question, for example by supplying a missing word in a sentence.

The following is an example of a small segment of programmed instruction in physics, that Skinner supplied in his 1958 article. The word to be supplied is in parentheses after the sentence.

1. The important parts of a flashlight are the battery and the bulb. When we "turn on" a flashlight, we close a switch which connects the battery with the _____. (bulb)
2. When we turn on a flashlight, an electric current flows through the fine wire in the _____ and causes it to grow hot. (bulb)
3. When the hot wire glows brightly, we say that it gives off or sends out heat and _____. (light)
4. The fine wire in the bulb is called a filament. The bulb "lights up" when the filament is heated by the passage of a(n) _____ current. (electric)
5. When a weak battery produces little current, the fine wire, or_____, does not get very hot. (filament)
6. A filament which is less hot sends out or gives off ____light. (less)

95

7. "Emit" means "send out." The amount of light sent out, or "emitted," by a filament depends on how _____ the filament is. (hot)

What are the advantages of such an approach? Skinner (1958) lists several: "The student is always alert and busy." "Like a good tutor, the machine insists that a given point be thoroughly understood, either frame by frame or set by set, before the student moves on." "Like a skillful tutor the machine helps the student to come up with the right answer. It does this in part through the orderly construction of the program...." "The machine, like the private tutor, reinforces the student for every correct response, using this immediate feedback not only to shape his behavior most efficiently but to maintain it in strength in a manner which the layman would describe as 'holding the student's interest.'"

One of the major differences between the questions composed in programmed instruction and those composed by test-makers is the attitude toward incorrect answers on the part of the student. In Skinner's view, "It is a salutary thing to try to guarantee a right response at every step in the presentation of a subject matter." Incorrect responses on the part of the learner represent practices of giving incorrect information, and are to be minimized. In the college classroom, however, a test where everyone gets nearly all questions right is usually seen as failing in its job of sorting and ranking people.

Following Skinner's enthusiastic endorsement of teaching machines and programmed instruction, there followed an era which may be called the golden era of programmed instruction, primarily in the 1960s. A good many programmed books were produced, and a large number of empirical trials of programmed instruction in comparison to "conventional teaching methods" were carried out (Lockee et al., 2004). As Lockee et al. point out, such research is very difficult to draw conclusions from, since there can be tremendous variation within both "programmed instruction" and "conventional methods" with respect to what is done. Nonetheless, there was a great deal of enthusiasm for programmed instruction as the wave of the future. Skinner (1986) writes, "I was soon saying that, with the help of teaching machines and programmed instruction, students could learn twice as much in the same time and with the same effort as in a standard classroom." But the empirical evidence for this ratio was hard to pin down.

Ironically, interest in programmed instruction seemed to fade, just prior to the widespread availability of the invention that would make it vastly easier to provide: the personal computer. Skinner wrote in 1986 that "The small computer is the ideal hardware for programmed instruction," and noted that the teaching machines he wrote about earlier are housed in the Smithsonian. Although "programmed instruction" may seem to be a fad that has passed, in many ways it has morphed into "computer-assisted-instruction."

Problems with programmed instruction

What are the disadvantages of programmed instruction? I have worked through many programmed books, sometimes to great advantage. But it appears to me that there are some good reasons why ordinary expository prose was invented. There are some advantages to the arrangement of ideas into complete sentences (without blanks in them) and into paragraphs and bigger units rather than into small "frames." Sometimes there is continuity in the flow of ideas that gets interrupted when you have to create or fill in blanks every other sentence or so. While learning fact after fact may be easier in traditional programmed instruction, it has appeared to me that when grasping how points fit together into an argument, or how sequential events create a coherent narrative, very frequent questions can be annoying or distracting.

As the physics instruction example above illustrates, programmed instruction sometimes asks questions over information that has not been explicitly taught. For example, frame 6 says, "A filament which is less hot sends out or gives off ____ light. (less)" But the learner is really asked to rely on an educated guess or prior information to get this answer – the program has not explicitly made this point before the question is posed.

Another problem of programmed instruction has to do with the assumption that it is quite reinforcing to see the answer to the question you've just answered, and see that you got it right. This is sometimes, but not always true. Even in computer programs in which after a certain number of correct answers a cartoon animal does handsprings across the screen, how strongly is the learner reinforced? There is no question that electronic screen events can be highly reinforcing; seeing many children with big attention difficulties be spellbound by video games demonstrates this clearly. But finding a very quick way of providing screen reinforcement, such that the learning task is not experienced as interrupted by the reinforcement screen, or the reinforcement is not seen as interrupted by having to go back to learning, is still a problem in any sort of machine-directed instruction.

Alternate reading

In the brand of psychoeducational tutoring that we have devised, we have used a format of "programmed" books that has worked very nicely. In this format, there is a section of text presented, usually considerably longer than the frames of the type that Skinner used, but still able to be read aloud in a minute or two. Then, after each section, there's an "A or B" multiple choice question, often asking the learner to identify the main idea of the section. The information the learner needs to answer the question is always present in the section the learner has read. Often the two choices are constructed so as to be correct statements, but with only one of them the answer to the question that was raised. Providing a slightly longer presentation before asking the question hopefully enables the reader to integrate several sentences, thinking about how ideas combine to make an integrated whole, rather than have the fragmentation of text that programmed instruction has sometimes had.

As for the problem of how to provide adequate reinforcement for taking in and understanding a frame (or as we call them, a section) of text: we have reverted to perhaps the most basic social reinforcer: a genuine utterance of enthusiasm and approval from a human tutor. When the student gets the answer right, the tutor may say, "I agree!" or "Yes!' or "I think you got it!" When the student reads a difficult passage well, the tutor might say, "Nice reading!" When the student volunteers an interesting observation about what has just been read, the tutor might say, "Huh! Interesting point! Let me make sure I understand...."

Part of the original enthusiasm for programmed instruction was from the idea that part of the benefit of individual tutoring could be achieved by the use of machines. In our version of programmed instruction, the presentations are from books and from a real-time in-person tutor, either face-to-face or connected by phone. Thus the inventions of Gutenberg and Alexander Graham Bell are the technology we've used, in a reversion to an emphasis on human contact versus high-technology solutions.

Here's an example of the modified programmed format, in the first few sections of *A Programmed Course in Anxiety-Reduction and Courage Skills* (Strayhorn, 2012).

1. This is a book about reducing fears and aversions. What do we mean by these words?

Most people know what the word *fear* means. It's the same as being frightened, scared, or anxious. It's almost the same as being worried. When we're scared, we tend to think things like "I'm in danger; I've got to protect myself!"

Sometimes people feel scared without knowing exactly what they're afraid of. This has been called "free-floating anxiety." But for most of us, there are certain situations that make us scared. And usually there are certain bad things that we think might happen in those situations. Those bad things are called the feared outcomes.

What's one of the ideas stated in this section?

A. Fear is connected with the thought of being in danger and needing to protect yourself,

Or

B. Learning relaxation is an important way to reduce unrealistic fear?

2. What is an aversion? It's like a fear, but an aversion can involve any bad feeling, not just fear. For example, someone has an aversion to a certain food. When he thinks of this food, he doesn't really feel scared, but rather disgusted. Or someone else might have an aversion to doing math. The idea of doing math doesn't make the person feel scared, but more frustrated and confused. Someone else has a strong aversion to criticism. The criticism

tends to make the person feel angry rather than scared. An aversion is an association between a certain situation and a bad feeling.

The main idea of this section is that

A. We work to reduce aversions in the same ways we work to reduce fears, or
B. Aversions are like fears, only they can involve any bad feeling, not just fear?

3. The first step in dealing with fears and aversions is to figure out which ones we want to reduce, and which we want to hang onto. Some fears and aversions make us better off, and some make us worse off. We want to choose carefully whether we would be better off with or without the fear or aversion.

A main point of this section is that

A. An example of an aversion is someone who hates doing homework, or
B. some fears or aversions are harmful, and some are useful, and it's important to tell the difference between the two?

***

This modified programmed format can be useful for narratives as well as for expository writing. Here's a section from the "Journey Story" contained in *Programmed Readings for Psychological Skills* (Strayhorn, 2001). The story is meant to teach students to identify twelve different ways of thinking about situations, which is an important step toward doing the "twelve-thought exercise."

639. No matter where they looked, they could not find the travel box anywhere. Lilly thought, "I guess this means we're stuck here on the planet Cuckoo-Baffab until we find it. Maybe we'll be here for the rest of our lives. I sure would like to be able to go home. But if I have to, I could live here for

the rest of my life. At least I have my dad and my brother and Dr. Kuolo with me. And the people here are nice. I guess I could handle that."
Was she

A. not awfulizing,
or
B. blaming someone else?

640. When Sam saw that the travel box was gone, he thought, "It would have been a lot smarter of me to fold it up and take it with me. Nobody could have taken it. I wish I'd done that. Next time I'll try to think more before I act. But I don't want to punish myself too much, because that wouldn't do any good."
Was he

A. learning from the experience, and not getting down on himself,
or
B. celebrating luck, and blaming someone else?

641. Bo said to himself, "I wish whoever took the travel box had just left it there. But I guess I would have taken it myself if I had found it in the middle of nowhere. Anyway, it won't do any good for me to blame that person, whoever he is."
Was he

A. not getting down on himself,
or
B. not blaming someone else?

642. Suddenly they heard the noise of a whirring machine. Someone was riding toward them on one of the vacuum cleaners. It was Dr. Kuolo! It was funny to see her on this thing.
The squoos jumped up and down with great glee when they saw their trainer and friend, and Dr. Kuolo said to them, "Oh, you great, noble animals! You have stayed just where I wanted you to stay!" The squoos

looked proud, as if they were saying to themselves, "Hooray for us! We did something good!"

Were they

A. celebrating their own choice,

or

B. celebrating luck?

643. Dr. Kuolo said, "I notice that the travel box is missing. That's a shame. But come on, we don't have a minute to spare. The great battle is to take place when the cuckoos cuckoo four times, which is just a while from now! I came back because I've already taught the Bafs how to make the machines. They're turning them out like hotcakes. I need to get the squoos. Come on. Let's go back through the land of the Bafs, toward the battleground. We need to focus on getting there quickly!"

Was she

A. goal-setting,

or

B. blaming someone else?

644. "Hold on, Dr. Kuolo," said Sam, "not so fast. We've gotten to know the Fabs really well, and we think they're nice people. We don't want you teaching the Bafs how to build a weapon that will wipe them out. What's going on, anyway? I think we deserve an explanation."

"Well, let's see," said Dr. Kuolo. "I could explain here, or you could all come back with me and bring the squoos too, and I can explain on the way back. I think the second one would save time, because there isn't a moment to lose."

Was she

A. blaming someone else,

or

B. listing options and choosing?

* * *

Chapter 9: Programmed Instruction and "Alternate Reading"

Some experience with alternate reading

In our telephone tutoring program, it's not unusual for grade school aged children to read three or four programmed texts, each in the neighborhood of 100,000 words, with no pictures, on subjects such as anxiety-reduction, friendship-building, anger control, and self-discipline. The chance that such children would read these books, or comparable books without comprehension questions, on their own if we simply handed the books to them and suggested reading them, is approximately zero.

Why do they succeed in the telephone tutoring situation? Because the reading is turned into a social activity. The student reads one section, and the tutor reads the next, aloud. Because the student gets some approving acknowledgment for each section that is comprehended, as measured by whether the student gets the comprehension question right. Because the length of the sections appears to be about right for the feeling of a back-and-forth turn-taking between tutor and student. Because the questions require enough attention that the student can't get them right if their attention is "off in the clouds," (or in the cloud of the Internet), but the questions are not designed to trick the reader or to ask for memory of details, but for overall understanding. Thus the questions are hopefully neither too easy nor too hard.

The experience of reading several books aloud seems to do something almost magical for students' reading skills. We commonly observe that at the beginning, students tend to skip words, skip lines, and read words incorrectly much more often than they do after they've been at it a while. The auditory feedback of hearing the printed page tends to prompt the student to go back and self-correct errors rather than letting them slide by. In addition, the model of an adult who is trying hard to model good reading-aloud skills lets the young reader hear how it's done well.

An unachieved goal: production and expression versus recognition

Lest it sound like alternate reading is a miracle, we should mention an observation we are grappling with. It is very possible for children to read or hear every section of a certain chapter, to get the comprehension question correct for each section. We sometimes then ask these same children, "What did you learn from this chapter?" or "How would you summarize this chapter?" or "Tell me one of the points that has been made anywhere in this book," or some other open-ended question asking not for recognition of a correct answer, but production and expression of the ideas that were communicated. These questions render the students speechless often enough that we realize that alternate reading plus A or B questions do not result in total retention.

From the very first book written in the modified programmed format, there was another alternative to the A or B multiple choice questions: the use of "reflections." Here's the way this was explained in the Introduction to *Programmed Readings for Psychological Skills*:

For a higher challenge level, the learner can do the "reflections exercise" with each numbered vignette. A reflection is an utterance that paraphrases in your own words what you have just heard (or read) in order to make sure you understood it correctly. You pretend that you have heard the author speak to you, and you speak back. If you start your sentence with one of the following phrases, you can be pretty sure you are using a reflection:

So you're saying _____?
What I hear you saying is _____.
In other words, _____?
So if I understand you right, _____?
It sounds like _____.
Are you saying that _____?
You're saying that _____?

One useful way for two people to work together with the Programmed Readings is to take turns reading vignettes and reflecting. The student reads the vignette and answers the comprehension question, and the tutor reflects. Then the tutor reads the vignette, the student answers the comprehension question, and the student reflects. This way the tutor gets a chance to model taking pleasure from reading in an expressive voice, to model doing good reflections, and to model not getting fatigued. You can often get a lot further taking turns than you could if the student read every vignette.

Here are some examples of reflections, for the first several vignettes of this book:

1. So you're saying Jack felt good about persuading Jed not to kill a bug, huh?

2. What I hear you saying is that Peg handled it well and had a good time by herself when she couldn't go to her friend's house?

* * *

Doing the reflections exercise with each section gives the student great amounts of practice in not just recognizing, but in producing and expressing, the important ideas of the texts. Some learners who have done reflections after each section have made very impressive gains in reading comprehension.

The problem is that the reflections exercise is a great deal more mental work than simply answering the A or B comprehension question. Some of our students can tolerate that much mental work, and others would rebel against it. The logical solution would be one of moving up a hierarchy: using the A or B questions at the beginning, and at some stage graduating so as to include reflections as well. So far we usually find ourselves compromising by using the A or B questions only.

The "Tell me what you've learned" question, admittedly, is a very difficult one, even for highly intelligent adult learners. How easy would it be to stand up without preparation and summarize what you learned in a course in chemistry, history, or psychology? How easy would it be to summarize what you've read in this book so far? Judging from my own experience, the "Summarize it" question may be difficult even for people who have *written* books, not just for those who have read them!

The true test of whether the student has absorbed written instruction well is neither the multiple-choice question nor the "Summarize it" question, but the question of whether the student applies the learnings to real life. Does the student feel good about acts that exemplify psychological skill? Does the student tend to generate several options when there are important decisions to make? Does the student tend to gravitate toward figuring out what to do, rather than blowing off steam, in frustrating situations? Does the student feel good about doing something kind for someone else? Is the student able to stretch his or her work capacity? These ways of assessing learning are quite difficult to measure.

Despite this unfinished business, alternate reading with two-choice comprehension questions seems to be a wonderful way to promote learning. Usually it seems to be the best compromise on how much mental work to ask of the student while reading.

The major objection to one-on-one educational methods of all sorts is that there is not enough time, it's inefficient, it's too costly, etc. But when the student is learning the skills most important for happiness and success, and when the tutor learns not only those skills, but the crucial skills of supporting and encouraging the positive development of another person, our attitude is that whatever time it takes is time better spent than almost any other alternative use of time. This is a major departure from the philosophy of early programmed instruction. We are not trying to automate learning, or to remove human input, in order to make it more efficient and less labor-intensive. Rather, we are trying to increase the human interaction element of learning, on the grounds that tutoring can provide meaningful and fulfilling interaction for both tutor and student.

Chapter 10: Psychological Skills Exercises

The "big idea" of psychological skills exercises

If we really believe that mental health is a set of skills, then it logically follows that we need a set of exercises with which to practice those skills.

In math, we have problems to solve. In piano, we have scales as well as songs to practice. In singing, we have vocalization exercises. In chess, we have problems in which we find the best move. In tennis, we practice the various strokes. For physical fitness, we have stretches, wind sprints, bench presses, and many others. For test-taking, there is an industry that produces practice tests and exercises for most of the high-stakes tests that our society has produced. For any skill that we can think of, there are exercises to practice that, if chosen and performed correctly, can increase our level of skill. Many people want to be more proficient at various skills; fewer people are willing to devote many hours to patient practice, especially if they have to do these practice exercises on their own. Working out at a gym during an appointment with a personal trainer is probably easier for most people to do than to work out at home; practicing piano during a scheduled piano lesson is easier to accomplish than practicing in between lessons.

The idea of exercises to increase mental health skills is in some ways revolutionary, or paradigm-shifting, or at least nontraditional. Many people resist the idea that courage and joyfulness and nonviolence, for example, are even skills, much less that we can do exercises to increase these skills.

Without speaking further of psychological skills exercises in the abstract, let's look at some examples of these, and think about what psychological skills they can foster.

The celebrations exercise

What have you done lately that you are glad to have done? What skill does that exemplify? Simply answering these questions, with as concrete and specific narration as possible, constitutes the celebrations exercise. Typically a tutor and a student will take turns with celebrations, and the tutor will go first.

For example: "Today I saw someone I didn't know well sitting by herself at lunch. I asked, 'May I join you?' and she said yes. We chatted a good bit; it turns out we're both interested in singing, and we talked a lot about that. It was friendship-building and joyousness. And also courage, because it took some of that for me to get the nerve to ask if I could join her.... Now it's your turn!"

"OK, my turn. Yesterday, Sunday, I did a lot of homework in the morning, and I was looking forward to relaxing after I got it done. But just at the moment that I was ready to relax, my mom asked me to cut the grass, even though it was really hot out. I went ahead and did it quickly, and then had even more fun relaxing. So it was productivity, and compliance and kindness, and some fortitude."

What is the point of this exercise? First, each time one narrates a positive example of a psychological skill, running the image through the mind, one is doing a "fantasy rehearsal" of that skill. Second, if one can feel good about having done that example, one is getting positive reinforcement for it, also making something like it more likely to be chosen again. And third, the more one can direct attention to one's positive choices and feel good about them, the happier one feels and the less likely to become depressed one gets.

Celebrating others' choices

This is like the first celebrations exercise, only now the participants search their memories for positive actions of other people. The feeling of gratitude tends to grow if the participants choose positive actions others have done that affect them. The narrations still constitute fantasy rehearsals. One can find positive models in history, fiction, observation of real-life people, the news, and anywhere else.

Skills stories

This is like the celebrations exercise, only the participants make up the stories that illustrate various skills. Typically they start at the top of the productivity, joyousness, kindness... list and take turns making up brief stories to tell each other. The principle of fantasy rehearsal is what makes this exercise useful: conjuring up images of positive psychological skills tends to strengthen those skills in the repertoire.

The divergent thinking exercise

Someone called someone else on the phone; why did the person do that? Someone felt surprised; why? Someone did something fun; what was it? Someone was awakened in the middle of the night by a sound; what was it? Someone was taking a trip when a problem came up; what was it?

Questions like these can have many, many answers. In the divergent thinking exercise, people take turns thinking of possible answers to a question like this.

The phone caller was a telemarketer trying to sell someone a credit card. The phone caller was the person's spouse, calling up to just say, "Hi, I love you." The caller had seen the person commit a crime, and was calling up to blackmail the other person. The caller was the person's son, calling to ask for money. The caller was a poll-taker, asking who the person would vote for in an election. The caller was a telephone tutor. And so forth. All answers are "correct."

The point of the divergent thinking exercise is to rev up the random idea generator in the mind, to get practice in thinking of many options, not just one. Often we are conditioned to think that there is only one right answer to a problem, and we need to get some corrective practice with questions to which there are many answers. The divergent thinking exercise is a great warm-up for brainstorming options, listing choice points, and the pros and cons exercise.

Brainstorming options

The tutor and the student pick a hypothetical choice point situation, and take turns generating options for what the person(s) could do. Generating options is a crucial subskill of decision-making, both individual and joint.

Here's an easy example of an individual choice point: Someone wants to get in better physical shape. What options can you think of?

Here's a harder individual example: Someone really dislikes going to school. What are the person's options?

Here's a fairly easy joint decision choice point: One person wants to practice playing the drums, but a family member in the same house wants to study for a test. Their rooms are next to each other and the noise bothers the studier.

Here's a harder joint decision situation: A girl likes to chat and have friendships with lots of different guys, but her boyfriend feels very jealous when she does so. What options could either or both of them try?

Listing choice points

It's often easier to think of options for a choice point than to think of choice points themselves. In this exercise the tutor and the student take turns thinking of choice points, suitable for use with the brainstorming options exercise. The key is that any situation people can find themselves in is a possible answer. Recognizing that one is at a choice point and a decision is called for is often a key to making a good decision.

The pros and cons exercise

Once one has generated options, a next step in the decision process is to evaluate them. One way to do this is to predict the good or bad consequences that could occur (which are called advantages and disadvantages or pros and cons) and to think about which option has the highest pro to con ratio.

For example: Someone has a friend who has turned mean lately, and has said some very insulting things to the person. The person considers the option of avoiding the person, not responding to texts or calls, and spending time with other people. What pros and cons can you think of?

The guess the feelings exercise

In the guess the feelings exercise, the two people tell stories about people having certain experiences, and feeling certain ways. The feeling can be guessed from the essential clue: what the person thought. For example:

My flash drive failed. Did I feel proud of myself, or angry? Here's the clue: my thought was, "Hooray for me that I have everything backed up!"

The sequence is:

1. Here's the situation that I or someone else experienced (in reality or fantasy).
2. Here are your two choices, to guess how the person felt about this situation: for example, did he feel irritated, or proud?
3. Here is the clue that will let you answer that question: the person's thoughts about the situation.

One of the things the learner hopefully gets straight early on is that the game is not to stump the guesser, but to make it easy for the other person to guess the feelings.

When the learner does this exercise, it becomes clear that we can influence our feelings by choosing our thoughts. This is the big idea of cognitive therapy.

The twelve-thought exercise

Here are twelve different possible ways of thinking about any situation that one encounters.

1. Awfulizing. "This situation is bad."
2. Getting down on myself. "I did something bad." or "This shows that I am bad."
3. Blaming someone else. "Someone did something bad." or "Someone is bad."
4. Not awfulizing. "I can take it. It's not so bad as to defeat me permanently."
5. Not getting down on myself. "I choose not to spend my time punishing myself."
6. Not blaming someone else. "I choose not to spend my time going over how bad the other person's actions were."
7. Goal setting. "Here's what I want the outcome of this situation to be:_____"

8. Listing options and choosing: "Here are some options for achieving my goals:_____ ... Here are advantages and disadvantages____.... I pick this one (or these)."
9. Learning from the experience: "The lesson in this for the future is _____."
10. Celebrating luck; "I'm glad that it so happened that _____."
11. Celebrating someone else's choice: "I'm glad this person did _____."
12. Celebrating my own choice: "I feel good about doing _____."

All of these thoughts are appropriate at various times. The idea is to become flexible enough to choose a way of thinking based on what will work best for any given situation. Often people who have trouble with emotional regulation, or anger control, or anxiety, or depression, are in habits of overdoing or overgeneralizing one or more of the first three.

For the twelve thought exercise, you think of any situation. Then tutor and student go in order, making up each of the twelve thoughts as applicable to that same situation. They take turns. For example, suppose the situation is "I lose a chess game." The first person may say, for not very overgeneralized awfulizing, "What a bummer! I thought I had it won!" The second may say, for getting down on himself, "I made a real blunder. I put my king and queen where he could fork them with the knight. Big mistake." The first may say, for blaming someone else, "I really don't like his smug, self-satisfied attitude." The second may say, for not awfulizing, "I can handle this. It's just a game. It's no big deal." And so forth.

This exercise capitalizes on the big idea of cognitive therapy: our emotions and behaviors are very much influenced by our thoughts, over which we can exert voluntary control. The twelve thought exercise has helped many people, both children and adults, to realize that there are many ways of thinking about any given situation, and that they are free to choose their thoughts on the basis of what will work best.

The four thought exercise

The twelve thought exercise is great for getting more thoughts into the repertoire and for developing flexibility. But it's too long to go through in most real-life situations. However, if one practices the four thought exercise, one can develop a reflex of using these thoughts as a default in just about any unwanted situation. The four thoughts are:

not awfulizing
goal-setting
listing options and choosing
celebrating your own choice.

In doing the four thought exercise, the tutor and student take any situation and generate all four thoughts, in order, about that situation. They take turns, but in a little different way than in the twelve thought exercise. One does all four thoughts with one situation, another does all four thoughts with another, and so on.

Doing the four thought exercise with hundreds of hypothetical provocations, or situations that might trigger anger, is a great way to practice the skill of anger control; doing this exercise with many possibly scary situations is a great way to practice anxiety-reduction.

The tones of approval exercise

There are several variations of this. In the introductory version, the trainer says things with any of three different tones of voice:

neutral
small to moderate approval
large approval.

The student simply identifies which tone the trainer used.

In a second version, the trainer says things with the various tones, and the student imitates, trying to use the same tone that the trainer used.

In a third version, the trainer gives various phrases and various degrees of approval, and the student tries to say the phrase with the requisite degree of approval.

Tones of voice are very important in interpersonal relations, and this exercise helps the learner to be more conscious of them and to use them to be more reinforcing of others when desired.

The reflections exercise

One person is the talker, and the other is the listener. The talker's job is to talk, about anything, and to stop talking frequently to wait for a response from the other. Each time the talker stops, the listener responds with a "reflection," or a paraphrase of what the talker has just communicated. The easiest way I've found to teach people to do reflections is to ask them to fill in the blanks in any of the following sentences known as "prompts for reflections":

So you're saying _____?
What I hear you saying is _____.
In other words, _____?
So if I understand you right, _____?
It sounds like _____.
Are you saying that _____?
You're saying that _____?

There are several purposes of the reflections exercise. First, it is a simple concentration exercise. The listener has to "tune in" and pay attention to the talker, in order to reflect accurately. Second, it is a useful technique in conversation, to be able to check one's understanding of the other, or to let the other know that one understands.

Listening with four responses

In conversation, a good listeners would sound very unusual if they did a reflection each and every time the other person paused. But they would *not* sound unusual if they varied their responses among the following four:

reflections
facilitations (utterances like: yes. Uh huh. I see. Humh. OK. Oh. Right....)
follow-up questions (e.g. What happened after that?)

positive feedback (e.g. That's an interesting idea.)

In this exercise, there are a talker and a listener. The listener, this time, responds not just with reflections, but with whichever of the four listening responses seems most appropriate at any time, trying to vary among all of them.

The social conversation role-play

The tutor and student play the parts of people other than themselves. For example, they are students who sit together at lunch. Or one is George Washington and the other is Harry Potter. Or one is taking a walk in the neighborhood, and encounters another neighbor.

In the role-play, they have fun making up any things to tell about themselves and their experience that they want to. They shift back and forth between the roles of talker and listener. They try to use lots of the four listening responses. They also try to speak with tones of enthusiasm.

The joint-decision or conflict-resolution role play

The two people pick a hypothetical conflict or joint decision from a list. They role play a conversation that resolves the conflict or joint decision. This exercise is also called "Dr. L.W. Aap," because the letters in that mnemonic remind us of the 7 criteria they try to have their conversations meet, as follows.

1. Defining. Each person defines the problem, without commanding or criticizing the other person.

2. Reflecting. Each person does a reflection to make sure he or she understands the other person's point of view about the problem.

3. Listing. Together, they list options for what to do. They list a total of at least four options.

4. Waiting. They wait until they are finished listing options before starting to talk about their disadvantages.

5. Advantages and disadvantages. After they are finished listing options, they talk about the advantages and disadvantages of the options that seem best (and not the bad characteristics of the other person).

6. Agreeing. They agree on something, even if they can agree on nothing more than the plan to continue to think about the problem and resume the discussion later.

7. Politeness. They do not interrupt each other, raise their voices, or insult each other.

What if this exercise alone were carried out thousands of times by almost all people, starting in early childhood? I think that the world would be much less violent and more harmonious.

STEBC fantasy rehearsals

This is an extremely versatile exercise – useful for any psychological skill. You simply imagine yourself handling a situation well – with just the thoughts, emotions, and behaviors that you have decided are best. And then you celebrate having done so. STEBC stands for situation, thoughts, emotions, behaviors, and celebration.

One can do silent fantasy rehearsals. But even more useful, I find, is to do them aloud. And still more useful is to write them down and to read them repeatedly.

Before doing these, it's obviously important to first make a good decision about how best to respond to the situation. One doesn't want to do repeated rehearsals of misguided behaviors. Often some supervision by a professional is useful for this exercise.

UCAC fantasy rehearsals

UCAC stands for urge, celebration, alternative, celebration. These are particularly useful for impulse control problems. For example:

Urge: I'm working on homework, and I'm getting the urge to bite my fingernails.
Celebration: Hooray! I caught that urge before acting on it!
Alternative: Instead, I'll spend a few seconds relaxing my muscles.
Celebration: I'm really glad I did the alternative I chose, rather than biting my nails!

* * *

There are many more psychological skills exercises that are fun and useful. These exercises have been the subjects of two books that I have written. This chapter has provided a sampler.

Hypothetical situations are sometimes even better than real life ones

There are some real advantages to using hypothetical situations rather than real life situations. The anger control manual contains several hundred provocations and conflicts to practice with, for example. It would be difficult for most people to generate that many practice situations on their own. It is also very useful to practice with situations that do not arouse great emotion – to activate the "cool" system dominated by rational thinking and not the "hot" one driven by emotion. (The frontal cortex versus the limbic system?) By practicing the skill of calm rationality with hypothetical situations, one can develop habits that would be much more difficult with strong emotion-provoking situations. In addition, hypothetical situations tend to bypass much of the defensiveness and shame that people have to deal with when they work on situations that they have actually handled poorly. The mental maneuvers that are practiced with hypothetical situations are generalizable to real-life situations. Finally, hypothetical situations do not necessitate such a high degree of confidentiality and secrecy as when, by contrast, psychotherapy clients disclose just what situations they have handled poorly and exactly how they have handled them poorly.

Psychological skills exercises as performance measures

What we do in mental health intervention depends on outcome research, and outcome research in turn depends on how we measure outcome. So far, research has depended upon Likert scales – people saying whether something happens, for example, "never, sometimes, often, or very often." Or, for another example, whether someone is "1, normal, not at all ill; 2, borderline mentally ill; 3, mildly ill; 4, moderately ill; 5, markedly ill; 6, severely ill; or 7, extremely ill." Where is the demarcation line between marked illness and severe illness? Of course, no one can say exactly. But if Likert scales are all we have, we have to put up with their problems.

Performance measures, on the other hand, ask someone to do a specific task, and measure how well the person can do it. An IQ test is a classic example of a performance measure. It holds out enormous advantages over asking people to rate on a Likert scale where someone falls on a scale of not at all smart to extremely smart.

Various psychological skills exercises seem to lend themselves to standardized questions and performance measures. We can generate standard situations for brainstorming options and see how many of a standard set of reasonable options the person comes up with. We can use the same method with pros and cons. We can ask people to generate both parts in a role play or a dictated dialogue for social conversation or for joint decision-making, and rate the resulting dialogues according to criteria for quality. We can ask people what ethical principles or values they subscribe to, and record what they say about these, and attempt to quantify how much they are able to articulate their ethical ideas. How much such measures would correlate with real-life observations of behavior is an open question. For generating options, some work already exists that suggests that better adjusted people can generate more and better options; that training can improve option-generating ability; and that training in option-generating can improve the quality of life (Chang et al., 2004) Even in this widely studied area, however, much more work remains to be done.

Hypothesis: Much more of mental-health-promotion time should be devoted to psychological skills exercises

How would people change in their overall quality of life if they went from very little competence in a good number of psychological skills exercises to high proficiency in these exercises? Would such a movement produce more good than alternative ways of spending time working toward improved mental health? These are important questions that may someday be answered empirically. I would hypothesize that working toward great proficiency in these exercises, and then continuing to practice them, may turn out to be one of the best avenues toward mental health promotion.

Chapter 11: The Content of a Psychoeducational Curriculum

In this chapter, I will touch upon some of the big ideas that should be on the agenda of psychoeducation.

The preschool years

The preschool years, including toddlerhood, present an ideal opportunity to start psychoeducation. Before the child learns to read, the child can receive many models of psychological skills. Activities that can be fun ways of conveying psychological skills include story-reading, singing, dramatic play, and social conversation, as well as carefully chosen doses of "adult-directed activity" and "rule-governed activity."

The brains of preschoolers and toddlers soak up the models going on around them, as they learn, for better or for worse, very rapidly, how to act in this world into which they've very recently come. They imitate the real-life behavior they see going on around them, but also the behavior they see encoded into television shows and movies, books, stories, video games, songs, dramatic play, and other media. Perhaps the most fundamental principle of psychoeducation in this stage is this: show the child positive models, both in stories, songs, and plays, and in real life.

Story reading

The "Primer Stories" in the *Manual for Tutors and Teachers of Reading*, (Strayhorn, 2009) and the *Illustrated Stories That Model Psychological Skills* (Strayhorn, 2003) can be read to children starting from a very early age. Story reading with young children is in itself a psychological skill, for whoever is doing it. The adult should select stories that present imitation-worthy models, often, and present bad models, if at all, very seldom and never in a glamorized way. The stories should be of the right length for the particular child's attention span. The reader should put lots of expressiveness and enthusiasm into the reading performance. The reader should give the child lots of eye contact, and, if appropriate, physical contact. If the child stops paying attention, the adult does not reprimand, but withdraws and waits for the child to return attention to the reading. If the child never returns attention, the adult does something else, with or without the child. If the child does return attention, the adult tries to reinforce this with tones of voice and other social reinforcement. At the end of the story, the vocal tone of the reader reinforces the child's attending until the end, for example by an enthusiastic statement such as, "And that's the end of the story!" The adult usually allows the child to ask for "another one" rather than being the one to ask the child to listen to another one, working toward the situation where the child considers hearing a story a treat rather than a job. The adult should try to avoid having any aversion to reading the same stories many times; young children develop some of the repetition-tolerance skills they need to become proficient at something, by doing the same thing repetitively.

Modeling plays

The *Plays that Model Psychological Skills* (Strayhorn, 2003) were originally designed to be performed for young children by older persons, using toy characters. These model for the child how to do dramatic play, and how to incorporate prosocial plots into the dramatic play. The adult gets the plot in mind, and acts it out for the child. Using stimulus control, if the adult wants the child to watch and not take part, the adult has the toys out of the child's reach. After a play has been put on, and the adult wants to let the child participate in spontaneous dramatic play, the toys are now placed in the child's reach – usually on the floor. The same considerations of enthusiastic tones, selection of positive models, avoiding negative models, and picking plays of a length to fit the child's attention span, apply to plays as they do to stories.

Spontaneous dramatic play

In my opinion, a parent who does not perfect the art of spontaneous dramatic play with a young child is missing out on a tremendously fun and useful activity. Dramatic play allows the child to practice constructing hypothetical social situations, which is central to the act of social decision-making. It allows for practice in social skills. It allows practice in creative imagination. If siblings can learn to do dramatic play together in a fun way, the sibling relationship is greatly enhanced. Language skills are fostered. The adult can show the child prosocial models, and can use differential reinforcement to bring out the child's generation of prosocial alternatives for behavior. And finally, dramatic play can provide endless hours of fun.

It's sometimes difficult to find dramatic play toys that 1) do not have weapons or aggressive postures or are otherwise disposed to fighting; 2) have a good mixture of people and things, where the people can interact with the things; 3) are not characters of stories the child is very familiar with from movies, so that the toys are more of a blank slate on which the child can compose new plots; 4) do not seem too babyish or too advanced for the child's age, and 5) do not pose a choking hazard if the child puts things into the mouth.

To signal that you are speaking for a character, you pick up that character and move it up and down, despite the fact that our whole bodies do not move up and down when we speak!

Part of the art of spontaneous dramatic play is, as much as possible, to stay in role, i.e. to speak for the characters rather than from your own persona. A good adult (or older child) play partner knows how to be non-directive, how not to command the child to answer questions or carry out certain actions. Instead, the adult often uses "tracking and describing," or simply putting into words the actions the child's characters are carrying out. For example: "There goes the farmer into the tractor. Mr. Pig goes into the farmer's cart. There they go, taking a trip to the barn...." Tracking and describing from the point of view of a character follows both the "role of a character" rule and the "tracking and describing" guideline. For example: one character that the adult manipulates says to another, "Hey look, they're building a little fence." The adult has another character say back, "Yes, and there goes the horse into the fenced in area. Mr. Horse, do you like being in there, or do you mind it?"

In the dramatic play, the adult (or older child) tries to model positive actions and imitation-worthy talk. If the child's characters put the adults' characters in a bad predicament, the adult can take the opportunity to model problem-solving thought out loud. If the child's characters are critical or mean to the adult's characters, the adult's characters can model a very appropriate response to the difficult situation. The adult can keep in mind the 12 thoughts, and can model not awfulizing, goal-setting, listing options and choosing, learning from the experience, celebrating, or whatever other thoughts seem appropriate.

When a stimulus-seeking child has his characters enact cruel or mean behavior, the adult's characters respond with calm, careful deliberation, or with relatively long periods of silence. When the characters enact kind behavior, the adult's characters are enthusiastic, peppy, and fun. Thus, the adult uses differential reinforcement. For example, a child I played with had a character attack the others, knocking them around, while I sat silently; seconds later, the child's characters were medical responders, and I joined enthusiastically in the effort to nurture and help. The adult doing dramatic play may read either the plays, or the "play plots" in *Plays that Model Psychological Skills,* to get into mind prosocial plots to model in case there is a lull in the activity. When the child's characters do prosocial things, it should usually be the adult's characters, rather than the adult from his or her own persona, who reinforces the child's characters for their helpfulness or kindness. The adult uses differential reinforcement to aim for a turn-taking rhythm, where the adult and child each take turns making utterances and listening to the utterances of the other. For children who are too controlling and bossy, it can be useful for the adult to have a gentle conversation about the goal of letting the other person do more; these conversations are best to have before the play begins; if the child does make strides in the right direction, the adult may break from the rule of speaking from the characters and thank the child right in the midst of the dramatic play – briefly. If the adult and the child play together often and regularly, the child will often serialize the plots, returning the next session to where the story left off previously, and this is great. The adult should keep in mind all the things the child is getting from this activity, including the organization of thought, the maintenance of a focus of attention, practice of social conversation, practice of prosocial behaviors, seeing models of prosocial behaviors, being able to think about situations that are not actually present, enjoying the fruits of one's own imagination, cultivating an activity that siblings can enjoy with each other, and other advantages.

Pre-reading activities for preschoolers

Pre-reading activities for the preschool years can be fun for the child and can make the task of learning to read much easier when the child undertakes it. The set of songs on a CD called *What the Letters Say* (Strayhorn, 2001, also on the Internet at https://optskills.org/songs/) that I recorded are meant to be played repeatedly, and ideally, danced to. Getting the letter sounds into memory can be much easier when children hear the sounds spoken in isolation, in the context of songs. A second prereading activity is the Letter Stories, (Strayhorn and Fischer, 2002) a set of stories in which the letters are characters with arms and legs and faces, who communicate with people by saying their individual phonetic sounds, and then collaborating to make words. Those children who have enjoyed hearing these stories repeatedly have gotten a very pleasant introduction to the art of reading recognition. In addition, the plots of the stories are meant to model prosocial behaviors.

Musical activities with preschoolers

Among our psychological skill armamentarium are some songs that I recorded, some composed by me and others by unknown authors. These songs, which are on a CD called *Spirit of Nonviolence* (Strayhorn, 2001) and also on the Internet (at https://optskills.org/songs/) celebrate nonviolence, friendship-building, and other psychological skills. A variety of activities can be done with these, or with other songs selected so as to model positive patterns of thought, emotion, or behavior. A list of "oldie" songs modeling positive patterns is presented in my book, *The Competence Approach to Parenting* (Strayhorn, 2001). The simplest activity is just to listen. After some listening, adults and children can sing them together. They can sing them in turn-taking, where the adult sings one line and the child sings the next. They can dance around while playing them or singing them. For those who think that they can't dance, any movements that someone attempts to make roughly in time with the music definitely constitutes dancing, and any movements made while music is playing, for these purposes, still constitute dancing! Dancing around while playing modeling songs is a particularly useful activity for children who have been expected to sit for a good while.

The "dance and freeze" activity is fun, and it also exercises self-control. The child or children and the adult start the music, either playing it or singing it. While doing so, they dance around enthusiastically. Then they stop the music, with a pause button or by stopping singing, and during the silent period they hold perfectly still, starting dancing again when the music starts again. This activity is even more fun with a strip of crepe paper in both hands to wave around while dancing

Social conversation skills should be nurtured early

Social conversation skills can be thoroughly instilled in the preschool years, largely through modeling. Parents or caregivers can frequently tell young children about their own experiences, using age-appropriate vocabulary and length of utterance; children will eventually reciprocate. When children tell about their own experiences, adults can respond with reflections, facilitations, follow-up questions, and positive feedback, with tones of enthusiasm and approval. Getting, early in life, experiences of enjoying social conversation and doing it well, is probably an enormously protective factor for mental health. To name just a few mechanisms: proficient use of language assists in all intellectual and academic activity; the ability to take pleasure in conversation provides a source of reinforcement that protects against depression; positive relationship-building through conversation is an antidote to oppositional and conduct problems.

There is no developmental stage that one has to wait for before starting to model appropriate social conversation for a child. Parents or caregivers can start the modeling process at birth (or even in utero) and let the child respond whenever development permits.

Adult-directed activity and rule-governed activity

The psychologically competent preschooler is comfortable with, and proficient in, child-directed activity, adult-directed activity, and rule-governed activity.

Spontaneous dramatic play is an example of child-directed activity – they child is free to determine the direction of the activity. Social conversation can be child-directed activity.

When an adult asks questions, the child answers, and the adult says whether the answer was right or not, that's an example of adult-directed activity. If during the preschool years the child can have positive experiences with adult-directed activity, and achieve positive emotional associations with it, this is a very favorable development, because school consists of a very large fraction of adult-directed activity. Even very young children can have fun with adult-directed activity. For example, a one year old might enjoy the game of "What does the dog say?" "Ruff ruff!" "Yes!" and so forth. Many of the earliest activities in the reading manual can give a child experience in adult-directed activity early. It can be fun for a two year old to play the blending game: i.e. the adult and child look at Sesame Street figures, and the adult says, "I'm thinking of one of these; can you guess which? Here's your clue: it's Buh-er-tuh.... Right, it's Bert!"

When a child looks at a picture book, points to the pictures, and the adult names the picture, that's child-directed activity. When the adult points to the picture and the child names it, that's adult-directed activity. The idea is for the child to have pleasant experiences with both of these.

The major rule-governed activities preschoolers encounter are games and sports. The game of tag is a simple rule-governed activity. When the child sits in a swing, picks a number, and the adult holds the swing and moves it back and forth while counting to that number, and gives a big push on arriving at that number, this is a cooperative game with a rule. "Hot and cold," where one person looks for a hidden object, and the other gives clues by saying "warmer" when the child gets closer, and "cooler" when the child moves farther away, is another cooperative game with rules. Tic-tac-toe is a rule-governed activity that can help a young child learn to plan ahead; I like to join the child in playing against the computer rather than playing against the child. Perhaps it's not too far-fetched to imagine that positive experiences with rule-governed activities help the child to deal with the rules of school, or complying with the rule of law later on.

Chapter 11: The Content of a Psychoeducational Curriculum

Psychoeducation in the school-aged years

Reading

Reading is a crucial psychological skill.

A separate chapter has gone into more detail about the rationale and strategy for reading instruction and its place in psychoeducation. To summarize: First, we should recognize the importance of reading as a crucial skill in coping with the world. Lack of reading skill makes school vastly less pleasant for children, and the negative emotion stirred up can have repercussions in quite complicated ways. It is a shame that so many children suffer from reading problems, because learning to read is a fairly straightforward, though time-consuming, task, even for those children who seem to innately lack talent in it.

Good "hierarchy-ology" makes reading instruction fun.

It's essential to use good "hierarchy-ology": to pick challenges which are neither too hard nor too easy for the individual learner. It's important, for many learners, to shore up the foundation skills of reading: oral language development, phonemic awareness, and spatial awareness. For children who have a hard time with any of these, the tutor should find the right place on the hierarchy of difficulty for these skills, and move along the hierarchy at the learner's best pace. Next, letter-sound correspondence is taught, which is not hard if the child has already practiced a lot with saying the sounds in isolation in phonemic awareness exercises or letter songs. When the child can say a standard sound for each of the 26 letters, the child is ready to start "sounding and blending" words in word lists: saying the individual sounds of a word, and then the word itself. There are two hierarchies for sounding and blending: first, the lists are arranged in order from easier to harder, and second, within any given list the tutor can make it easier by doing the "sound and blend after me" activity before doing "sound and blend on your own." As soon as the learner has made some progress in reading recognition, text-reading becomes part of the agenda, and continues along with sounding and blending. Sounding and blending by syllable, where the learner says the sounds of the individual syllables, rather than those of individual phonemes, help the learner to become competent with polysyllabic words. Eventually the learner graduates from sounding and blending exercises. Long after that, the learner continues to develop reading fluency by alternate reading aloud, comprehension probes, and attention to using expressive tones of voice. Periodic testing of reading ability can actually be fun for the learner, because the test scores document progress and give cause for celebration. The *Illustrated Stories* and *Plays That Model Psychological Skills* are used for reading practice.

The skills concepts: vocabulary guides thinking.

The Sapir-Whorf hypothesis, or linguistic relativity, is a famous idea derived from anthropological observations. The idea is that since words are a major aid to thinking, the words that people know both reflect and to some extent determine their ways of dealing with the world. Every area of specialized knowledge develops its own vocabulary; experts in those fields know those words. A chess player knows about *forks* and *skewers*; a musician knows about *keys* and *measures*; a pharmacologist knows about *tolerance*; a ballroom dancer knows about *promenade position*; a tennis player knows about *topspin*; an investor knows about *price-earnings ratio*, and so on.

What are the most important words to teach, if we want people to be expert at psychological skills, if we want them not to be "emotional illiterates?"

An answer that the mental health community has emphasized is teaching "feeling words": angry, sad, ashamed, guilty, surprised, proud, compassionate, liking, fun, and so forth. And this is indeed part of the psychological skills curriculum, and it comes close to the beginning, with fairly high priority. With such words people can think better both about what is going on within both themselves and others.

But there's an even higher priority, and this is where we begin: teaching the words for the psychological skills themselves, the desirable patterns that people need to learn to do more often. The short list consists of productivity, joyousness, kindness, honesty, fortitude, good decisions, nonviolence, respectful talk, friendship-building, self-discipline, loyalty, conservation, self-care, compliance, positive fantasy rehearsal, and courage. If a child learns nothing more than the meanings of these words, and somehow gets motivated to go forth and do lots of positive examples of these, the child has internalized a succinct guide to good mental health with this alone.

How can we teach young children words, such as fortitude and positive fantasy rehearsal, that even many adults don't understand? First, it's important to realize that neither the number of syllables in a word, nor its initial unfamiliarity, presents a big barrier to learning a word. I cite as evidence having listened to many young children telling me about stegosauruses and tyrannosaurus rexes! The key ingredient to learning the skills concepts is lots of very concrete examples. In our case, these examples are stories that model these skills.

Thus, we accomplish vocabulary learning at the same time as we give the learner lots of positive models of the skills. The strategy is to present a story modeling a certain skill, and to let the learner guess which skill the story is an example of. This strategy is used with the primer stories, the *Illustrated Stories*, and the stories in the first chapters of *Programmed Readings for Psychological Skills*. In addition, the learner is taught the jingle to remember the psychological skills – the "What Are the Qualities?" song.

As soon as the learner begins to grasp the concepts of the psychological skills, these ideas are strengthened and used in the celebrations exercise. The tutor and student generate examples, frequently, of things they have done that they are glad to have done, and decide which skills these actions are examples of.

These activities are placed at the beginning of the psychological skills curriculum because they are so important. The heart of psychoeducation, and the key to happy, kind, and successful life, it can be argued, is simply to use the opportunities life gives us, to do as many positive examples of psychological skills as possible.

There is a three-step process in psychoeducation, for which the psychological skill terms provide a prime example. First, learners are given examples, and practice classifying those examples, using the terms that have been taught. For example: here's a story of someone who introduces herself to someone and has a very interesting conversation with that person; is this an example of friendship-building or fortitude? Second, learners generate hypothetical or fantasy examples of their own; this exercise is called "skills stories." And third, learners use the concepts to help them enact positive examples in real life, and to notice and celebrate those examples. This is called the "celebrations exercise."

The three steps are classification of models, generation of models and examples, and enacting real-life positive examples. This process is basic to the entire process of psychoeducation.

Self-discipline as a central skill

How do we expect a learner to get any sort of productive work done, in the face of constant temptations from electronic games? A crucial idea to get across early in life is that people can achieve long-term goals only by resisting certain short-term temptations. The ability to do this is the skill of self-discipline.

Study of this skill comes early in the psychoeducation process, because it is necessary for the conduct of psychoeducation itself. What if the student doesn't "feel like" having a tutoring session when the appointed time comes? If students can recognize the temptation not to participate, and overcome it, then the students can celebrate their self-discipline triumphs – but only if the students know what self-discipline is and can realize that they have passed up a temptation in the service of a long term goal.

Self-reinforcement, a.k.a. celebrating your own choices

Imagine two people, both of whom have to do some unpleasant and tedious work, and both of whom successfully complete the task. The first one thinks, "What a stupid thing to have to do." The second one thinks, "Hooray, I used productivity, fortitude, and self-discipline! I took that unpleasant task that I was dealt, and used my skills to handle it successfully! I even used some joyousness, as I celebrated completing each part!" If these two do the same sorts of responses over and over with different situations, the second will have a tremendous advantage in life. The second will probably get much more work done and feel much happier doing it.

The celebrations exercise

For this reason, we try to teach students early in the process to do the celebrations exercise with the tutor. The tutor and the student take turns (with the tutor going first) telling each other about things they are glad they have done, and they identify which skills the positive behaviors were examples of. At the same time that the students and tutors are reading many stories modeling psychological skills, the students learn to look for, and feel good about, the positive models they are enacting in their own lives.

It's one thing for a tutor and student to come up with some perfunctory report of a positive behavior, just to get the celebrations exercise out of the way. It's another thing for the tutor and student to really thoroughly accomplish the goals of the exercise: that the student (and tutor too) really notice more of the positive things they do, that they feel more pleasure over those positive examples; and that they actually do more positive examples. Therein lies some of the artistry of tutoring.

Part of the art of accomplishing the goals rather than just going through the motions comes from the tutor's explaining to the student what the goals are. "To be able to recognize and remember and feel good about the good things you do is a very important skill. We do the celebrations exercise to try to develop that skill. The people who are really, really good at this skill find life so much more rewarding than those who are not good at it. If both of us get better and better at this, we will have done something amazing." Pep talks like these may help the student to realize that what's at stake here is the quality of existence, not just getting another task out of the way.

Thoughts greatly influence feelings and behaviors, and we can choose our thoughts.

Why do two people experience the same situation, but feel very differently about it? Part of the reason is that they interpret, or think about the situation differently – they are using different self-talk. For example, both people awaken to find that snow is on the ground. One thinks, "Oh, no, it's going to be slippery and I'm going to have to shovel the sidewalk." When that person shovels the sidewalk, he thinks "This is futile. As soon as I get this shoveled off, more snow will come again." The second thinks, "Isn't that newly fallen snow beautiful!" As he shovels the sidewalk, he thinks, "I'm already getting some great exercise today!" The two people have vastly different experiences because of their different self-talk.

Learning, through many concrete examples, about how self-talk influences emotion, is the purpose of the Guess the Feelings exercise, described in the previous chapter.

Ways of reducing unrealistic fears

Unwanted or unrealistic fears and aversions often get in the way of carrying out psychologically skillful patterns. Anxiety disorders come in first place in prevalence estimates for psychiatric disorders. And yet most people, including many who have gotten drug treatment for anxiety, have never been exposed to the rudimentary ideas presented in a chapter of *Programmed Readings*. The first is that some fears and aversions (such as a fear of poisonous snakes, or an aversion to eating dirt) are realistic and useful, and others are unrealistic and impairing; we need to be able to tell the two apart. Every successful learning-based strategy for fear-reduction involves some "exposure" to the feared situation – you have to stay in the scary situation long enough to practice new responses to it, other than panicked attempts to escape it. If one responds to the situation by rapid escape, the diminution in fear that follows can reinforce the escape and increase the wish to escape the next time. Thus brief exposures terminated by escape can actually increase fear rather than decrease it. We are much less likely to choose escape over choosing long-enough exposure if we work our way gradually up a hierarchy of scary situations, from least to most. Our exposures are much more effective when we choose fear-reducing self-talk (such as, "I feel good about this courage skills triumph!") as contrasted to fear-enhancing self-talk (such as, "I can't stand this!" We also can practice various methods of relaxation, including muscular relaxation; these help us directly create a physiological state incompatible with fear. Exposure and practice can take place effectively through fantasy rehearsal methods as well as by getting into the real-life feared situation.

In summary, We can reduce unrealistic fears through prolonged-enough exposure, well-chosen self-talk, moving along a gradual hierarchy, relaxation practice, and fantasy rehearsal. These basic ideas can be communicated to grade school children through the chapter on fear-reduction in *Programmed Readings*; they can learn about fear-reduction much more thoroughly later on in our full-length manual on this topic.

The twelve thoughts

Because the twelve-thought system for classifying cognitions is so useful for all sorts emotional and behavioral regulation skills, learning the terms for the twelve thoughts comes early in the curriculum, in about the middle of *Programmed Readings*. I'll repeat them here:

1. Awfulizing
2. Getting down on yourself
3. Blaming someone else
4. Not awfulizing
5. Not getting down on yourself
6. Not blaming someone else
7. Goal-setting
8. Listing options and choosing
9. Learning from the experience
10. Celebrating luck
11. Celebrating someone else's choice
12. Celebrating your own choice.

The learner is introduced to these through a story in which the characters think or say one of the twelve thoughts very often. The learner's task is to answer an A or B multiple choice question to correctly classify the thought.

With many concepts, as I mentioned earlier, we move through hierarchical stages where first the learners identify or classify, when presented with examples. Later the learners practice coming up with their own examples. Finally, the learner creates positive examples in real-life experience of using the concepts to make good choices. *Programmed Readings* gets the learner through the first of these stages with the twelve thoughts. When the tutor teaches the student to do the twelve-thought exercise, they move to the second stage.

The four ways of listening

The same movement – from classification of examples, to generation of hypothetical examples, to enacting positive examples in real life – is very useful in teaching people to be better listeners for one another. Many people have trouble with shyness, with not knowing what to say. This problem is greatly alleviated if the person knows how to respond to what the other person says. We teach four ways of listening: reflections, facilitations, follow-up questions, and positive feedback. We start by letting the learner read dialogues and classify the utterances the listener makes in them. The learner will later carry out exercises to practice producing these responses: the reflections exercise and the listening with four responses exercise.

Ethical dilemmas

Many of the hard choices people make occur when two principles are in conflict with one another. It's at least something of an aid to decision-making to think clearly about which principles are involved. Programmed Readings presents vignettes where two of the principles are in conflict with one another, and asks the reader to identify which two: for example, is it compliance versus loyalty, or joyousness versus self-care?

In Kohlberg's (1975) theory of moral development, the highest stage involves not acting out of fear of punishment, following authoritarian rules, or engaging in expedient exchanges, but acting on "principle." Kohlberg and his colleagues believed, with some evidence, that discussion of ethical dilemmas seemed to advance youth faster along the scale of moral development. I posit that acting on principle is facilitated by being taught a set of principles, realizing which are at stake in given situations, and recognizing the situations in which those principles conflict.

Assertion

Assertiveness training, a.k.a. assertion training, was one of the major psychoeducational movements emerging from the behaviorism of the late 1950's, 1960's, and 1970's (Wolpe, 1958, 1969; Smith, 1975). Such training sprang from very two very common clinical observations. The first was of people who were afraid to displease others, afraid to assert their own wishes, silent and passive in the face of others' taking advantage of them, and often developing anxiety and depression and relationships ruined by silent resentment. The other observation was of people who were grabby, obnoxious, unempathic, or disposed to temper outbursts and violence to get their way. The goal of assertion training is a golden mean between these two extremes: being able to make one's wishes clear, take strong stands, insist on being treated fairly, and negotiate well, but to do it with consistent emotional control, as politely as possible. The assertiveness movement visualized an interpersonal world where people spoke candidly, calmly, and rationally in order to get mutual needs met, where people acted neither overly dominant nor overly submissive.

One of the major tasks of assertion skill is being able to generate polite and gentle ways of refusing requests or making requests. In *Programmed Readings*, we start the three stage process by asking learners to see examples of people's being assertive, and discriminating or classifying which of two responses is more gentle.

Joint decision-making and conflict resolution

If both parties in a negotiation, or joint decision, or conflict-resolution conversation can be assertive, that is certainly better than if they are passive or aggressive. But it's necessary to get beyond a simple repetitive calm statement of wishes and wants, and to develop skills of a more creative problem-solving process, if people are truly to maximize their joint happiness.

The process of joint decision-making that we teach has seven criteria. First: the people state their own points of view about the problem without insulting or criticizing the other, or commanding the other to do anything. Second, each person does a reflection (So what I hear you saying is ____) to make sure that he or she understands the other's point of view. Third, they list several (e.g. four or more) options as to what their joint plan can be. Fourth, instead of criticizing the option and arguing about it immediately after it is posed, they wait until they have accumulated a list of options before they start evaluating them. Fifth, once they start evaluating the options, they speak of the advantages and disadvantages of the options, instead of the flaws of the other person. Sixth, they find a way to agree on something, even if it's only to resume the conversation later. And seventh, they are polite with each other throughout the whole conversation.

We refer to these as Dr. L.W. Aap conversations, with Dr. L.W. Aap a mnemonic for

1. Defining
2. Reflecting
3. Listing
4. Waiting
5. Advantages
6. Agreeing
7. Politeness.

What if joint-decision conversations between world leaders, family members, co-workers, and all others were closer to the Dr. L.W. Aap format? It's hard to imagine this without imagining a much happier, less violent world. As I've said before: What if part of every child's education involved role-playing, and writing, many, many Dr. L.W. Aap dialogues, from an early age and throughout education? Could the practice gained in many hypothetical situations generalize to the real-life interpersonal conflicts, the mishandling of which cause so much misery?

Decisions about compliance

The skill of compliance does not consist of blindly following all rules and obeying all requests and orders. It involves making rational decisions about when to comply and when not to. *Programmed Readings* starts the three stage process with the skill of compliance by giving examples of good and bad reasons for noncompliance, and asking the learner to discriminate between the two.

62 skills

Programmed Readings ends with more examples of skills, only this time classifying them by the full system of 62 skills, for which the 16 are group headings. This longer classification system allows a more fine-grained analysis of the positive maneuvers that constitute mental health, even though it has a major disadvantage of being hard to hold in memory. This list is reprinted in Appendix 2 of this book.

Friendship-building

Typically the next manual students read in the psychological skills curriculum is *A Programmed Course in Friendship-Building and Social Skills*. Positive relationships are crucial to mental health, and this manual seeks to help learners to cultivate them.

The subject of friendship-building begins with the idea that people will not find perfect people to be friends with. A large part of success is finding something to enjoy in other people and neither being too irritated by, nor inclined to imitate, the negative aspects, within reasonable limits.

A very important social skill is the art of greeting and parting rituals – knowing how to say the things synonymous with "Hello" and "Goodbye," in ways that let the other person feel valued. Eye contact, smiling, using the person's name, and using an enthusiastic voice all make the words of greeting or parting convey that value message.

Putallaz and Gottman (1983) examined the way in which socially accepted and rejected children start socializing. The finding was that the rejected ones tended to interrupt the other children, trying to drag their attention away from what they were doing, toward the newcomer. They tended to disagree, ask informational questions, say something about themselves, and state their feelings and opinions. The accepted ones tended to scope out the situation and join in the activity without requiring people to stop attending to what they were already doing. This idea seems readily teachable; cultivating the habit of making social initiations well is of course something more than getting the idea of avoiding annoying interruptions.

A more important key to preserving good social relationships is avoiding doing some other things that tend to alienate people: getting very angry or upset over little things, being too bossy, being too argumentative and contradicting. The art of tact, of saying things politely, even when being assertive, and the art of reinforcing the other person are also important social skills.

Social conversation is a fundamental friendship-building skill. Many shy students have difficulties in figuring out what to talk about and ask the other person about. The friendship-building manual provides a sort of menu for conversation topics, remembered by the mnemonic PAPER: places (Where are you from? Where do you live?), activities (What do you like to do? What did you do last week end?), people (Do you have brothers or sisters? Do you know _____?), events (Did you hear about the tornado? I heard that ___ happened?), and reactions and ideas (What do you think about _____? What are your beliefs about _____?). Knowing how to listen is probably even more important than having things to say, and in the friendship-building manual, we review four listening methods: reflections, facilitations, follow-up questions, and positive feedback. And in social conversation, the tones of voice with which one speaks may often be even more important than the content. We teach students, as well as tutors, to discriminate three degrees of approval and enthusiasm in the tone of voice: neutral, small to moderate approval, and large approval. After classifying examples, the student is ready to practice producing examples in practice sessions, and thence, hopefully, to more skillfully modulate tones of voice in real-life conversation. A book can tell about this skill, but of course it is best practiced when people can hear one another. Another crucial social conversation rule is to stop talking often enough and yield the floor to the other person. There are two ways to avoid talking too long. One is to be sensitive to the nonverbal signals the other person sends – by looking around at other things, drumming their fingers, opening the mouth to try to speak, and so forth. The second is simply to be aware of how long you have been talking, and to yield the floor at least before a minute has gone by. Another social conversation skill is being a good interviewer as well as a good interviewee, knowing how to seek, and find, the topics of conversation that are maximally interesting and fun for both people. The art of humor is much more complex than the other skills. Many people who have had social skills sufficient to get into positions of power or influence have been fired, resigned, or otherwise gotten into trouble by stepping over an invisible line and making inappropriate jokes. The ability to generate and appreciate humor is a skill that can benefit, at least somewhat, from conscious study.

The skill of inviting other people to spend time with you is multifaceted. It partly involves the courage to risk rejection. It partly involves figuring out details: how far ahead of time, what would the other person enjoy doing, should the invitation be by text or voice, if the person is not free at one time should one try for a different time. It involves having a lighthearted attitude that lets the other person know that all will be well whether they accept or not. And often the biggest hurdle is just getting up the energy to extend invitations rather than putting up with loneliness.

Social relations involve important balances. For most people, how much they like another person depends largely upon how kind, how nice, the other person is to them. Yet kindness often needs to be balanced with assertiveness, with sticking up for one's own rights. People often enjoy people who can take social risks – who can say and do things that are off the beaten path, creative, and a bit wild. But this style needs to be balanced with carefulness not to offend or scare people or otherwise make them uncomfortable. Achieving such balances is not at all easy, partly because people have such different preferences and tolerances.

Especially for children, but also for some adults, the social aspect of games and sports deserves special attention. If the goal is friendship-building, then it's good to consider games to be for fun, to keep things in perspective, and to be gracious both in victory and in defeat, putting a higher priority on the relationships involved than on the final score. Someone who disputes every call, accuses the other of cheating, screams in anger or cries upon losing, or gives up prematurely sends messages of "Don't play with me again."

Conflict resolution and anger control

One of the first tasks in learning conflict-resolution and anger control is to come to the belief that harmonious joint decisions and nonviolence are really desirable. We live in a world where proficiency in violence is still a chief means toward power, and where much admiration is lavished on those who are good at particular brands of violence. We look for strengths in leaders (which often translates into the willingness to send other people into danger). Consistent nonviolent and respectful conflict-resolution strikes many people as boring. Without violence the "action and adventure" movie genre would be doomed, as would of course the horror genre, as would mixed martial arts, boxing, and American football.

A second big idea in the field of anger control is that the following is NOT true: "You must express or release or channel your anger, because keeping it bottled up does great harm." Here's a more enlightened view: We want to learn to deal with the situations that cause anger (which we can call *provocations*) in the most rational and effective way possible. Anger control and conflict resolution skills consist in finding the best ways to deal with provocations. Different provocations, of course, demand different sorts of responses. But if the learner adopts the goal of figuring out how to best respond to provocations, and not the goal of releasing anger, the game is half won.

How, other than by screaming and violence, can people respond to provocations? We can divide such responses into thoughts, emotions, and behaviors. With respect to thoughts, the twelve thoughts provide a set of options, and the four thought exercise provides a default template. In fact, simply taking a long list of provocations and practicing the four thought exercise with each of them represents a simplified approach to learning anger control. But there is a lot to learn about how to do the four thought exercise well.

The four thoughts are not awfulizing, goal-setting, listing options and choosing, and celebrating your own choice. In doing goal-setting well, it's good to have in mind various types of goals. In provocations, human beings are tempted to set goals of getting revenge, or of making the other person feel pain just because it feels good to do so. (Enjoyment of the infliction of pain is called sadism. The pleasure that comes does not necessarily need to be sexual in nature.) These goals are irrational. However, the goal of punishing the other person's misbehavior in order to make it less frequent is closely related to those goals, and life is complex because sometimes punishment is the best way to handle a provocation. Sometimes the dominance motive is rational: there is a wish to improve one's position on the "dominance hierarchy," to establish the precedent that one will not always submit to the will of another. The dominance motive, however, is responsible for much bullying. Similarly, self-defense, which sometimes requires the use of force or violence, is a motive that can be rational. We have to be very careful about punishment and dominance and defense motives, that they don't rapidly turn into needless cruelty. Another set of motives or goals is often very conducive to nonviolence: the goals of **a**voiding harm, affirming to oneself one's **s**elf-discipline, **p**roblem-solving, **e**mpathy and understanding of the other person, and **k**indness even in the face of provocation. I refer to these as the ASPEK goals, and a very useful anger control exercise is to formulate an example of each of these in response to lots of provocation vignettes.

Not every provocation needs to lead to emotions of anger. How else might someone feel, in response to a provocation by someone else? One can feel determined to handle the situation well, curious about what's going on with the other, cool and calculating, sympathetic to the other person, humble and recognizing one's own imperfections, or proud of handling the provocation well. It's a useful exercise to generate the thoughts that might lead to these alternative ways of feeling.

What are the options for how to behave in the face of provocations? People are not born knowing how to generate nonviolent options proficiently. A menu for nonviolent options can be remembered by the mnemonic Ida CRAFt (together with a fair amount of work in memorizing!) (The letters in capitals are used twice.)

1. **i**gnoring
2. **d**ifferential reinforcement,
3. **a**ssertion,
4. the **c**onflict-resolution paradigm (trying to meet the 7 Dr. L.W. Aap criteria),
5. using any of several options for response to **c**riticism,
6. appealing to authority or the **R**ule of Law;
7. **r**elaxation;
8. getting or staying **a**way from the other person,
9. **a**pologizing,
10. **f**riendliness and kindness,
11. use of nonviolent **f**orce,

12. and using calm and rational tones of voice.

Interestingly, in my work with families where anger or violence is problematic, the "away from the other" option is an extremely useful one. When the level of anger exceeds a certain point in either person, the chance that further dialogue will be beneficial becomes very low. The best thing for people to do at that point is to walk away from each other, particularly to separate rooms. It's very useful to plan and even role-play such strategies ahead of time, so that people don't get even more angry that the other person is cutting off communication.

Being criticized is a special case of provocations that most people are very ill-equipped to handle. Again the strategy of getting familiar with a set of nonviolent options is useful. Sometimes, when criticism is constructive, the best response is "Thank you." Other responses worth studying are planning to ponder or problem solve, agreeing with part of criticism, asking for more specific criticism, doing a reflection, making an "I want" statement, silent eye contact, explaining the reason for one's actions or rationally debating the critic, and criticizing the critic. Again there's a mnemonic: These are the "T-PAARISEC" options. Again, lots of practice with these options is required before they reach a level of habit strength that enables them to be used in the "heat of the moment."

We have previously described the Dr. L.W. Aap criteria for good conflict-resolution conversations. (They are: defining, reflecting, listing options, waiting until listing is over before evaluating options, advantages and disadvantages, agreeing on something, and politeness.) Even though in real life, it is hard to find someone who can meet all 7 criteria with you, it is extremely good exercise to do many Dr. L.W. Aap role-plays – it fosters a rational approach to conflict resolution that is helpful even when the other person is not meeting any of the 7 criteria.

Violence is a method of getting power. A learner is reluctant to give up power, without having other methods of getting it. Accordingly, it's useful to study nonviolent methods of getting power – for example, the power that comes from acquiring wealth, becoming an expert in some field, being able to speak persuasively, being able to walk away from a deal, being able to tolerate another's hostility, having lots of allies, having ethics on your side, and so forth.

And finally, violence is most likely to occur in a negative emotional climate – a situation where people criticize and command and contradict and threaten each other often. But people can improve the emotional climate of social groups simply by saying certain things to each other more often: things like, "Thanks for doing that!" "Good luck with ____ (what you're about to do!" "Good morning!" and so forth. Studying a list of these things and fantasy rehearsing saying them can go a long way toward creating happier and less angry environments.

Thus the approach to anger control and conflict-resolution that I advocate involve lots of study, memorization, and practice of response patterns that compete with screaming, threatening, and violence. The key is highly repetitive practice of the positive response patterns through role-playing and fantasy rehearsal.

The skill of self-discipline

It's important to realize what self-discipline is. It's the ability to pass up something pleasurable or do something uncomfortable or painful in order to achieve a worthy goal. That goal usually involves getting greater happiness than would have been obtainable by giving in to the temptation. Self-discipline is NOT subjecting oneself to painful or unpleasant experiences that have no payoff. It is not becoming a workaholic and foregoing recreation and fun.

Since self-discipline exists in order to help us attain worthy goals, an important first step is choosing worthy goals to strive for. What is really worthwhile to accomplish? Finding goals that one can believe in is the first step in self-discipline. Would accomplishing this make both me, and other people, happier? Are there other goals that would bring about more happiness? These questions are crucial to consider while choosing goals.

Once the goal is chosen, it's good to make it as concrete and specific as possible. What exactly would have to happen, to achieve this goal? Writing down the goal and reading the written goal statement helps keep one focused. An "internal sales pitch" is worth thinking about and writing down:

what are the reasons to achieve this goal? Why is it worth working toward? What is a list of payoffs that would result?

Next, one does well to make concrete plans for how to attain the goal. What are the various steps or stages? Who is involved? What is the list of tasks that need to be carried out? What is our guess about how long each should take? In addition to a master plan, daily plans are worth writing and checking.

In planning for accomplishing the goal, what are the self-discipline choice points? Now we begin to anticipate the situations where we will be tempted to goof off or do something easy, but attaining the goal requires doing something less fun. We decide: what would we like to do, think, and feel in those choice points? What is the pattern that will produce success?

At this point we can begin to do lots of fantasy rehearsal workouts, mentally practicing "self-discipline triumphs." We imagine ourselves feeling very good about making the goal-directed choice rather than the immediate pleasure-directed choice.

Then, as we work toward the goal in real life, we start accumulating self-discipline triumphs. We try to celebrate and feel proud about each one of them.

Meanwhile, we monitor our progress toward our goal. How much closer are we than we were before? We also celebrate any progress.

As we do this, we may find something wonderful happening. We may find that the actions that once required lots of self-discipline to carry out actually become enjoyable. For example, the person who had to force herself to give a speech comes to enjoy public speaking; the person who pushed himself to run finds that he comes to enjoy running more and more; people who forced themselves to practice a musical instrument start loving to play it; the person who used self-discipline to avoid doughnuts finds himself loving salads, and so forth. I call this "advanced self-discipline."

Another thing that may happen over time is called the development of greater work capacity. The person who had an aversion to working for longer than a certain period of time becomes able to stay focused for longer and longer times. This may occur by the same exposure and habituation and self-reinforcement mechanisms that people use to reduce other aversions.

Chapter 11: The Content of a Psychoeducational Curriculum

The person who pursues a self-discipline-requiring goal does well to use certain other principles. Stimulus control means not giving yourself easy access to the things that tempt you. For example, the alcohol-avoider decides not to keep alcohol in the house; the weight-loser gets bags of potato chips out of easy reach; the writer works on a computer that doesn't have internet access; the person studying for a test turns off her cell phone. To use the principle of daily routines, you try to harness the force of habit to do self-discipline requiring things at the same time each day. Organization skills both require self-discipline (because putting things and tasks in order often isn't fun) and facilitate self-discipline (because it's easier to accomplish goals when the project and all used to accomplish it are organized). Key organization tactics include use of an appointment calendar, a daily to do list, and a well-developed filing system. Additional key tactics include not acquiring too much clutter, setting a regular time for handling papers and emails, and creating and updating a "memory" file holding information that needs to be preserved.

It's good to distinguish daily to-do items from daily "resolutions." For to-do items, the idea is to order them in priority, start with the highest priority task and proceed in priority order, and work for a reasonable amount of time, not necessarily getting to all the to-do items. For resolutions, the idea is to establish a habit of keeping as close to 100% of resolutions as possible, and to avoid the habit of making resolutions only to break them. For example, if one is trying to lose weight, it's a bad idea to make a resolution of "Nothing with sugar today, and nothing in between meals," and then change that to, "OK, only one piece of candy, but that's it," and then change that to, "Only three more and then I'm really done," and so forth. The problem with this is that one gets reinforced (by the pleasurable temptation one has given into) for resolution-breaking. It's therefore better to consider carefully which resolutions one can keep, not to make resolutions lightly, to write them down, and to try very hard to keep each one.

An interesting idea about self-discipline is that it's a depletable resource. For example, spending time being polite to rude people may temporarily reduce our capacity to resist overeating; working to concentrate on boring ideas may temporarily reduce our capacity to resist playing video games. If self-discipline is depletable, a major question is, how can it be restored? Sleeping is a classic method. I hypothesize that if self-discipline has been used up by having to sit still, exercise may restore some of it; it it has been used up by physical labor, rest may restore it. If it has been depleted by annoying interactions with people, solitude may restore it; if it has been depleted by solitary work, socialization may restore it. And if it has been depleted by high stimulation work (such as work in an emergency room), a quiet, low-stimulation environment may restore it; if it has been depleted by low-stimulation work (such as grading papers) a highly stimulating situation may help restore it.

Choosing wisely among the thoughts in our twelve-thought classification system is extremely useful in the cultivation of self-discipline, as well as for almost all other skills. For example, if one is attempting the self-disciplined act of turning off a video game, it's easier if the thoughts are of goal-setting (my goal is to stay cool, get off the game without looking back, and move quickly to the next activity) and celebrating one's own choice (hooray, I'm doing it, I'm in the process of creating a self-discipline triumph). It's harder if the thoughts are of awfulizing (what a bummer, I was only a little way off from accomplishing something big!) and blaming someone else (why does that parent of mine always have to spoil my fun by commanding me to get off the game?)

Self-discipline is about accomplishing goals. A crucial ingredient in accomplishing goals is "time on task." It's a very simple idea, but very often overlooked, that we're more likely to succeed when we're willing to invest more time and effort into the goal. It's useful for people frequently to ask two questions: 1) what is my highest priority goal? and 2) how much time per day am I devoting to working on this goal? There are many, many people for whom the cultivation of a certain psychological skill – anxiety reduction, joyousness (versus depression), kindness (versus aggressive behavior) – is clearly the most important goal for life, but for whom the amount of time devoted per day is zero.

One major way of devoting time to cultivating a skill is simply reading instructions on how to do the skill well. Many people assume that when they have read a book, there is no reason to read it again. But we need constant reminders of important ideas, and re-reading is an important pathway to keeping important ideas in mind. Thus whatever goals we set, it's good to establish a habit of reading and re-reading the books that tell us how to achieve those goals.

Skills of anxiety-reduction and courage

Fears and aversions very frequently interfere with our enjoyment of life or our ability to function well. (I use the word *aversion* to refer to a bad feeling that is associated with a situation, when that feeling isn't necessarily fear.)

We feel fears and aversions for a very good reason: to protect us from danger. Most of the built-in fears and aversions we have are extremely useful. We fear walking off cliffs and have an aversion to the taste of most poisons for a good reason – the avoidance of these things enables us to survive. But it would be very difficult to design a brain that automatically had only useful, helpful fears and aversions, and no useless, unrealistic ones. The brain needs fine-tuning by our teaching it to feel fear or aversion when it is useful, and not when it is harmful. How do we decide which is which? That decision process starts with thinking about danger. We think about four types of danger: physical, social, economic, and goal-related. Danger is proportional to how bad something is that might happen to us, and how bad that thing is; we can call these the probabilities and utilities (or disutilities) of outcomes. Figuring out that what we fear is either not very bad or not at all likely often helps to reduce fear in itself. Even if it doesn't, it gives us the go-ahead to use other techniques to try to get over the fear.

Where do unrealistic fears come from? Partly, we inherit the tendency to be cautious or fearful. But another process is important to understand. When we get into a scary situation, feel great fear, and rapidly escape from the situation, the escape is reinforced by a diminution of the fear. (It's called "negative reinforcement" because it's the cessation of something unpleasant rather than the starting up of something pleasant.) Reinforcement strengthens the behavior that it follows. So the fear-reduction following escape leads the person to have a stronger urge to escape, the next time the person encounters the same situation. And since the urge to escape is experienced as fear, the fear has grown greater. Thus brief exposures followed by escape tend to increase fear. Sometimes fears can start small and grow to be quite large, by this mechanism.

Other fears originate with traumatic events – for example, a child is bitten hard by a dog, and fears dogs thereafter. For some fears and aversions, we can't come up with an explanation for their origin. Fortunately, we don't need to know where fears come from, in order to reduce them. Many people spend many hours in a vain attempt to answer the question, "Where did my anxiety come from," assuming that discovering the answer is the only key to reducing the anxiety. There are concrete steps to reduce anxiety that one can take without ever figuring out how it originated.

One of the most important steps one takes in getting over unrealistic fears is to ponder, and clearly decide about, a crucial choice point that I call mastery versus avoidance. If I'm afraid of dogs, one option for me is just to avoid dogs for the rest of my life. If I fear social interactions, I can choose to be solitary. If I fear elevators, I can take stairs. These are examples of the avoidance choice. On the other hand, I can do the work necessary to reduce these fears, to master them – this is the mastery choice. Some people do not really want to work toward mastery; they really want to avoid the scary or aversive situation. Mastery takes hard work and self-discipline, and unless someone really wants it, it's very difficult to get.

If, on the other hand one really desires mastery, the full set of Oh Ram Prism methods is useful. To review, these are:

1. Objective-formation, or goal-setting. We set clear goals for how to handle the scary or aversive situation.

2. Hierarchy. We arrange the scary situations in order of difficulty, and work with the easier ones first, gradually working our way up.

3. Relationship. We cultivate a good relationship with the person or people helping us (assuming that person is worthy of it); if we are on our own, we try to "be our own best friend."

4. Attribution. We attribute to ourselves the power to conquer the fear or aversion.

5. Modeling. We take in models (in real life or in stories) of people successfully handling, or even enjoying, the scary situation.

6. Practice. To practice handling the scary situation, we have to "expose" ourselves to it, and to practice something other than escaping the situation. Ideally, one practices thoughts, emotions, and behaviors that are carefully selected. It's very important that such practice can occur in fantasy as well as in reality, and the fantasy practice is often much easier (lower on the hierarchy) than real-life practice.

7. Reinforcement. The more we can get rewarded for practicing handling the scary situation, the better. A very important source of reinforcement is our own self-talk. Saying things to oneself like "Hooray! I'm doing something very brave now!" is very important for anxiety-reduction.

8. Instruction. There's a great deal to learn about fear-reduction, and people with unrealistic fears should invest the time necessary to learn it. Reading an instructional book should be part of fear-reduction work.

9. Stimulus control. Stimulus control means arranging for the environmental stimuli that make success most easy, particularly at the beginning. For example, having a kind, supportive, encouraging person available when you start exposure and practice makes success easier.

10. Monitoring. You monitor your progress as you go along, keeping track of which situations you are able to tolerate successfully, and what the SUD levels are. SUD levels are ratings of fear or aversion – SUD stands for Subjective Units of Disturbance (or Distress, or Discomfort).

When setting the goals for how one wants to handle a scary situation, several other aspects are useful to keep in mind.

1. Probabilities and disutilities. If the situation is not actually dangerous, we want to remind ourselves of the low probabilities and/or disutilities that lead to that conclusion.

2. Allies. To what extent do we want to make the journey to fear-reduction alone, or to what extent do we want to get help from supportive other people? It's often easier to do it with support.

3. STEB and STEB revision. STEB stands for situation, thoughts, emotions, and behaviors. The more thoroughly we can map out how we would like to think, feel, and behave in very concrete and specific situations, the easier it is to adopt these new patterns.

4. Tones of voice. If we can practice speaking to ourselves, and others, in a non-frightened tone of voice, fear-reduction is easier. Calm, relaxed tones are one option, but excited and fun-loving tones are also an alternative.

5. Breathing. Paying attention to breathing patterns, and doing the exercises that teach us how to avoid hyperventilation, are important to include, since hyperventilation often plays a big part in anxiety.

6. Activation or arousal versus relaxation. Controlling our own level of arousal is an important skill. We can do lots of practice of getting excited and getting relaxed, either using biofeedback or using our built-in gauges of how relaxed we feel. Learning to relax muscles is an important technique that many have found very helpful in regulating arousal.

7. Doing, not feeling, as the criterion for success. People working on fear-reduction should, particularly at the beginning, define success as *doing* the things that a non-fearful person can do, not necessarily feeling calm and relaxed while doing so. The feelings usually fall in line eventually where the behavior leads. If one worries too much about how one feels, it's possible to get into a vicious cycle that goes: "Oh, no, I'm feeling scared! I had hoped not to! This means I'm failing! Now I feel even more scared!" Instead, a better thought pattern is, "I'm feeling scared, but I'm doing it anyway! That's called courage! Hooray for me, for this courage skill triumph!"

     A mnemonic for these seven aspects of setting and pursuing the fear-reduction goals is PAST BAD.

Chapter 11: The Content of a Psychoeducational Curriculum

As you can see, both the anger control curriculum and the anxiety-reduction curriculum involve lists of things to remember, complete with mnemonics. This is for a reason. Learning words, remembering their meanings, remembering the lists, gets one into a thinking, calculating, verbally reasoning mode, that provides a nice alternative to the wordless emotional state that often constitutes great anger or great fear.

In reducing fears, it often takes some work to decide what one is really afraid of. For example, several children are afraid of going to school. They are not necessarily able to tell you why, the first time you ask. They often need to ponder this question, for example by imagining the school day and noticing what parts of it provoke the greatest fear when imagined. When they do this, they may recognize different situations to which the fear is actually attached: one has a revulsion to vomit, and is afraid that a classmate may vomit; one has a fear of failure and humiliation on schoolwork; one is afraid of rejection from peers; one is afraid of picking up germs; one is realistically afraid of being bullied, and so forth. Psychoeducational tutoring is not meant to provide conversations where the child comes to insights about fears, but rather to teach the child that it's useful to decide upon what is really feared the most about a situation, and give some examples of the results of this thought process.

Once one does decide upon an unrealistic fear or aversion, it's good to construct a hierarchy, so that one can practice with the easiest situations first and gradually work the way up to the harder ones. There are a number of ways of making up situations that will be less scary than the original one. You can imagine someone else's experiencing it, rather than your doing so. You can imagine that the scary thing is smaller or less intense. You can imagine a story with a happy ending. You can see the scene from far away. You can have the characters be cartoon characters, or imagine the scene with funny aspects. You can imagine powerful allies with you as you encounter the scene. You can imagine the scene as occurring in a movie, TV show, or book, rather than in real life. Similarly, you can vary the intensity and distance and other aspects to make hierarchies for real-life exposures.

Once you have made a hierarchy of scary situations, it's good to ponder how you do want to think, feel, and behave in the scary situation.

What do you want the replacements to be for the previously-habitual scary patterns?

When deciding upon replacement thoughts, the twelve-thought categorization is useful. Particularly, the four thoughts, i.e. not awfulizing, goal-setting, listing options and choosing, and celebrating your own choice, form a great default pattern for handling scary situations. An extremely useful exercise for anxiety-reduction is to take the list of scary situations found in an appendix to the anxiety-reduction book, in the "Fear and Aversion Rating Scale," and to do the four-thought exercise with each of them, aloud.

It's also good to ponder the question, "How would I like to feel in the situation that is now unrealistically feared?" The answer is not always cool, calm, and relaxed. For example, someone who is afraid of social interaction may find it more pleasant, as well as more realistic, to aim for feeling excited and energized in a pleasant way. Someone who has a fear of feeling humiliated by vomiting decides that he would rather feel humor and silliness and hilarity (with wise-cracking behaviors) rather than feeling dreamy and relaxed. Someone who has a fear of bees and wasps would rather feel fierce and valiant; another person would rather feel compassionate; a third would rather feel alert and vigilant in a cool and calculating way.

Once one has decided, "How would I like to feel instead," it's useful to recall, or imagine, situations in which one felt that way, and to use these "resources" as ways of transferring those feelings to the previously feared situation. For example, someone is afraid of public speaking. The person recalls instances of feeling show-offy and having fun during childhood, acting out skits around a campfire with friends. The person brings those feelings to mind as clearly as possible, and then imagines having similar feelings while giving the speech.

Even though one can feel excited in a pleasant way as an alternative to fear, it remains true that being able to regulate your level of excitement and arousal, particularly to lower it at will, is a very useful skill. Basic psychological skills education should include some training in relaxation/meditation techniques. The chapter on relaxation and meditation techniques in the anxiety-reduction book describes several methods. Two important preliminaries to most of these methods are getting enough exercise beforehand (sitting meditations are not fun when you've already had to sit too long already) and cultivating a positive attitude toward the use of the technique.

The muscle relaxation technique entails paying attention to the difference between tension and relaxation in muscles, and spending time getting the muscles as relaxed as possible. A variant of muscle relaxation is "breathe and relax," in which you search for any muscle tension each time you inhale, and you let off that tension each time you exhale. In the "mind-watching" technique, you let your mind do whatever it wants; you save out some of your consciousness to observe what the rest of it is doing. You try to have the observing part feel serene and benevolent toward yourself, even if scary or guilt-producing or otherwise upsetting images come into awareness. This nonjudgmental awareness of what is going on in your own mind is a part of what some people call "mindfulness." Another technique is meditation by repeating to yourself, silently and rhythmically, a word, called a mantra. In some research on this technique, participants used the word "one" (Benson & Klipper, 1975). In all the techniques in which you focus your attention on something, it's an important part of the technique to expect times when your attention will wander, and to simply gently bring your attention back to the focus when you realize it has strayed, without getting down on yourself or awfulizing. Rather than repeating a word, you can slowly repeat a movement, such as a dance move or exercise-like movement. This is particularly useful for people who have had to sit too much already. Another technique is visualizing relaxing scenes, whichever have the most pleasant and relaxing associations for the individual. Biofeedback often makes relaxation much more fun; in this, we use some device to measure a physiological parameter (such as skin conductance level, fingertip temperature, muscle tension, or heart rate) and play around with increasing and decreasing these levels. Techniques of imagining acts of kindness, wishing for good outcomes for oneself and others, imagining pleasant dreams, imagining positive examples of psychological skills, and reading and contemplating inspiring quotations all draw upon the idea that images of the best that humanity is capable of tends to be good for the psyche. The last technique is simple rest: sit or lie down, and do whatever seems restful to you (not counting TV, video games, or other sources of electronic stimulation!)

Breathing faster is part of the "flight or fight" response. This behavior evolved as an instinctual response to danger, because literally fleeing or fighting generates lots of carbon dioxide that needs to be blown off by rapid breathing. But when we are scared in situations where we don't exercise, breathing faster blows off more carbon dioxide than is optimum. Sometimes the unpleasant feeling of "too low carbon dioxide" gets interpreted by the brain as "I'm not getting enough air." The result is even more rapid breathing, and a vicious cycle that leads to what's experienced as a panic attack or hyperventilation episode. At other times, the person goes along in a state of too low carbon dioxide without a full-blown panic attack, but a very unpleasant state of anxiety. If one can learn to recognize the "too low carbon dioxide" state in its beginning stages, and nip it in the bud by breathing more slowly, this skill can dramatically reduce or eliminate panic attacks and improve anxiety. I recommend two exercises to improve this skill. In the first, the person holds the breath, just to the point where it begins to feel unpleasant, notes, "this is the feeling of too high carbon dioxide," and cures that unpleasant feeling by taking a deep breath or two. In the second exercise, the person hyperventilates for 10 or 15 deep and fast breaths, feels the slightly unpleasant feeling that this induces, notes, "this is the feeling of too low carbon dioxide," and cures that feeling by breathing very slowly for perhaps half a minute or a minute. It takes practice to correct bad breathing habits; it doesn't do to just say, "OK, when I start to have a panic attack I'll slow down my breathing." One needs to create a reflex where one habitually reacts to the "low carbon dioxide" feeling by breathing more slowly. Changing habits takes practice.

Anxiety-reduction goals are greatly fostered by becoming an expert in fantasy rehearsal. The more one can fantasy rehearse positive responses to the unrealistically feared situations, the easier real-life exposures will become. I speak of two types of fantasy rehearsals: coping rehearsals and mastery rehearsals. In a coping rehearsal, you imagine yourself being scared or having the other aversive feelings as you encounter the situation; you imagine yourself sticking with the situation and having the fear gradually go down; you imagine yourself feeling very proud about your act of courage. In a mastery rehearsal, you imagine that a miracle (or lots of hard work) have happened, and the formerly unrealistically feared situation is no longer the slightest bit scary. You imagine yourself handling it with comfort and perhaps pleasure, and you feel glad that the situation no longer elicits bad feelings. Both of these types of rehearsals are quite useful. When rehearsing, the STEB mnemonic helps us remember to visualize the situation vividly and to include the thoughts, emotions, and behaviors of the new desirable response.

In combating anxiety, one of the most helpful resources is a positive emotional climate in relationships. In a positive emotional climate, people have fun with each other, approve of one another, are kind, and are ready to help. In hostile, negative emotional climates, anxiety is higher because danger, particularly "social danger," but perhaps physical danger as well, is more likely to be present.

Overcoming social anxiety is particularly useful, because it enables one to seek out and establish relationships with positive emotional climates. A large part of overcoming social anxiety consists of skill-building. The social interaction skills we discussed earlier are major aids. Another ingredient is correcting certain thought distortions – for example, recognizing that people are not usually preoccupied with judging and mentally criticizing you, and that people may care a lot less about judging your worth than you may have thought they do. Another example is recognizing that even if someone, or a group of people, do judge you negatively, this is not an awful event, particularly if the people use misguided criteria for judging, as they so often do.

A special type of anxiety is worry. It's very useful to take the energy that one would expend on worrying, and try to direct it toward more useful decision-making. I recommend sitting down and listing the areas of worry, and using the SOIL ADDLE steps of decision-making for each one. These steps are:
1. (Situation) you think about the important aspects of the situation you face;
2. (Objectives) you clearly specify your objectives in dealing with the situation;
3. (Information) you get information that will help you decide;
4. (List) you list options for what to do;

5. (Advantages) you think of the **a**dvantages and disadvantages of options;
6. (Decide) you **d**ecide;
7. (do) you **d**o what you've decided;
8. (Learn from Experience) you **l**earn from the **e**xperience.

Carrying out these steps in writing tends to elicit productive, organized thought about the situation. Worry often occurs when the situation is so complex that it's difficult to hold in memory all the important aspects of the decision process. Another anti-worrying technique is to use checklists to systematically check how safe and secure you are with respect to each of the four types of danger we mentioned earlier: physical, social, economic, and goal-achievement-related aspects of life. Worrying is sometimes the product of the knowledge that "There may be something important that I'm forgetting to pay attention to." If one can attend to the important things in an organized way, worry may be reduced.

Reducing compulsions has very much in common with reducing fears and aversions. In fact, it can be argued that compulsions are repetitive behaviors, the reinforcers for which come from the temporary reduction of an unrealistic fear or aversion. For example, compulsive handwashing is reinforced by a brief reduction in the unrealistic fear of having one's hands contaminated; a compulsion not to step on lines or cracks on the sidewalk is reinforced by a brief reduction in the unrealistic fear of the consequences of stepping there; compulsive checking of having turned the stove off is reinforced by a brief reduction in an unrealistic fear of burning the house down; and so forth.

The strategy for reducing compulsions involves repeatedly putting oneself in the situation that induces the fear or aversion and not letting oneself do the compulsion; this is called "exposure and ritual prevention." Just as with other fears, it's good to make a hierarchy of exposures and start with the easiest. Just as with other fears, it's useful to pay attention to self-talk. It's useful to pay attention to the SUD level, but to put even greater importance on the act of staying in the trigger situation without doing the compulsion. Helpful self-talk is important; it's good to reinforce oneself for the courage triumph that the practice session entails. And last but not least, fantasy rehearsal can be extremely useful as a method for practicing handling the situations that trigger compulsions, in a more convenient and less painful way than starting right away with real-life exposures.

Obsessions are also related strongly to fears and aversions. They may often be thought of as greatly feared mental images. For example, someone has the image of himself doing a forbidden violent or sexual act, and feels fear or guilt or revulsion over picturing such a thing. But trying very hard to banish a thought from the mind seems to stubbornly return that thought to consciousness. This is called the "white bear problem," so named after Leo Tolstoy's narrating that when he was a child, his older brother would challenge him to "stand in the corner and not think of the white bear." Tolstoy confessed, "I remember how I used to stand in the corner and endeavor, but could not possibly manage, not to think of the white bear." (Birukov & Tolstoy, 1911).

How do people who are not bothered by obsessions act when images of antisocial behaviors pop into their minds? I believe that most of them simply continue doing what they are doing, without getting too worried about the thought that has intruded. People with obsessions can do fantasy rehearsals, imagining that an unwanted thought has come to mind, and imagining themselves deciding what is their best use of time at the moment, and doing that activity, whether or not the intrusive thought continues to occupy a place in consciousness. The real-life experience that one can act in ways that are wise and good, despite having mental images of behaviors that are unwise or bad, provides reason not to fear the mental images. Another approach to obsessions is simply to observe the intrusive images, note one's SUD level, and continue to observe them, working not toward complete comfort with them, but with the ability to tolerate them enough that it is possible to do wise and good things without their being too distracting.

The anxiety curriculum is the place I've chosen to go into greatest detail about nonpharmacologic techniques of avoiding insomnia and making sleeping pleasant. A number of sleep hygiene rules promote a conditioned association between being in bed and sleeping: one should not spend lots of time in bed reading, watching TV, talking on the phone, or doing other things. If one finds oneself tossing and turning unpleasantly, one should get out of bed and do something else for a while, something useful but not too exciting or reinforcing, perhaps something a little boring – such as reading one of my books. If one is kept awake by worries, I recommend getting up and writing about the decisions that the worries are grappling with. A very important guideline is to increase the amount of exercise one gets, so as to be very tired by bedtime. Keeping the bedtime and waking time regular is an often-advised, seldom followed, but very wise guideline. One should consider cutting back on scary and violent entertainment, particularly if disturbing images come to mind when lying in bed awake or if nightmares come. Working on relaxation techniques and using some of these while in bed, particularly the pleasant dreams technique, may be very useful.

Nightmares can greatly interfere with our enjoyment of sleep. To reduce nightmares, cut down on violent and scary entertainment; practice re-fantasying the scary content of the nightmares, in such a way that the story becomes a pleasant one; practice lots of other pleasant dream-like narratives while awake; read stories that model gentleness, kindness, and harmony among people; imagine stories in which you have such powerful allies to protect yourself (nonviolently) from predators that you do not need to hurt or otherwise disable them; imagine narratives in which you have the magical power to change bad and scary predators into good and loyal and nonviolent allies.

Work block, or the inability to get oneself to quit procrastinating, is a very painful problem. We can conceive of it as an aversion to working, or negative feelings with a conditioned association to the stimulus situation of a certain type of work. The aversion is reinforced and usually increased every time one tries to get working but escapes by procrastinating again; the escape behavior is reinforced by a temporary reduction in aversive feelings; this reinforcement experience increases the urge to procrastinate on the next occasion. We can deal with work aversion using the same techniques that we use for other aversions. Here are two techniques I've found particularly useful. The first is attention to self-talk, i.e. turning off the internal critic, and revving up the self-reinforcement for any productive activity. A second technique is recruitment of an ally, i.e. arranging with a person for an appointment to do work at a particular place and time; the two people reinforce each other for putting in the time and effort. But all the other techniques can be useful: muscle relaxation, moving along a hierarchy, fantasy rehearsal, etc.

Similarly, test anxiety and picky eating can be dealt with using the stockpile of anti-anxiety techniques we've mentioned.

Becoming a successful student

Performing up to one's potential in school is a very important psychological skill. Grades and scores, whether given by teachers or derived from standardized tests, are doubtlessly very imperfect indicators of how much a student has gotten from a course. Some students, usually spurred on by a parent, go overboard in the quest to look perfect before a college admissions committee, at great expense to their own mental health. Many students fall prey to the delusion that if they don't get into one of the few "elite" colleges, they are failures and consigned to life of being a loser. Others seem to opt out of the academic game altogether, at even greater expense to their life trajectory. A middle course is wise. In this middle path, one tries to learn as efficiently and enjoyably and successfully as possible, investing large, but reasonable amounts of effort into academics, seeking to enjoy the time spent studying, while not forsaking other enjoyable activities that give life balance.

It's easier to spend time on academic work if one has made an "internal sales pitch" -- a list of reasons why success is desirable. There are several good reasons. As long as you have to play a game, it's more fun if you are winning it. You learn skills important for job success, and for escaping poverty. You learn to tap into sources of pleasure that can enrich your experience throughout your whole life. Enjoying reading and writing means that you need never be bored. Writing helps you organize your thoughts. Math helps you think more effectively. Learning self-discipline and increasing your work capacity helps you succeed in any goal. Getting good grades can win admiration from other people. You can learn skills that may allow you to do lots of good for humanity. Keeping in mind the reasons for being a successful student makes achieving the goal more likely.

Academic success demands a lot of effort, and you should try to rig it that your effort pays off. This means that if you are in a learning situation where the work is too hard or too easy, you should try to get into one where the work is close to the "just right" level of challenge. Your effort will have more payoff if you pay attention to any measures of progress that your educators give you – test scores, grades. You may sometimes need to come up with other ways of measuring your progress, because tests and grades are sometimes not accurate enough.

There are certain skills that you will want to make automatic, so that you can do them as if by reflex, without needing to do a lot of laborious thought. For example, it is useful to become fluent in the basic math facts, e.g. 15-7 or 54/9. You will want to be able to read aloud a text appropriate for your age level, clearly and fluently, with few misreads. You will want to be fluent in both handwriting and typing. You'll want to master the spellings of the several thousand most commonly used words in the language. You'll want to know the meanings of more and more words as you get more and more educated. There are ways of measuring all these skills; enterprising students can figure out their own ways of measuring them over time. If you measure, you can see your progress and feel good about it. Doing repeated time trials is a great way to measure progress, particularly when they are not in public and there is no chance of feeling embarrassed.

The best students keep constant track of how well they are succeeding in school, for a very important reason: they want to adjust and fine tune their strategies so as to achieve success in the most enjoyable way. If they are not succeeding, they change something quickly. In response to bad grades, there are various strategies: they may simply spend more time studying. They may change where and when they put in their time working. And they may change what they do while studying – what they do with their eyes, hands, and mind.

In adjusting how they study, the best students figure out how to divide their time between taking information in, for example by reading, and testing themselves to see if they remember the information. One way of testing one's own recall is to do the reflections exercise with each paragraph of reading – to look up and say what one got out of that paragraph.

Another really useful way of testing oneself is to write down questions (and their answers) while reading, or making a "catechism." Then, you go back, read the question, answer it mentally or aloud or in writing, and then check it against the answer you wrote. If anything is unclear, you go back to the text and reread. This technique alone can turn a struggling student into a successful one, if the student has the self-discipline and writing fluency to be able to use it.

Another technique for learning from reading is to frequently ask the question, how do the various parts of this written work fit together? How do they relate to one another? Where does what I'm reading now fit into the whole work?

A prime way to improve study efficiency is to eliminate distractions. A student who attempts to do homework while watching television is in trouble; often it helps to work at a computer that has no internet connection so as to avoid temptations.

Students who have trouble in math, physics, chemistry, and other problem-solving subjects should take note of a "well-kept secret": you should read the explanations of how to do a problem in a textbook, and work carefully through any worked-out examples the book gives. Many students go straight to their homework problems, without taking the time to read the very clear explanations of how to do them.

When writing, I recommend dividing the task into stages: generating ideas, deciding which to include, deciding what order to put them in, and deciding how to word and punctuate them. If beginning writers try to do all these tasks at once, they are likely to overload working memory; if they concentrate on one at a time, they have a better chance to do each task well.

It's important not just to learn, but to get credit for what you do. For this reason, successful students tend to be very aware of grading rubrics – the algorithms whereby grades are generated. They pay close attention to what tests will cover and what they will not. They put their effort into what is necessary to get the grade. They are also careful to remember to turn in their work. Going through the steps necessary to remember to record an assignment, do the assignment in time, transport it to the classroom, and hand it in is for some students the major grade-limiting set of steps for being successful, and not the learning itself.

When academic work is unpleasant, it is often because one is not competent enough at it. Thus the "avoidance versus mastery choice point" comes up often. Do I want to try to avoid math, or do I want to master the essential math skills, starting with the most basic ones? Do I want to adjust to hating writing, or do I want to master every step in the process and make it fun?

To overcome test anxiety, fantasy rehearsing being in the test situation while actually rehearsing a practice test is a key technique. All the other anxiety-reduction techniques should also be considered. These include relaxing muscles, choosinguseful self-talk, and recalling times when you have felt the way you want to feel in performance situations and visualizing feeling the same way during the test.

A very important technique is to adjust the frequency of review to match the steepness of your forgetting curve. Suppose a course has ten units. The person studies each unit, and learns it well, but never reviews it afterward. But then the person has to perform well on a final exam over all ten units. If the person has a super retentive memory, the person may stroll into the final exam and ace it. But what if the person tends to forget each unit about two weeks after learning it? The person will have a monumental task of pumping everything back in to memory just before the exam. Different people have different forgetting curves. If you tend to forget more quickly, it behooves you to review more often. It is much easier to bring material back to memory if you review it just as it is starting to fade from memory; it is much harder when it has been mostly forgotten. By carrying out quick reviews, someone can bump the forgetting curve upward and hang on to what was learned much more efficiently. When in doubt as to what the exact shape of your forgetting curve is, it's good to err on the side of carrying out quick reviews often, by skimming over text chapters or re-testing oneself on the questions and answers one generated on the text.

Most students do not realize how much the process of learning and remembering can be disrupted by sleep deprivation. Again, people differ greatly, but lots of them become lots smarter when they can get more sleep. The sleep hygiene rules mentioned in the anxiety book are important.

Some of the major obstacles to becoming a successful student are the common time-wasters that tempt students away from more productive activity. Television, electronic games, the Internet, and fiddling with smartphones all can be rewarding and fun activities, but they spell doom for many students' chances of academic success. Sports and extracurricular activities, likewise, can be quite valuable activities, but both parents and students must keep in mind that there are only a limited number of hours in a day. If one needs to spend more time on academic work, it's necessary to spend less time on something else.

The word "shaping" means helping someone to achieve a goal or to do a complex behavior by reinforcing successive approximations to it. Students can learn to do internal shaping, by using reinforcing self-talk as they do each of the tasks necessary for academic success. With enough self-reinforcement, the job of being a successful student becomes much more pleasant.

Task-switching

Task-switching refers to a set of tasks or challenges that are examples of "executive functioning" and which rely upon prefrontal cortical activity. Such challenges require you to pay attention to similar stimuli, but to alternate between different directions about how to respond to the stimuli. An example is the Stroop Task, where you look at words for colors, printed in other colors, and switch between reading the word and saying what color the word is. The literature on task-switching (Strayhorn & Strayhorn, 2010) provides evidence that people with ADHD and other conditions that reduce executive functioning, on the average, do worse on task-switching. Also, there is evidence that practice in task-switching can improve performance on these challenges. What we wait for is evidence as to whether practice in task-switching can strengthen executive functioning so much that real-life decision making, planning, and execution of plans are done so as to improve the quality of life. Our manual (Strayhorn & Strayhorn, 2010) provides math facts exercises for task-switching, on the theory that at the very least, the student who practices task-switching in this way should improve in math fact fluency.

Chapter 12: Skills and Guidelines for Tutors

What does one have to know in order to be an excellent psychoeducational tutor? As you read this chapter, you may want to keep in mind how much the skills of tutoring overlap with excellence in 1) any other job, 2) friendship, 3) parenting, 4) marital relations, and 5) any other thing that human beings do together.

In order to make this chapter somewhat self-contained, there some overlap with and repetition of ideas presented elsewhere in this book.

1: Commitment

Psychoeducational tutors are asked to think hard, before taking on the job of tutoring, whether they can be successful. For success, they need to stick to the job for at least a year – in marked contrast to other jobs where one can be successful by working only a few months. They make appointments with the family and call the student on the phone for 30 minute sessions, 6 days a week. They spend time learning lots of things about how to make these sessions as worthwhile as possible. They commit to use the curriculum that the program furnishes rather than making up their own; nonetheless there is lots of room for personal judgment and the expert use of their own personalities. They keep records of what they've done, and report them to the administration of the project once a month. They reply in a timely manner to communications from supervisory staff. And they manage to maintain high morale in their students and themselves.

The financial rewards for all this conscientiousness and caring are not the major draw. (The opportunities for meaningful service and valuable learning are the major draws.)

Donating "only" 30 minutes a day, day after day, may not sound like much, but it means that many spur of the moment things tutors might do will have to be interrupted by their sessions. The job of psychoeducational tutor is not easy. It requires lots of patience, steadfastness, organization skills, and being able to psyche oneself up into an upbeat mood regularly and on schedule.

Chapter 12: Skills and Guidelines for Tutors

The job of psychoeducational tutor is a chance to do lots of good for a child. It's also a chance to do harm. Suppose a tutor forms a close relationship with a child and the child comes to depend upon the regularity and dependability of the sessions for emotional support and psychological growth. If the tutor terminates the job prematurely, the child may have a hard time switching to a different tutor. Tutors are not interchangeable. Many children make strong attachments to individuals, not to a "program." Candidates who are not sure whether they can keep the commitment may want to try substituting for other tutors. They can also study the manuals and come to in-person or electronic meetings, and let the idea percolate. But they should not start up with their own students until they have soul-searched enough to know they want to stick with the commitment.

Here's a checklist for tutors, regarding threats to keeping the commitment of tutoring.

Is there a chance of your spending time abroad?
May you get a leading part in a play?
May you run for office?
May you take an extremely demanding course load?
May you take on a new job that is draining and difficult?
May you get into a relationship with someone who wouldn't appreciate your taking out tutoring time?
Is there someone whom you may need to take care of, whose care would demand so much time that you couldn't tutor?
Are you a "spontaneous" rather than "planned" type of person, who can't predict exactly what will go on in your life very far ahead of time?

People can still tutor even when the answers to some of these have been "yes," but it takes more dedication and sacrifice to do so. Tutor candidates should consider carefully, because it is very important not to have to tell the student "good-bye" prematurely.

2: Consistency, and communication about any lapses

Part of the commitment that tutors make is to have sessions consistently. It is extremely disappointing for supervisors to ever hear that the sessions have not been going on for a while, without their knowledge. If something on the tutor's end, or on the student's end, is going to interrupt the regular schedule of the sessions, supervisors need to hear from tutors as soon as possible. Administrators need to do what they can to patch the interruption, perhaps by arranging a substitute tutor. This involves another work skill for tutors, that of keeping administrators informed about what is going on.

Suppose a tutor is going to take a vacation, and the child would like a little break. The tutor works out with the family to restart the sessions after vacation, without bothering the supervisor with this. This is not OK! Part of the job of the tutor is keeping the supervisor informed about what is going on. If tutors need to miss one or more days of tutoring, they should let their supervisor know as far ahead of time as possible.

What does far ahead of time mean? A week or more is best. A day ahead is better than saying that a substitute is needed "today," and even that is better than no communication at all.

To repeat, even a notification at the last minute is vastly preferred to none at all! Tutors should NOT just cancel sessions without letting a supervisor know.

It's important to avoid a communication blackout. There may be times when, for example, the family's phone that the tutor has been calling will malfunction. If the phone is the only way the tutor knows to connect with the family, and the family doesn't know the tutor's phone number or email address, the child may go without the tutoring for several days or longer, and the continuity and dependability of the tutoring will be severely weakened.

There is a good way to prevent this. Tutors should get every available piece of contact information from the family: every phone number, parents' work phone numbers, every family member's email address, and the family's mailing address. If there are restrictions on the use of the parents' work phone numbers, these should be noted. Likewise, tutors should give the family every phone number and email address with which they can contact the tutor. If the phone goes unanswered when a tutor calls at the appointed time, the next move is to go straight to the file of contact information data and leave messages via all other methods of communication. If these don't get answered, it is "even" possible to send a non-electronic letter to the family!

3: Quitting a job proficiently

When anyone starts a job, it is good to have a good and mutually acceptable plan for how it will eventually end. In ideal circumstances, tutors would be able to keep working with their students as long as their students need work. However, some students need psychoeducational tutoring for a matter of years, and tutors may not be available for that long. The key proficiency of quitting well is to give plenty of advance notice, to family, child, and supervisor. Let the supervisor know as soon as there is any possibility that you may be quitting. Tutors should let administration know at least a month ahead of time, so that they can help to train and prepare their successors, and so that, if desired, tutor and successor may overlap with each other. Two months is much better. Tutors should let their students have plenty of time to get used to the idea that you are leaving.

But if drastic life changes strike, and if tutors need to resign immediately, they should at least let administration, family, and child know, in a final conversation with each. To simply stop calling without returning phone calls is highly unprofessional and unethical.

If tutors conduct a "good termination" with the child, with plenty of advance planning, it's good if they can build in the possibility of staying in touch once in a while over the long term. If it is possible for them to stay in touch with students after they finish the tutoring, e.g. by calling once every three months, that is great. If they can offer to students the option of calling them and chatting when the students get an urge to, this too softens the pain of separation for the student. I have yet to see a child abuse this privilege.

4: Communicating with supervisors

If tutors and supervisors all come together in a building and work in physical proximity of each other, they can just knock on office doors when there is an important issue on which to communicate. In the virtual workplace that the Organization for Psychoeducational Tutoring inhabits, electronic devices are crucial for communication. So many electronic messages are sent and received in this world that emails or other messages from supervisors may seem lost in an overwhelmingly large set.

Despite this problem, tutors need to respond quickly when an administrator sends an email or leaves a voice message or sends a text (or all three) asking one or more questions. If tutors cannot reply to questions right away, they should at least let supervisors know that the message was received and when an answer will be coming. Being able to communicate is very important for an organization. An organization where employees do not respond promptly to employers' questions or requests can't run well.

5: Appointment-keeping

Tutor candidates who haven't yet been able to accomplish the habit of keeping appointments very dependably should deselect themselves from the tutoring before beginning. Because the development of a strong, stable relationship between the tutor and the student is so key to the tutoring, it is critical that tutors assess their ability to "wear the ball and chain" of daily appointments before committing themselves.

It has been said that "Eighty percent of life consists in showing up." The basic unit of psychoeducational tutoring is the "session." An appointment is made between tutor and student (or student's parent) for a certain time. The tutor calls at that time, give or take a minute or two, (that is, neither early nor late) and either the student or the parent answers, with the student ready for the session. If one is to be a tutor, it is crucial to have excellent habits of "appointmentology." Here are the rules of appointmentology.

1. Well over 95% of the time, simply keep appointments without changing them. Make the commitment to the time and keep it within a minute or two.

2. If you discover that you can't keep an appointment, let the person you have the appointment with know, as far ahead of time as possible – that is, as soon as you discover that you can't keep the appointment. Do NOT wait until the appointment time and let the person know then.

3. If you can't keep the appointment, see if you can reschedule for a different time that day (first choice) or reschedule for the next day (second choice). If you can't get in touch with the family, leave messages by every channel that you have: land line voice mail, cell phone voice mail, and email. Be proactive about getting all these numbers and addresses as soon as you start the tutoring – don't passively wait for someone to give them to you. Be prepared so that you can make valiant efforts to contact the family before the time of the session.

4. Try never, never to be a "no show," with no-showing defined as having the family expect you to call and your simply not calling. No-showing is the cardinal sin of appointmentology.

5. If you should ever do a no-show, contact the family as close as possible to the instant you have realized this. Apologize sincerely and reschedule. No-showing and then not being in contact is an even worse violation of good appointmentology than a simple no-show. Also please let your supervisor know what happened, being proactive in notifying the supervisor yourself rather than having the family notify the supervisor first.

6. In order to reduce further the chance of no-shows, give the family your phone number and email address, and encourage them to contact you if by some improbable set of circumstances you should ever no-show. If they contact you at the time of the session, apologize and hold the session. If they contact you after the appointment time, apologize and reschedule for as soon as possible.

7. Put a great priority upon your establishing and keeping a reputation as someone who can be counted on to call when you have committed yourself to call. If you know yourself well enough to know that you can't keep such commitments with very, very infrequent exceptions, please deselect yourself from being a tutor before you even begin!

* * *

One of the mistakes most frequently made with phone appointments is to wait until the time of the appointment to cancel or postpone. Tutors will likely be annoyed if they have passed up a movie or dinner with friends to keep a phone appointment, only to find out at the time of the appointment that the family has known for the last few hours that they could not keep the appointment. For the same reason, if tutors can't keep an appointment, they should reschedule, not at the appointed time, but ahead of time, so that people are able to plan their schedules accordingly!

Here's a very important word to wise tutors: ***Use the alarm clock function of your cell phone!*** Phone appointments are easier to forget than in-person appointments, because one doesn't have to get ready, take transportation, etc. Tutors should use technology to help themselves remember, and alarm clocks on phones or wrist watches are perfect reminders.

People who select and hire tutors should note carefully whether tutor candidates keep phone appointments during the screening and interviewing and training process. Difficulty keeping those appointments is a clear sign that a candidate should not become a tutor.

It is usually easier for tutors to follow the rules of appointment-keeping if they let the force of habit and routine work in their favor. If at all possible, tutors and families should get into a set routine of appointment times.

What if the problem is not the tutor's appointmentology skills, but those of the family? The standards for families are much less stringent than those for tutors. Tutors will have to forgive appointmentology violations by families that they would not accept in themselves. Still, if families cannot keep appointments at least 80% of the time, in most cases tutoring can't be continued. If this is the case, tutors should keep careful records of what appointments were made, kept, and canceled. Tutors should communicate with a supervisor about what to do. In most cases the supervisor will communicate with the family and see if a plan can be made to salvage the tutoring. The choice to terminate tutoring because of missed appointments is not something tutors should make on their own – it is a major decision, and should be made at the highest levels of the organization.

Chapter 12: Skills and Guidelines for Tutors

Even though tutors have to be tolerant and kind in the face of appointment breaches, they should not "enable" the families to get sloppy with appointment keeping skills by over-indulging requests to change the time. Suppose that a tutor calls at the appointed time, to be greeted with a request like, "Could you call back in half an hour?" Usually the response to this should be, "No, but we can reschedule for tomorrow." Tutors have set aside time and have planned, often at considerable sacrifice of their own convenience. Their clients should appreciate this fact and not take it for granted. If necessary, tutors should politely explain this to the child and to the parents. Families may need to be reminded, by an administrator, that both tutor and student affirm the importance of the activity by sticking to the plan for the appointment time.

What if the family is in the middle of something, and wants the tutor to call back in ten minutes? Usually the response should be that this is fine, but the session will have to end at the usual time. In other words, tutors should not the need to go over the end time because they acceded to a request to start a little late. If the family can't get going on time, the session will be shortened a little bit.

It's a different situation when the family contacts the tutor ahead of time to change the appointment time. Suppose the appointment time is at 5:30 pm today, and a tutor gets a text message at 10:00 am asking if it would be possible to change the time to 7:30 pm. Now the tutor can reschedule if it's convenient, and not reschedule if it isn't. But the tutor in the call-ahead case is not reinforcing the child or family for bad appointment-keeping skills.

It's important to negotiate postponements or reductions or reschedulings of appointments with the parent, not the child. Tutors must avoid getting a child into the habit of successfully postponing an appointment because the child is in the middle of a video game! So if you call, and if the child asks the tutor to call back in ten minutes, the tutor should say that postponements are arranged with the parent, and the tutor should talk with the parent or guardian or caretaker about what's going on.

6: Promoting a positive emotional climate

What do we mean by "positive emotional climate?" We mean a relationship where lots of approval, and very little disapproval, goes back and forth; where people are kind to each other; where people listen to each other; where people enjoy making each other happy; where people are a source of enjoyment for each other.

The emotional climate of a relationship depends upon both people. But each makes his or her separate contribution. Tutors want their own contributions to emotional climates to be as positive as possible.

Lots of people have experienced relationships where people seem to communicate their caring about the other person by teasing, being sarcastic, or giving good-natured insults to the other person. We strongly recommend *not* doing this in tutoring sessions. We recommend avoiding irony, but just saying what is meant, and giving approval in straightforward ways. If tutors give gently teasing jabs at their students, they may find that students respond to this precedent by insulting them very disrespectfully. Tutors should set a precedent of dignity in communications with the student.

A very important job of a tutor is to project a spirit of optimism, enthusiasm, joyousness, and approval. In face-to-face interaction, tutors can provide positive reinforcement and approval to children by patting the child on the back, giving a thumbs-up gesture, nodding, smiling, and all sorts of other signals that are impossible to do over the phone. Over the phone, they must rely upon the auditory channel. Between the semantic content of what they say and the musical inflection of their voices, the latter is more important in setting the emotional tone of the session.

We can rate the amount of approval conveyed in the musical tones of someone's voice (this is separate from the semantic meaning of the utterance). We can use a rating system with three gradations:

neutral

small to moderate approval, or

large approval.

Neutral tones are monotone, not excited, rather robot-like. Small to moderate approval tones are cheerful, happy, peppy, and upbeat. Large approval tones convey a real feeling of great positive excitement about something the child did. Tutors are advised to use a lot of small to moderate approval in their sessions, as a baseline way of being. They should give larger approval to reinforce larger accomplishments. They should not use neutral or disapproving tones for very long without a really unusual and cogent rationale for doing so. The "tones of approval" exercise is one the tutor will usually eventually teach the student; it's important for the tutor to get really good at tones of approval before the tutoring starts.

Tutors who are not in the habit of using lots of upbeat, cheerful, enthusiastic tones of voice will need to remind themselves, every session, to charge up their enthusiastic voices. There's a prize for all this effort: tutors will find that revised habits of vocal tones will have effects beyond the tutoring, changing their own interactions and their own lives. They will find that people tend to be more enthusiastic and approving back to them.

In the psychoeducational tutoring enterprise, enthusiastic excitement often makes the difference between the child's being able to continue in the tutoring and to persevere in the process, rather than complaining and whining and eventually dropping out. Projecting joyousness in the tone of voice is one of the supreme skills of the expert tutor.

7: Maintaining authority

The tutor calls the shots for the session. Tutors should avoid the pattern where the child feels that he or she has the power to arbitrarily refuse to do something if he doesn't feel like doing it. Tutors want to get the precedent going from the very beginning that they *announce* when each activity begins and ends, and what it will be. The student can have input by asking the tutor to do a certain activity, not by telling the tutor.

In keeping with the need for the tutor to be in authority, tutors should usually not ask children if they want to do an activity. They should not say, "Would you like to sound and blend another list?" They should not say, "Do you want to read from the self-discipline manual next?" Instead, they should simply announce what is coming next. If a child obviously dislikes a certain activity, the tutor can end it sooner, but should not end it immediately after the child's complaining about it.

The tutor should explain that no one activity lasts very long, and the ability to do something you don't feel like doing for at least a short time is the very important skill of self-discipline. This skill can be the key to success and happiness in life.

The tutor can explain to a student that if there's an activity that is tough, the student can build up his or her toughness by gradually increasing the ability to endure that activity. Sometimes it's useful to explain that when people start an endurance activity like running or swimming or biking, or a strength activity like weight-lifting, at the beginning they get tired quickly or can't lift much. But as they get in better shape, they are capable of going for much longer than they would have thought possible at the beginning, and they get stronger and stronger. When you put demands on yourself, you gradually grow in your strength and endurance. If tutors can help their students see things from the point of view of "I'm getting stronger and stronger," versus "I have to work when I'd rather play video games," that attitude difference can be crucial to success.

In keeping with the idea of maintaining authority, tutors should not let the child dictate when the session is over. Usually they should plan on a session of a certain length and stick with that. They stop at the end of the time. And they are generally the ones to point out that it's time to finish, not the students.

Tutors should not use the ending of the session as a reinforcer, for example by saying, "You did so well, we can stop now." They should avoid sending the message that an early end to the session should be a reward – the session is a privilege for the student. If the student says, "When do we stop," the tutor might say something like, "There are a few minutes left. Let's see if we can do x sections before we stop the alternate reading, and a quick exercise."

The above is not meant to imply that tutors have to be rigid. If the child is sick or has a big performance coming up after the session, for example, the tutor may choose to have a much shorter session. If the child says, "When can we stop," usually it's good to ask, "Are you wanting to stop sooner than usual?" and to find out why. This is best done at the beginning of the session, not in the middle or near the end.

Short sessions can be very useful in keeping up the precedent of having the session on time, when there are some demands from life that get in the way of a full session. If at the beginning of the session tutors get what sound like reasonable requests for a short session, they should feel empowered to accede to this request. I recommend touching base briefly with the parent about shortened sessions. Tutors should teach the child and the parents to make such requests at the beginning of the session, or better still even farther ahead of time, not in the middle of the session.

Tutors should avoid ending sessions contingent upon the child's complaining about feeling tired or bored. If the student dislikes working so much that the end of a session is a reinforcer to the child, this reinforcer shouldn't follow the behaviors of complaining of fatigue or generating fatigue. Reinforcers should follow goal attainment or a certain amount of time working toward goals. Try to end after the allotted time.

However, the child's complaints, if they arise, should be taken into account. Tutors should discuss these with their supervisor. One option is to try to build more fun activities into the sessions. Perhaps some of the activities are too hard for the child and need to be made easier – or vice versa. Perhaps the expectation for the length of the session needs to be cut down. Or, perhaps tutoring is not for this child, and we need to terminate and deliver it to a child who does enjoy it.

Tutors should continually ask themselves whether the session demands are suitable to the children they are working with. Rather than waiting for complaints, they can simply ask the child, after several sessions, whether the child feels that the sessions are too long, too short, or of the right length. They can ask the child whether the amount of work done in the sessions is too much, too little, or just right. If the child communicates that the work is too much, we should take that seriously. We may want to cut down on the amount of work temporarily, and try to build up the student's work capacity so that eventually the child is capable of a session the same length as most other children his age. We may want to be very open with the child and the parent about this goal.

8: Alternate reading

Alternate reading consists in taking turns reading from the programmed manuals. These manuals are divided into brief sections that are followed by a comprehension question.

The tutor reads a section aloud and the student answers the comprehension question. (A "section" is one of the numbered parts of programmed texts. Each time there's an A or B multiple choice question, one section ends and the next one then begins.) The tutor reinforces the student's correct answer (by saying, "Yes!" or "I agree!" or some such) or very briefly explains why the other answer is correct. Then it's the student's turn to read the next section. The student again answers the question, and the tutor gives feedback. (Thus the student answers all the questions.) Then it's the tutor's turn to read again.

Why have the tutor read half the sections, instead of giving the student twice as much practice reading aloud by having the student read all sections? The tutor's reading aloud lets the tutor model for the student how to speak clearly and how to use appropriate intonation. If tutors can read as expressively as an actor does when recording an audiobook, they show the student how to do this. Also, tutors' reading time gives the students a chance to relax. For many of us, being read to gives something of a feeling of being nurtured. Plus, by taking turns reading sections, tutors set the precedent for turn-taking that is vital to all sorts of tutoring activities.

Alternate reading can be a very pleasant and relaxing routine. I find that the more I do it, the more it feels like a form of meditation. It's low-pressure, but it engages the mind and the attention. It's a rhythmic sort of activity, with the turn-taking routine, and that rhythm feels somewhat like the rhythm of repeating a mantra or focusing on one's breathing and so forth. Hopefully both student and tutor can eventually get into the relaxing meditation-like feeling involved in the alternate reading.

Some tutors get the urge to quiz the student further, after a section of alternate reading, as if the child's answering the fairly easy comprehension question is letting the child get off too easily. Also sometimes tutors feel impelled to ask the student to explain why the answer he or she gave is correct. Tutors who get either of these urges should please, almost always resist them! We want the alternate reading to be relaxing. Tutors don't need to make it more "rigorous." More questioning than is already built in runs the risk of slowing down the enterprise and making it less pleasant. It's also usually more relaxing for tutors if they just sit back and stick to the script and not feel that you have to improvise a lesson plan on the spot. If the child is reading the sections and answering at least 80% of the questions correctly, something is probably sinking in.

If the child is learning to read, we can start alternate reading by taking turns with the panels of the primer stories in the *Manual for Tutors and Teachers of Reading.* Then the child is often ready to take turns on the panels of *Illustrated Stories that Model Psychological Skills* and *The Letter Stories.* Some children need some easy books intermediate in level between the primer stories and Illustrated Stories; the *Big Blue Book* and the *Big Red Book of Beginner Books* have served us well for bridging that gap.

In reading illustrated stories, it's great to take turns on the panels – i.e. the pictures with captions in the upper left, upper right, lower left, and lower right. Usually each page has four panels. Some children get on a roll and would like to read an entire illustrated story to the tutor. If so, it's fine to let the child read the whole story. Maybe the tutor can "sort of" take turns by reading the child a story that the child is less familiar with, so as to help lay down some memory traces that will help the child read the story alone soon.

Programmed Readings for Psychological Skills (Strayhorn, 2001) is usually the first programmed manual to read, because it contains such important concepts, and because the reading difficulty level is lowest of the programmed manuals. *A Programmed course in Friendship-Building and Social Skills* (Strayhorn, 2003) is the next easiest manual to read. The manuals on psychological skills exercises, anxiety reduction, and anger control are next higher in difficulty; the ones on self-discipline and being a successful student are perhaps a little higher. *Reading About Math* (Strayhorn, 2012) is at a high elementary reading level; the math level spans the range from very basic elementary level to elementary algebra. It's good to read all these manuals with students, and to read parts of them more than once.

After the student has finished *Programmed Readings*, the student is ready to read some novels that we have made "skill questions" about, one question per page. So far we have skill questions on the *Boxcar Children,* numbers 1, 2, 3, and 7; *The Wheel on the School, Mrs. Frisby and the Rats of NIMH, Charlotte's Web,* and two collections of Donald Duck and Uncle Scrooge comics. The skill questions help the student review the concepts covered in the manuals, particularly *Programmed Readings.* The novels may be more entertaining than some of the more expository skill writing. If so, tutors can let the more entertaining reading reinforce the more self-discipline-requiring reading, by having some skill-book reading followed immediately by some novel-reading. The questions are collected in the volume called *Psychological Skills Questions on Novels* (Strayhorn & Strayhorn, 2014).

In the novel-reading, you take turns reading by pages, and each page counts as a "section."

What if the child, or the parents, want to read books that are not in the official curriculum? In general, we want the intervention to be standardized, so that there is only a finite set of curricular materials. If you and the family want to nominate a certain book to be incorporated into the standard set, tutors may please get in touch with supervisory staff. It the book is good enough, we may be able to dig up time to construct psychological skill questions on it and make it part of our "skill-ized" book set. But tutors should not just go along with any request they get from the family or student. They should talk it over with supervisors and let us examine the book and talk it over with the family.

Suppose that in alternate reading, tutors find that their students answer every question, or nearly every question, correctly. What should we infer from this? We infer that the writing is not over the student's head (and that's good) and that the writer has done a good job of making the answers unambiguous (and that's good too!)

We should NOT infer that the writing is "not challenging enough" or "too easy for" the student. Our educational system sometimes convinces people that if people can get all or nearly all questions right, the challenges are not "rigorous" enough. I have heard of college professors and teaching assistants lamenting when the class got too high a fraction of test questions correct (rather than celebrating that the instructor successfully got across what he or she set out to teach!) If the goal of asking questions is to create a competition that will rank order the performance of learners, as in a foot race, making up tests where most people miss many questions makes sense. But if the goal is to help individuals to maximize learning, this attitude can be quite pernicious. Wrong answers tend to create "false memories"; this is one reason that the writers of programmed instruction want to facilitate as close to "errorless performance" in the learner as possible. Also, if as an educator your goal is to get across a certain point, you have succeeded when the student demonstrates understanding it, and you have failed when the student is mixed up on it. Thus the ideal is 100% success.

Some of the parents of our students have overheard their children getting the answers nearly all correct, and have inferred that the student already knows what we are teaching, and thus any problem in the child's behavior must result from lack of motivation rather than from lack of knowledge and skill. Of course, this inference is totally incorrect, partly because with good programmed instruction you can get correct answers on material you had no knowledge of before. On a more complex level, I believe that it is an error to make a hard and fast distinction between "motivation" and "skill." If, for example, one improves in the *skill* of celebrating one's own kind acts, one thereby increases the *motivation* to do kind acts. If one practices generating multiple options to the point of automaticity, one usually gets more urges, or has more motivation, to think before acting.

Any incorrect inferences that parents make about the negative meanings of correct answers of course do not represent a reason to blame or disparage parents, but represent an agenda item for the parent education component of the intervention. We try to get across to parents the notion of nearly "errorless learning" at the beginning of tutoring, but that doesn't mean that all of them will remember it!

There's another inference we are tempted to make from the student's correct answers to the end-of-section questions: that the student will necessarily remember the material and be able to apply it. Unfortunately, this inference is not correct either. Some older students have felt that *Programmed Readings* is "too easy" for them. Yet often those same students may draw a total blank when after reading this easy book, they are asked questions like, "How do you do the 12 thought exercise?" "What are the four ways of listening that the chapter on ways of listening discusses?" "What are the steps of conflict-resolution that are remembered by 'Dr. L.W. Aap'?" or even, "Which of the 16 skills and principles do you remember?" And there is often even more of a blank look in response to the question, "How would you summarize the ideas in this book?"

The fact that people don't automatically remember and apply concepts just from reading and understanding them once is one of the main reasons for psychological skills exercises, where the student can repetitively practice using the concepts with hypothetical situations.

But it will also be good if tutors can communicate to students that there is a lot more to "mastering" the content of a book than just getting the questions right. Remembering and applying the ideas constitute a much higher level of challenge. If the student seems insulted by the easy nature of the questions, tutors should consult the supervisor about incorporating challenges for the student to summarize what was learned rather than just answer A or B. The art of doing these challenges well is not easy. Tutors should ideally make the degree of challenge for each student not too hard, not too easy, but just right.

9: Chatting with the student

One of the three main parts of the psychological skills session is chatting. Tutors should remember that they are not counselors or therapists (even if by training, they are!) The conversations they have with the student are not aimed at solving the problems in the student's life. The tutor and student simply have fun getting to know each other better and talking about life. If the student doesn't feel like social conversation, as many students will not, especially at the beginning, it's fine to skip this part of the session – for the time being. But the goal of pleasant social conversation should remain on the agenda. It's often a source of pleasant interaction for both tutor and student; it can reinforce each of them for the work they are doing together. Plus, social conversation is a very crucial psychological skill. It's great to get very much practice at doing it well.

In attempting to promote social conversation, tutors often get the urge to ask the child a lot of questions. Usually this doesn't work. How have you been doing? OK. What have you been up to? Not much. How was school? OK. Did anything interesting happen at school? No. Did you learn anything interesting? No. This isn't what we mean by pleasant social conversation!

What should tutors do to promote social conversation, as a substitute for grilling the student with questions? One answer is: model for the child how to volunteer information about their own experiences. For example: "I did something fun since I talked with you last. There was an old friend of mine, whom I hadn't seen or talked with for years, and I just picked up the phone and called her up. She was surprised to hear from me!" Or for another example: "I saw a very interesting movie last night. It was a story about …" Or for another example: "After our session tonight, guess what I'm going to do -- I'm going to write a paper, for a course I'm taking. The topic is …"

Some tutors assume that all students will enjoy talking about their school days. With this assumption, they repeatedly ask the student about school. Tutors should keep in mind that some students hate school and attempt to block out from memory the occurrences of the school day as soon as they get out of it. Whether this strategy is a good one for the student is debatable. But if the goal is to get started into fun chats, tutors shouldn't keep asking about any subject matter that the child doesn't seem to want to talk about. To extend this principle, before tutors ask too many questions about their students' friends, they should gingerly get a feeling for whether the student has any friends in the first place.

Sometimes one of the best ways to encourage social conversation with many children is for tutors just to go about their work of alternate reading and psychological skills exercises, interrupting this work every now and then by telling about their own experiences, and just waiting (sometimes many sessions) for the child to interrupt the work by telling about his own experience. When the student does interrupt, the tutor can listen carefully and enthusiastically, and thus encourage the student's chatting further.

Another fun way of promoting social conversation is "ice-breaker" exercises. In "Two Truths and a Tale," tutor and student tell three things about themselves or their experience to the other, two of which are true and one of which is made up and not true. The listener guesses which are true and false. But the emphasis is on exploring what the person discloses, not on correct guessing. In the "Would You Rather" exercise, tutor and student refer to a list of questions, or make them up, such as "Would you rather be transported 500 years into the future, or into the past?" or "Would you rather be a music superstar, or teach nonviolence in a way that keeps one person from getting killed, even though you never get to find out who that person is?" Another is the Sentence Completion Exercise, where tutor and student take turns completing sentences such as "I hope that ..." or "It makes me feel good when ..."

9a: Listening skills

A major part of the chatting activity is for tutors to model good listening skills. When the student talks, the tutor should try to use 1) reflections, 2) facilitations, 3) follow-up questions, and 4) positive feedback. These are four ways of listening that are explained to the student in *Programmed Readings, Friendship-Building*, and *A Programmed Course in Psychological Skills Exercises.* When tutors use these listening responses in conversation with the student, there are at least two positive effects: first, the tutor helps the student to enjoy chatting more. Second, the tutor teaches the student how to be a good listener, by giving the student models. Here are some examples:

Reflections:

Sounds like you felt really good about doing that.
So if I understand you correctly, even though you felt like yelling at your sister, you didn't do it, and you used self-discipline?
In other words, you're saying that you find yourself thinking about your celebrations several times during the day!
What I hear you saying is that you can't decide what to do about this kid, and you're still going back and forth between a few options, huh?

Facilitations:

Cool!
Oh?
Uh huh!
What do you know!

I see.
Humh!
OK.
I understand.
Awesome!
Yes...

Follow up questions:

What happened then?
Why do you think she did that?
Tell me more, please.
I'd like to hear more about that, please.
So what are your thoughts about that?
What kind of thing was it?

Positive feedback:

I'm glad you told me that.
Thanks for telling me about that.
That's an interesting point.
I'm really glad to hear that.
Good point!
That sounds like a smart idea.

Every once in a while tutors will want to ask a "new topic question": unlike a follow-up question, this one isn't about the same topic the student just talked about, but introduces a new subject for the conversation. Conversations where people do this too often never seem to get into any topic in depth. Sometimes new topic questions can be annoying when the person hadn't finished with the old topic, or when the new topic is not of interest. But when people keep these things in mind and avoid these pitfalls, new topic questions can add to your conversation rather than subtract. The same goes for "new topic statements," where you tell about some of your own experience that had not previously been the topic. It can interrupt things, but it can also let people try out a new subject of conversation and model for students how to tell about things they find interesting and fun to talk about.

When chatting with your student, tutors should be conscious of the tone of voice and the context in which they use their student's name. It's good to use the student's name when you are excitedly reinforcing the student, as in "Good, Johnny!" They should avoid using the student's name in a sort of nagging voice when you are correcting the student, as in "Johnny, you skipped a line," or "No, Johnny. It's the other answer."

If tutors use the student's name in the positive context and not the correcting or contradicting mode, the student's name will become a sound the student likes to hear, at least from the tutor. Since this sound is one the student associates with his or her own identity, creating a positive emotional association with it seems good.

When the student speaks, the tutor may respond with a whole range of emotions – from "Oh, my gosh! That's hard to believe!" (astonishment) to "OK, no big deal." (cool aplomb) From "Why do people do things like that!?" (righteous indignation) to "What a great idea!" (admiration) From "Hmm. OK." (noncommittally taking it in) to "Wow! What a great celebration! Hearing you say you did that is music to my ears!" (joy) Some tutors need to try very hard not to maintain the same bland level of emotion no matter what the child says. Resisting this habit and communicating a wider range of emotion during conversation makes the sessions much more fun for the student.

As a general rule, we should assume that excitement is reinforcing. Sometimes even the excitement of negative emotion, for example exasperation or anger, is reinforcing to stimulus-seeking students. This implies that tutors, (and even much more so, parents) should try to get excited about good things and stay unexcited about bad things that people do, even the people you talk about. Thus the most excitement should usually come in expression of positive emotion.

9b: Avoiding the role of the advice-giver

The role of the tutor is not one in which the student presents life situations and the tutor says what the student should do. Why not? First, most students don't even ask for advice or give any indication that they want it. Even if they do, much of the time tutors won't know the situation well enough to know what's the best thing to do. Hearing a full explication of the situation from student and parent, and probing the right questions, can be a delicate and time-consuming process. Even if the student talks about the situation a lot, the student may have distorted the facts, or left out some important ones. Also, if the tutoring role becomes one primarily of counseling or advising, parents and students can legitimately get mad at us if you give advice which the student attempts to follow and has things not work out right. Also, the advice a tutor might give may be in conflict with that given by a therapist or parent. We have a certain curriculum to teach, rather than being the student's adviser.

If a student starts telling a tutor about a problem situation in his or her life, the tutor should consider using reflections and facilitations. These are great ways of helping the student feel understood, without falling into the trap of feeling the need to give advice. Using reflections to make sure one understands what the student is saying is a way of listening while following the rule, "First of all, do no harm."

All this having been said, there are some exceptions to the rule of avoiding advice-giving, particularly when it's clear what the right or wrong thing to do is. The tutor does not need to keep secret any opinions about cruel or self-destructive options – it's more than all right to affirm the basic aims of increasing one's own happiness and those of others! Tutors should chat with supervisors when contemplating how strong a stand to take in favor of a certain life decision for their student.

10: Taking the role of an enthusiastic fellow learner

The tutor should avoid taking the role of the mental health expert. A better role to take is that of an enthusiastic fellow learner. Most tutors will not have carefully studied, or even read, the programmed manuals before reading them with their student – and this is fine. The tutor may be candid with the student that the tutor and student can learn together. The tutor can model for the student taking the role of an interested learner – by saying things like, "I see what this is getting at... it's _____. I can see how this would be useful." Or, "That sounds like a useful model of a way of thinking about things. I'm going to give that a try."

With both parents and students, tutors find their work easier if they emphasize the "fellow learner" role and avoid the "expert" role. There's a game that "experts" fall prey to, which goes: 1) let's ask the expert a very difficult problem, 2) let's allow the expert to answer (perhaps even listening to the answer), and 3) let's then prove to the expert that the advice won't work. If you don't position yourself as an expert, you can stay out of this game.

11: Competence in the psychological skills exercises

Although I just emphasized the "fellow learner" versus "expert" role for the tutor, it is very important for the tutor to learn to do psychological skills exercises proficiently.

One of the three main parts of the psychological skills session is psychological skills exercises. (The other two parts are alternate reading and chatting. For many children, reading exercises are a crucial part also.) Just as push-ups and running are exercises to build up your physical strength or health, exercises such as the celebrations exercise, skills stories, the four-thought or 12-thought exercise, the brainstorming options exercise, the reflections exercise, listening with four responses, the conflict-resolution role-play, fantasy rehearsals, and others are meant to build up psychological strength or health. Usually they present the opportunity to *practice* one or more psychological skills. Such practice counts toward the sometimes large number of practice hours that may be needed to become an "expert."

We'd like tutors to read at least one of the two full-length books I've written on psychological skills exercises. Tutors and students should eventually read (in alternate reading) *A Programmed Course in Psychological Skills Exercises.* Tutors should read this book on their own, first. There's another book on these exercises, entitled *Exercises for Psychological Skills*, which is meant for tutors and some advanced students to read.

Let's quickly remind ourselves of what is meant by some of the psychological skills exercises.

In the celebrations exercise, the tutor and student take turns telling real-life things they have done that are positive examples of psychological skills, and they identify which skills these are examples of. These recountings represent both rehearsals and reinforcements of positive examples.

In skills stories, tutor and student take turns making up concrete positive examples of the psychological skills and principles in little stories like those at the beginning of *Programmed Readings*. The principle, again, is fantasy rehearsal: imagining positive patterns makes them more likely to be chosen in real life.

In the four-thought exercise, the student takes a hypothetical situation and generates the following types of thoughts about that situation: not awfulizing, goal-setting, listing options and choosing, and celebrating your own choice.

In the twelve-thought exercise, the tutor and student take turns making up twelve different types of thoughts about a given situation. (The twelve are: awfulizing, getting down on yourself, blaming someone else, not awfulizing, not getting down on yourself, not blaming someone else, goal-setting, listing options and choosing, learning from the experience, celebrating luck, celebrating someone else's choice, and celebrating your own choice.) By learning labels for types of thoughts, the student can more easily do metacognition, or thinking about thoughts. We're hoping to help the child achieve the liberation of being able to choose which thoughts are most useful rather than being stuck in habits. The four-thought and twelve-thought exercises are educational approaches to much of what goes on in cognitive therapy.

In the option-generating exercise, the tutor and student take turns thinking of options for response to a hypothetical situation.

In the reflections exercise, one person talks, pausing often, and the other listens, using reflections of the form, "So what I hear you saying is _____." Then it's the first person's turn to talk and the second person's turn to listen.

In listening with four responses, one person talks, and the other listens, using not only 1) reflections, but also: 2) facilitations such as "yes," "I see," "Uh huh," "Oh," and so forth, 3) follow-up questions, such as "What happened next?" and 4) positive feedback, such as "That's an interesting idea!" Tutor and student alternate between talker and listener roles.

In the conflict resolution role-play, tutor and student role-play a very polite and rational conversation which resolves a hypothetical disagreement, attempting to meet seven criteria for conflict-resolution conversations. The seven criteria are 1) **defining** the problem, without criticizing or commanding the other person, 2) **reflecting** the other person's point of view to make sure you understand it right, 3) **listing** options together, 4) **waiting** until all the options have been listed before evaluating them, 5) thinking about the **advantages** and disadvantages of options, 6) **agreeing** on something, and 7) **politeness** throughout. The first letter of each of the bolded words makes the mnemonic Dr. L.W. Aap.

Over time, the goal is for tutor and student to do more and more exercises, proficiently. The tutor should keep track of which exercises the student has become proficient in, to what degree (three levels for each are defined in *Programmed Course in Psychological Skills Exercises*). We may independently test the student to confirm that the student has attained proficiency. One measure of our success is how many exercises the student can learn to do very proficiently.

One of the reasons we are excited about psychological skills exercises is that we think they may double as "performance tests of psychological skills." Which, for example, would be a more valid test of the skill of generating options when making decisions: 1) hearing a bunch of choice points and being asked to think of options, or 2) rating, on a scale of 10, how much you agree with the statement, "I can think of lots of good options for solving problems?" We think there's a reason why chemistry professors bother to make up final exams, rather than simply having their students rate themselves on the question, "On a scale of 0 to 10, how good are you in chemistry?" Most of measurement of psychological health has been stuck in rating scales, and one of our research goals is to contribute to changing that.

12: Fostering The effort-payoff connection

One of the strongest antidotes to depression, and promoters of happiness, is the feeling, or the knowledge, that your efforts are paying off.

Conversely, perhaps the most depressing situation is one in which nothing that you do can make any difference – no matter what you do, things will turn out the same. Another phrase for the effort-payoff connection is contingent reinforcement – the things you want are contingent upon what you do.

In our tutoring program, we ask our students to invest effort. We want the students to see the results of their efforts – to get a payoff from them, and to be aware of that payoff. This can happen in several ways.

The most immediate payoff is the tutor's enthusiastic approval of the student's effort – this is called social reinforcement.

A second form of effort-payoff connection occurs when the student gets important outcomes measured, and sees that the outcomes have improved. For many students, our checking their reading ability serves this function. It can be very exciting to see the level of reading skill going up over time. Testing the ability to do various psychological skills exercises, and helping the student realize that she is becoming able to do more and more exercises, is evidence that efforts are paying off. Measuring parent and teacher behavior ratings over time and communicating the results to the student is another way of using outcome measurement to foster the effort-payoff connection.

A third very important way of promoting the effort-payoff connection is our keeping track of how much work the student has done, and periodically celebrating certain milestone levels. When we are teaching reading decoding, the unit of work is points; various exercises result in the accumulation of points. For reading students who are working through the word lists, a useful metric is how many lists the student has mastered. But this is definitely subordinate to the number of points achieved. The reading student gets two word list points for sounding and blending a word, and one point for reading the word without saying the separate sounds. One text unit consists of one illustrated story, one play, one numbered section in a programmed manual, or one page in a "skill-ized" novel. Some students will master the word lists in 30,000 word list points, whereas others will require 300,000 points. We want to celebrate the process.

For work on psychological skills, the two main measures of work output, or process measures, are: 1) how many "text units" the tutor and the student have covered through alternate reading, and 2) how many psychological skills exercises they have done, counting each repetition of any exercise as one more exercise.

Keeping track of which exercises the student has "mastered" and to what degree is another very important measure of progress.

We want to keep track of sections and exercises so that the student has a sense of cumulative accomplishment. For most students, we will send the student something in the mail after certain round numbers of sections or exercises or reading points. A standard mailing is a certificate stating the number of work units accumulated so far, a two dollar bill, a post card with congratulatory words, and perhaps another book to be used in the program. Sometimes other tangible prizes are used. For older students, just a simple letter recounting the cumulative number of work units carried out is useful. It seems to be rewarding for students to get these in the U.S. mail, perhaps because of the increasing rarity of non-electronic communications. The certificates and prizes seek to help the student know that people (not only the tutor, but also the administrators of the program) are keeping up with how much work has been accumulated, and that this work is being celebrated.

The notion that extrinsic rewards decrease intrinsic motivation, and thus should not be used, has been the subject of much research. Some introductory psychology textbooks present the "anti-extrinsic-reward" side of the question convincingly. My own conclusion is that to reject the use of extrinsic reinforcers is mistaken and harmful. If you want to read more about the "pro-extrinsic-reward" side of the debate, please see Eisenberger and Cameron (1996), Eisenberger et al. (1999), and Strain and Joseph, (2004).

In addition to plowing through lots of psychological research, we can contemplate real-life observations such as that the widespread custom of paying people money for work seems to increase productivity rather than decrease it.

Keeping track of the student's cumulative accomplishment and celebrating it can make all the difference in the student's attitude toward the tutoring. We want the student not to think, "Now I have my session, so I have to work for a certain length of time." We want the student to think, "Here's a chance for me to add to what I've accomplished so far."

It is most likely that the student will feel like he is working toward a goal if the tutor continually makes the student aware of his or her progress and accomplishments. Even smaller achievements should be tied to the particular variable used to keep track ("Congrats, you finished that list – and now you have X points!" or "So far today we've read Y sections – that brings us to a total of Z!"). The student should be reminded frequently about what the next milestone you're shooting for is and how close the student is to reaching it. And the parent should be updated in the same way. You can provide key support for the parents' own system of reinforcement, encouraging them to celebrate the student's accomplishments and cuing them as to when to do so.

If a student isn't enjoying the tutoring, it may be the case that the student is clueless about how many units of work he or she has done, what the next milestone is, and how the next milestone will be celebrated. And if this is the case, usually the tutor is not communicating this information to the student.

The ways of monitoring, recording, and celebrating accomplishment can vary from student to student. Tutors should talk with their supervisor about this if they are unclear on what's the best way to celebrate milestones. We can be flexible. For some students, we may forgo all certificates, prizes, and letters, but there should be a very good reason for this.

When in doubt, tutors can just do a little arithmetic and figure out a milestone that will result in a celebration after about the first couple of weeks, a month after that, and about every three months thereafter.

The administration will do the work of sending certificates and prizes for tutors, unless tutors want to get in on this and arrange with supervisors to do it. Sending these prizes is a way for administrators to keep track of what progress is taking place. If we never hear that a prize or certificate or letter should be sent, it should be a red flag for us that the effort-payoff connection may not be fostered thoroughly enough.

13: Hierarchy-ology: picking the right level of difficulty

What is one of the major advantages of one-on-one tutoring over larger group instruction? In classrooms, the tasks students are assigned are often too hard for some, too easy for others, and just at the right level of difficulty for perhaps only a few. In tutoring, by contrast, the tutor can continually adjust the level of difficulty to fit the learner's current (and continually changing) level of skill. In our tutoring, we should take advantage of our ability to fine-tune the level of task difficulty.

Working at the right level of difficulty helps maximize the speed of learning, but it also does something else very important: it maximizes enjoyment. The book *Flow* by Mihaly Csikszentmihalyi (1990) gives evidence that a level of challenge not so easy as to be boring, and not so difficult as to be frustrating, is key to the experience of happiness and fun.

The makers of video games understand this principle thoroughly. A well-done video game will let you "level up" or "level down" so that the game's challenges are just right for the your skill. This is one of the reasons why video games can be so addictive, particularly, perhaps, for people for whom most of the other tasks of life are either too easy or too hard.

When we think about the difficulty of tasks, we want to think multidimensionally. By this I mean that a given task can require several different skills, and thus it can occupy several different places on the various hierarchies for the learner. For example, consider alternate reading. This task involves at least the following: 1) decoding the words that are being read, 2) understanding the meaning of the words being read, 3) paying attention well enough to combine the meanings of the words and understand what is being read, 4) continue paying attention over time, versus being depleted of attentional energy, 5) submitting to authority enough to follow the tutor's direction that alternate reading is the activity to be pursued, 6) making the speech apparatus say the words right, and 7) using good intonation, good acting skills, by putting expression into the reading performance. We could probably break the task down into even more components.

One corollary is that you can't infer that a task is easy overall because a certain part of it is easy. Maybe a student is good enough at decoding that she can read the words fluently, but she doesn't know what they mean. Maybe a student can read well enough to do the activity, but the work capacity is so low that sustaining work over time is the limiting factor. Maybe the student can do the activity, but is not yet skilled enough at submitting to someone else's directives that the child can do it without aversion.

A rough guideline to finding the right level of difficulty is the 80% rule. If the student isn't successful on at least 80% of the challenges he or she takes on, we should consider lowering the level of difficulty. If she is missing more than 20% of the questions you ask, or misreading close to 20% of the words she's trying to read, or having trouble with 20% of the problems she's trying to solve, then the student is probably at too difficult a level. If what the student is being asked to do is too difficult, the tutor should figure out a way to "go down the hierarchy" to tasks in which the student can be successful at least 80% of the time.

The ways of going down the hierarchy of difficulty are very much spelled out within the reading curriculum. "Sound and blend after me" is easier than "sound and blend on your own." Sounding and blending words in lists is usually easier than reading words of equivalent difficulty in stories. Doing phonemic awareness and spatial awareness exercises is easier than sounding and blending word lists. Within the set of phonemic awareness exercises, some are very easy and some are much harder.

In alternate reading, some of the manuals and "skill-ized" novels are much easier reading than others. We shouldn't be afraid to put a manual away for a while if it's too difficult. If the content is really important but the reading skills aren't there yet, the tutor can read selected sections to the student. The tutor can adjust the length of time spent on the various activities, to fit the attention span of the learner.

Some of the exercises can be made easier. For the example, the tutor can make the one called "the guessing game" quite easy if that's what the learner needs. For the brainstorming options exercise, we can pick very concrete situations with several obvious solutions to make it easier, and vice versa. The reflections exercise is lower on the hierarchy than the listening with four responses exercise. If the celebrations exercise is hard for the learner, you can do a "celebrations interview," asking about specific good things the learner may have done. A student who has trouble submitting to authority can be officially allowed to pick between several activities. These are a few of the many ways that we can adjust the level of difficulty. Whenever we go down the hierarchy, the move isn't permanent – we think about how to work our way back up, and sometimes can do so quickly.

Sometimes we take on older students whose reading level makes *Programmed Readings*, particularly the first stories, seem way too easy. But we want to get across the fundamental content that is present in this foundational book. Here's one way of elevating the level of difficulty. You explain to the older student that the ideas in this book are very important, and thus it should be read, despite the fact that the reading level will be lower than the student's grade level. You also explain that one way of increasing the level of challenge is for the student to focus on intonation and expressiveness. Reading this book aloud is no problem, but reading it with as good a performance as a great actor could muster is very difficult. Using such expressiveness is a very important skill.

14: Using and promoting self-care

Tutoring by telephone is a fairly non-dangerous occupation! Nonetheless, it's necessary for tutors to use caution to protect themselves. Here are some of the ways that come to mind:

First, and most important, no one should try to tutor, or communicate by phone or text all, while driving a car or doing any other task from which distraction could be fatal or harmful.

Second, if tutors use headphones or ear buds, they should not turn the volume up high enough to damage their hearing.

Third, tutors should keep cell phones a safe distance from their heads, in case the theory that some harm is done by the waves that conduct the information turns out to be correct.

At the time of this writing, the conclusion of several official agencies is that there is not sufficient evidence to believe that the energy given off by cell phones causes cancer or other health problems. For example, the website of the Federal Communications Commission (2015) states, "Currently no scientific evidence establishes a causal link between wireless device use and cancer or other illnesses." The National Cancer Institute Website (2016) reviews a number of studies and summarizes opinions: "The U.S. Food and Drug Administration (FDA) notes that studies reporting biological changes associated with radiofrequency energy have failed to be replicated and that the majority of human epidemiologic studies have failed to show a relationship between exposure to radiofrequency energy from cell phones and health problems. The U.S. Centers for Disease Control and Prevention (CDC) states that no scientific evidence definitively answers whether cell phone use causes cancer." However, there certainly are some scientific studies suggesting a causal link (e.g. Hardell et al., 2013, Morgan et al. 2015), as well as studies casting doubt on the causal link (e.g. Chapman et al., 2016, Lahkola et al., 2006). I believe that it's best to err on the side of caution. A pretty good degree of protection is gained by using headphones or ear buds connected to the cell phone by a wire. Apparently even putting the cell phone on speaker and moving it away from the head lowers the exposure a great deal. Using a land line or Skype or something other than a cell phone is of course another solution. Tutors should be aware of this issue, take care of themselves, and encourage the parents of their students to take care of them.

15: Confidentiality

In the ideal world, there would be no stigma attached to efforts to improve one's mental health, and people would perhaps advertise their affiliations with organizations like ours, just as people advertise their college affiliations with sweat shirts and car window stickers. However, it is very possible that some families and students would regard their participation with us as something they would like held private. Thus all information about our students, and even their names, are considered private information, and should be kept confidential. In communicating about them, use their initials or first names. Tutors should hold their sessions in private locations; they should keep the records of sessions in a computer file that doesn't have the student's name on it. They should not speak with people outside the organization about personal or potentially embarrassing details concerning the student, even without referring to the student by name. Of course, it is not necessary for tutors to conceal from friends and family members the fact that they are tutoring, and the progress their students are making. Plus, they can feel free to talk with their supervisor and others within our group. To keep in practice, they should stick to the custom of using first names or initials only when speaking in group meetings. If they have any doubt about confidentiality guidelines, they should ask a supervisor.

16: Dealing with lost books

What if the student answers the phone, but has lost whatever book you are working on? Tutors shouldn't give up on having a session if this is the case. Here are some options. The tutor can ask to speak to the parent or caretaker, and ask that person to look for the book or to verify that it is lost. If it is lost permanently, we can send another. If the family has Internet capability, we can send an electronic copy of the book and the child can read it from the computer file. The tutor can always read each section of the book to the child, and let the child listen and answer the questions. The tutor can do psychological skills exercises for most or all of the session. If there is any other book in our program that the student can find, tutor and student can do some alternate reading with that book, even if they've already read it before.

17: Reinforcing goal attainment rather than expression of fatigue

Especially for students who have problems with low work capacity, getting to finish a work task can be reinforcing. This is particularly true for the tasks the student experiences as tedious, such as sounding and blending word lists or practicing math facts or for some students, reading aloud. What happens if the tutor waits until the student starts complaining and saying "I'm tired of this," or "I want to stop and do something else" before you finish up with the task? Then the student is getting reinforced for complaining of fatigue. This reinforcement contingency is not good for the student's work capacity.

On the other hand, suppose the tutor has a good intuitive feeling of how much work on a given task is not too much or too little, and the tutor announces, "We'll do this until we get X points." Then, when the X points are accomplished, the tutor says, "You did it! You have X points. Now let's go to the next activity!" If finishing up the activity is reinforcing for the student, the student in this case has been reinforced for attaining a goal, not for displaying fatigue. This is good for the student's work capacity.

18: Constant awareness of differential reinforcement

Let's generalize. We just considered that signaling that it's time to stop working may be reinforcing for the student. Let's think about the fact that *everything* the tutor does, that the student perceives, is either reinforcing, punishing, or neither. And one of those three types of responses follows *every* behavior that the student does. The best tutors are constantly aware of this, and they try to make their most reinforcing responses follow the most desirable behaviors of the student. They try to make non-reinforcing responses follow the undesirable behaviors of the student. When they reinforce the positive more than the negative, "differential reinforcement" works correctly. When they inadvertently reinforce the unwanted behavior more than the desired behavior, differential reinforcement works to the child's detriment. Working to make differential reinforcement exert its effects in the right direction for the student is a major task for the tutor, as it is for a parent, teacher, therapist, or anyone else who works with other people.

19: Dealing with fear of failure and conditioned aversions to academic work and conversation

Each child is different, and tutors sometimes work with children who have had nothing but solid success in every academic venture. But so far, this is the exception, and many of the children we tutor have had very negative experiences with school, and have acquired very negative conditioned associations with anything resembling an academic challenge. And of course, working on reading, taking turns reading aloud, and so forth are very academic activities. This, however, is one of the major ways that our tutoring can help, because if we can undo negative conditioning and replace it with positive associations, we can have a major positive effect on a child's life.

Every introductory psychology textbook speaks of Pavlov and studies on conditioned responses. Many children's experiences fit this paradigm closely. An unconditioned stimulus is disapproval from other people or "looking stupid" in front of others; the unconditioned response is the visceral and emotional reactions of fear and shame and humiliation and defeat. The conditioned stimulus is being asked to try to read something or do some other academic task; when this is paired with the unconditioned stimulus enough, the academic challenge comes to elicit the feelings of fear and shame. Thus very unpleasant emotions are now the conditioned response to academic challenges.

The solution to this is to start with challenges that the child can be successful with, to give lots of approval and celebration for those successes, and gradually to work up the hierarchy of difficulty, maintaining a high ratio of success to failure. Now the conditioned stimulus (academic challenge) is presented unpaired with the unconditioned stimulus (disapproval and social humiliation), so that "extinction" can occur. But beyond that, the experience is creating a new conditioned association: the stimulus of academic challenge is being paired with the unconditioned stimulus of the tutor's tones of enthusiasm and approval and friendliness and the feedback of success, so that we are creating a new conditioned association between academic challenge and the emotions of fun, confidence, and enjoyment, with the physiological responses to match!

Likewise, some children have had negative conditioning with social interaction. Their conversations with people have been unpleasant enough, often enough, that fear and shame have become conditioned to the stimulus of, for example, someone's saying, "How have you been?" For this reason, many children at the beginning of tutoring will answer that question by saying, "OK;" the question, "What have you been doing," by saying, "Not much;" the question "How was school today," by saying "All right;" and so forth. All these utterances sometimes really mean, "I don't want to talk, and I'm trying to escape the aversiveness of your questions by giving you a one-word answer which won't reinforce you for asking."

One of the answers to this is for tutors to go lightly on the questions, and go more heavily on modeling telling the child about their own experience. Tutors can demonstrate through their own examples how to really enjoy telling someone about something. They should work themselves into the state of mind where they can't wait to tell the student about the "celebrations" they've been saving up. When they model social conversation, they should make sure to let a few seconds of silence go by every now and then to give the child a chance to speak. When the student does talk, the tutor should respond very enthusiastically and in a reinforcing way. The four ways of listening we speak of elsewhere (reflections, facilitations, follow-up questions, and positive feedback) combined with tones of approval, provide ways of reinforcing the student's social conversation.

The tutor is not the student's therapist or counselor. But if the tutor starts tutoring with a student who hates reading and other academic tasks, and/or who fears social conversation, and if after several months the tutor now is working with a child who enjoys both reading and chatting, the undoing of negative conditioning and instilling of positive associations may have had a life-changing effect on the student. Reading and conversing are two of the most important activities of modern life. The difference between enjoying these activities and hating them is a monumental one. A tutor can have sometimes have a huge effect on a child's emotional life without doing anything other than being a good tutor and a nice person to chat with!

Sometimes "therapy" with children, conducted in a misguided way, serves to make more negative the conditioned associations with conversation. If a therapist mostly "digs" for the child's negative feelings, the narration of the unwise behaviors the child has done, the reasons and motivations for the child's maladaptive behaviors, the difference between what the child did and what the child should have done, memories of negative events, and so forth, the child may be learning that the process of exchanging words with another person is painful, or may be strengthening such learnings that have already taken place. Sometimes when a therapist sees a parent and child together, the parent naturally expects that telling the therapist about all the child's problem behaviors and emotions is a way of solving those problems. Meanwhile, the child, who is hearing a narration of everything maladaptive he/she has done lately, may be mainly learning that it's wise to avoid the situation where people talk with each other.

It takes a wise therapist to figure out how to discuss "problems" with a child who isn't at all sold on the value of "discussing" in general! It can take careful maneuvering by a therapist to get private time with the parent to hear about the child's problems in a setting where the child isn't embarrassed or humiliated by the narration.

Fortunately, psychoeducational tutors don't have to deal with these complexities. Their conversations with children are not aimed at discovering, learning more about, or solving the child's problems. Tutors' conversations with students are simply aimed at enjoyment and celebration of the positive. Tutors get to chat with the child about whatever is most pleasant for the two to talk about, especially the good things they both have done. If the child spontaneously talks about problems, the tutor listens nondirectively. But if, like most children, our students don't like to talk about "problems," we have no need to oppose this tendency.

20: Calling things by their right names

Words are important. Our sessions are "tutoring sessions," not "counseling sessions" or "therapy sessions." Tutors don't have the burden of being expected to solve particular problems that students have, that tutors may or may not learn about. Rather, they are trying to deliver a certain curriculum, that may help the child be better equipped to solve and prevent a wide variety of problems. If the child's parent refers to what we do as counseling or therapy, tutors should very politely let the parent know that this is not the case. They can say something like, "Regarding the word *counseling*, I've been asked to let people know that the word *counseling* may come with expectations and legal implications that we're trying to avoid, so the word *tutoring* is what I use."

When tutors take turns with your student reading the numbered sections in a programmed manual, that is "alternate reading." When they do something like the reflections exercise, the celebrations exercise, the twelve thought exercise, brainstorming options, etc., that is an "exercise." In the research we have undertaken, variables we track are: which books have been read, how many "text units" have been completed in alternate reading, how many exercises have been done, and how many exercises have been mastered. In a sense, alternate reading is itself an exercise, but it's a special enough case that when we count exercises, we don't count it – we count it all by itself, and measure it by the unit of "text units." Each time a student does the celebrations exercise or the reflections exercise, etc., we add one more to the total tally of "exercises."

If tutors refer to books by their titles, and to exercises by the names they were given, communication will be clearer. The exception to this is that sometimes young students do better by fetching the "light blue book" or the "purple and yellow book."

21: Speaking clearly

One of the primary requirements of a good telephone tutor is a style of speaking that is easy to hear and understand. And sometimes it's a problem to understand the student, and the tutor will need to teach the student how to come across clearly. The following are some guidelines on speech clarity.

One obvious way to do this is to speak loudly enough. A second important guideline is to position the mouth in the best place relative to the microphone of the phone you're using. The listener's feedback will help to figure this out. Speak slowly enough, and even more importantly, have a little bit of silence between each word so that the listener can tell when one word stops and the next one starts. In other words, say each word separately! But the most important guideline is to *make consonant sounds forcefully*. It's not hard for people to hear the vowel sounds in your words. But if they are to distinguish between lass and laugh, one has to make the s sound or the f sound forcefully. If the listener is to distinguish between mad and mat, the speaker should make the final consonant sound with vigor. Tutors and students may both benefit from focusing some energy on the single most important way to have speech be understood: emphasize the consonants.

If the student is hard to understand, perhaps the tutor can teach the student these guidelines and go over them often. Here they are:

1. Speak loudly enough.

2. Put your mouth close enough to, but not overly close to, the microphone.

3. Speak slowly enough.

4. Have a little silence between each pair of words.

5. Emphasize the consonants.

22: Knowing when to leave personal matters private

There are times when tutors disclose to students some things about their personal lives: for example, in the celebrations exercise, tutors think of things they're glad they did, and tell their students about these things. Or in the guess the feelings exercise, tutors think of real-life incidents they've experienced, and what they thought about it, and how they felt about it.

When disclosing to students, we want to give positive models and not negative models of how to live well. Tutors don't have to present themselves as perfect people, and they can talk about how to handle mistakes they've made. But they should avoid telling the student about anything they wouldn't want, say, a job interviewer or the student's parent to hear. They shouldn't make the student a confidant or use the student to talk about their own problems. Whenever there is self-disclosure, we want to present positive models as much as possible.

Part of the responsibility of being a tutor is being careful about making information about yourself publicly available on the Internet that would be harmful to the tutoring if the student, or his or her parents, see or read it. This means thinking twice before pouring one's heart out in a "status" report. It means avoiding posting any risqué pictures of oneself; it means avoiding language on the Internet that contains the common taboo words parents try to get their kids not to say; appearing to endorse or promote the use of alcohol or drugs; thinking twice before ranting about religious or political issues in a disrespectful way that might be offensive to a student's family (although tutors obviously retain the right to make public their carefully reasoned and even impassioned views on the issues of the day).

In a similar spirit, tutors should make sure the recorded announcement of their voice mails sound professional.

23: Keeping the parents informed

One of the important jobs of the tutor is to cultivate a positive relationship not only with the student, but with the student's parent or parents. For young children, the tutor will usually need to speak with the parent after every session to give feedback on how the child did and to let the parent help in reinforcing the child for the child's accomplishments during the session. For some older children, and in circumstances where the routine of sessions is set to occur very regularly, tutors needn't speak with the parent each session; still, they should chat with the parent at least briefly about how things are going at least once a week. They should not be afraid to ask the parent if they are satisfied customers, or even to have them rate their satisfaction with what is going on, on a 0 to 10 scale (where 10 is highest).

Tutors must have some authority, in their dealings with parents as well as with the child. If they ask to speak to the parent and the parent is very busy at the moment and does not want to speak, they can accede to that request. But they don't want to let parents set the precedent that the tutor never speaks with the parent, but only the child. We need parents to help us celebrate when the child passes a certain milestone of work. We want to get parents' opinions on whether benefits are coming from the tutoring. We want parents to know if there are any problems with scheduling or appointment keeping. Ideally, we want parents paying great attention to the progress report at the end of each session, so that the parent can celebrate with the child the accomplishments the child made that day. And even more ideally, we want parents to watch for positive examples of celebration-worthy behaviors the students do, and report them to the tutors. So if the parent is preferring not ever to talk with the tutor, a supervisor probably needs to talk with the parent. If the parent is so stressed or busy that we need to make an exception to our expectations about the parent's participation, so be it, but we don't want to slip into lowered expectations out of our own diffidence rather than out of a conscious choice.

24: Handling criticism from a parent

This section is fortunately relevant only on extremely rare occasions. But we are not perfect, and parents are not perfect, and it has been known to happen that a parent has unleashed hostile invective upon a tutor. It's good to prepare yourself for this – if it doesn't take place in the tutoring, it probably will at some other point in professional or personal life.

In the psychological skills training materials are various units on responding to criticism. There are units on this in *Programmed Readings,*

Anger Control, Exercises, and Instructions. All of these mention that one option for a response to criticism is to make sure you understand the criticism, perhaps by using reflections or by asking for more specific criticism. I recommend speaking in a calm tone. If the criticism catches a tutor off guard, an option is "planning to ponder or problem-solve": this means letting the critic know that you will think about this more and deal more with it later. If there is some piece of information the critic is not aware of that is fueling some anger, an option is "explaining the reason": letting the critic know this information in a calm tone. It's not professional to hang up on the critic, unless one has said several times that one needs to get off the phone now and the critic keeps talking. Another option is "Thank you for bringing this to my attention." Almost all the time tutors should let critical parents know they'll talk the problem over with the supervisor. It's unprofessional to raise the voice, and professional to stay cool. Tutors should not get too upset or worried or anxious – one good thing about this operation is that it's difficult to do very large amounts of harm; we have yet to remove the wrong kidney from someone or drop a bomb on the wrong people. As soon as possible, talk it over with your supervisor and we'll do some problem-solving about what option to enact.

25: Dealing with it if the student doesn't like the tutoring

We've been very gratified at how large a fraction of students seem to enjoy the tutoring process and voluntarily want to continue it, especially given how much work it entails. But occasionally we will hear that the child doesn't want to do it, that the parents have difficulty getting the child to come to the phone, or we will experience that the child seems to be an unwilling participant.

One of the good things about this intervention (as contrasted, say, to school) is that no one has to force it on anyone. If the child dislikes doing it, a really good option may be simply to stop it. There are literally millions of students out there who would love to have this opportunity, and we want to deploy our tutors to children who want it and not to those who hate it!

That having been said, it's good to keep in mind that many children have gone through phases of resistance to tutoring, but have later decided to continue it for a long time. There are options to consider other than terminating the tutoring.

When the student isn't enjoying the tutoring, here is a checklist of things for us to consider.

1) How are the tutor's tones of voice? Enthusiastic enough?

2) Can we make the activities the student is doing more fun, while still being beneficial? Do more of the fun exercises? Read more of the fun stories?

3) Is what the student being asked to do too hard or too easy? Can we shift the activities to land closer to the correct challenge zone?

4) Are we making adequate use of prizes, certificates, and extrinsic reinforcement? Have we dropped the ball in this arena? Are we giving prizes that are not reinforcing, where others exist that would be very reinforcing?

5) Are the sessions too long for the child's attention span? Would we actually accomplish more by shortening them for a while?

6) Is the pace of the sessions right? Does the tutor tend to move things along fast enough to be interesting to a child with a short attention span? Are there enough varied activities in the session? Should we be doing more activities, with a shorter time for each?

7) Is there a fundamental mismatch of personality between tutor and student? Would the student do better with another of us?

So far we've talked about factors that we can change. Let's continue with the checklist of things to think about if the student is not enjoying the sessions.

8) Is there someone, for example an older sibling, who perhaps out of envy, is making fun of the student for having the sessions? If so, do the parents or anyone else have the power to squelch this?

9) Is there a parent who is not on board with the tutoring, who sends subtle cues to the child that it shouldn't be going on? When parents are in conflict with each other about many things, they are often in conflict about the tutoring also.

10) Does the ringing phone for the session pull the child away from activities like video games, television watching, playing with friends, or sitting down to supper? If so, can we persuade parents to think ahead so as not to allow other highly reinforcing activities to compete against the tutoring?

11) Do the parents seem to care about the milestones the student reaches, and celebrate them greatly, or are they very distant from them?

12) Is there so much noise and distraction from siblings, electronics, pets, and other things that the student can't pay attention to the session? Electronic screens are a major problem with many students. Often we need to ask parents to help the child get into a screen-free environment for tutoring.

13) Is it possible for the parents and the rest of the family to get into the content of the tutoring more thoroughly, and support it more, by for example learning the names of the skills, doing the celebrations exercise as a family, and so forth?

14) Is the child overburdened with so many demands on his/her time, from school, sports, lessons, etc., that the tutoring represents one more burden upon an overtaxed and chronically depleted child?

15) Is the child chronically restless from too high a ratio of sitting to physical activity? Could we arrange for the student to get more physical exercise before the session?

16) Is the child trying to do the session when medicine for ADHD is in the "rebound" period, where it is even more difficult for the child to focus and concentrate than if the child weren't receiving medication?

17) Are there very upsetting events going on in the student's life, and does it so happen that the tutoring is experienced as a burden during a difficult period rather than a support?

18) Are things so disorganized that the student can't keep up with the books, and/or that the phone often doesn't work right?

19) Is the child often trying to have the sessions while in a car or in some other unfavorable environment?

20) Does the parent delegate to the student the responsibility of appointment-keeping, when the student doesn't have the requisite appointment-keeping skills?

21) Do the parents exert so little authority with the child that they can't tip the balance to help an undecided child get motivated to make the tutoring work?

The tutor may not be able to change any of the home and family factors. If tutors communicate with supervisors about these things, we may be able to do some problem-solving with the family about them.

If, after examining all these things, we decide that we can't do anything to help the child be anything other than an unwilling, grudging participant in the tutoring, and frank conversations with the child reveal that the child sincerely wants out, we want to give the child his or her freedom. We are a new enough intervention that not many people deem us essential. We have the luxury of restricting our services to children who at least acquiesce to them. We cultivate the idea that it is not a tragedy if a child or family rejects us. There are other, better established, systems in society (e.g. the health care system, the educational system) to deal with whatever problems may exist. We want to discuss the situation with parents, arrive at consensus, and part amicably when it doesn't work out.

26: Record keeping and monitoring

At the end of each session, tutors write down very briefly what they did and how long they spent. If the session was the standard 30 minutes, there's no need to record the time – that will be the "default" time. The record should note what sections you read and which exercises you did. For students in the reading program, the record should note which lists were worked on and what text was read, how many points today, and how many points total cumulatively. This recording task should take less than a minute.

Here are some examples, for two different children, on in the psychological skills track and another in the reading track:

Psychological Skills Track

5/28/2012
Sections 209-230 in Programmed Readings
Celebrations Exercise
12 Thought Exercise
Cumulative text units 349
Cumulative exercises 40

Reading Track
5/28/2012
List 94 sounded and blended after me, sounded and blended on own, read off
Read from Rusty-bicycle through Helen-strawberries in Illustrated Modeling Stories
155 word list points today
5,281 word list points cumulatively
6 text units today
51 Cumulative text units

At the end of each month, tutors get an email prompting them to report some data for the month. The monthly reports are a very important part of the tutor's job. They should not take long. The information is crucial for supervisors in our keeping aware of what is going on.

27: Being aware of outcomes

For students using the reading manual, we will be doing tests of reading periodically; tutors should be tuned in to how the student's reading skill is progressing. For students who are learning psychological skills, we (meaning program administrators) will be attempting to monitor the child's level of psychological functioning, and see if it is improving over time.

What is psychological functioning? To define it succinctly, it is being good to oneself, and good to others. It is to figure out ways of making oneself happy, and making others happy. Of course, some environments make this easier and some make it harder. The sixteen skills and principles our program teaches – productivity, joyousness, kindness, honesty, fortitude, etc. -- are also central to the definition of good psychological functioning. As a student improves in psychological functioning, the frequency of problematic behaviors goes down and the frequency of positive behaviors goes up.

If tutors tune in to what is happening to their students' academic skills, psychological skills, and overall psychological functioning, they will feel a sense of purpose and direction greater than if they just do one session after another without stopping to think of where it all is leading.

28: Helping students tell what they have learned

If a student has been reading about psychological skills for many hours, and someone asks the student, "What have you learned from the reading that we have done," the somewhat depressing response we're likely to get is a shrug or a blank look or an "I don't know." After reading over 160 sections illustrating the 16 skills and principles, if a while later someone asks the student, "What do you think are some important principles about how to live well?" or "What are some guidelines about how to decide what to do and what not to do?" or something like that – we often get the same response. If after reading 300 or more sections on the twelve thoughts, if someone asks the student, "What are some different ways of thinking about things that happen to us? How many different types of ways can you think of?" the same blank look may occur.

The question, "What have you learned," is a very difficult question. It's much harder than specific questions about the particulars of what the child has learned. Most children aren't good at answering this question. I'm often curious to find out what skills children are working on in math, but lots of them, who are doing passably well in their math courses, can't answer the

"What have you learned lately" question with something like "We learned how to add and subtract fractions."

To understand the difficulty of the "What have you learned" question, please imagine that someone were to ask you, spontaneously, to get up and expound upon what you learned in a course you took in school a couple of years ago. Perhaps you are the type of learner who could stand up and give a coherent summary of the major learnings that you took away from the course. If so, you are an unusual person! "Please tell what you learned in your chemistry course" is a much more difficult question than "What happens to the electrons when sodium and chlorine react with each other?"

But we hypothesize that the student who has learned to answer the question, "What have you learned," or "Can you summarize what the book said?" probably will retain the learning better than the student who hasn't. For this reason, we have on the to do list to offer tutors some specific materials to work with that will help the student answer the "What have you learned" question.

These materials will give students examples of what people can say when asked what they have learned. Here's an example of a very competent answer to "Can you summarize this?" for *Programmed Readings for Psychological Skills*.

"There are these things called skills and principles, things like productivity, joyousness, kindness, honesty, fortitude. They're the names of good things to do. Just about every moment of our lives, we have the opportunity to do at least one of these. If we do a good example of one of these, we have reason to celebrate. Even situations we don't like give us opportunities to do a good example of a skill, for example fortitude or good decisions. If we feel good about each of our good examples, we will tend to be happy and make other people happy. It helps to get into mind lots and lots of specific examples of these skills. That helps us to pick good examples, ourselves.

"There are also 12 types of thoughts. Not awfulizing, goal-setting, listing options and choosing, and celebrating your own choice are examples of these. If we can get aware of what we do say to ourselves, and pick well among these thoughts, that will help us to have feelings and behaviors that will work well. We can make our feelings and behaviors better by choosing well what to say to ourselves.

"When people have fears, they are sometimes realistic and sometimes unrealistic. When they are unrealistic, there are several ways of getting over them. These include taking it gradually, staying in the scary situation long enough, relaxing your muscles, and choosing useful self-talk.

"There are also 4 ways of listening to someone else. If you choose well about when to use reflections, facilitations, follow up questions, or positive feedback, you can help people to enjoy talking with you.

"When people have disagreements, there are 7 things they can do that make it more likely that they will stay cool and come up with a good solution. These are things like defining the problem, reflecting to make sure you understand, listing options, discussing advantages and disadvantages, staying polite, and so forth. If you practice solving problems doing these 7 things, you will help yourself stay cool and rational when you have a disagreement or a "joint decision" to work out."

If we can help children to answer anything close to this in response to "What have you learned" or "Please summarize what the book said," questions, we will have accomplished a lot.

29: Being a positive example collector

Nearly every session should contain at least one narrative of a "positive example" of a psychological skill. In the celebrations exercise, the student reports the examples from real-life behavior. In the skills stories exercise, the student makes up stories that give examples of psychological skills. In the celebrating others' choices exercise, the student gives positive examples seen elsewhere. In fantasy rehearsals, the student imagines a desirable way of acting. If the tutor can write down all these examples, and produce a growing book of positive examples for the student, this is extremely useful.

We are very interested in another source of positive examples. We encourage parents to report to tutors, at the beginning of sessions, the celebration-worthy behaviors they have noticed in their children. This helps the parent to notice and reinforce positive examples; the child's hearing positive examples communicated is almost always reinforcing. For parents to increase their noticing and reinforcing of their children's specific positive examples of psychological skills is one of the most momentous changes that can occur in a child's life. Not all parents will want to take part in the noticing and reporting of positive examples.

All the examples that are collected should be *concrete* and *specific* as possible. "He played well with his brother" is not very concrete, but relatively high on the "abstraction ladder." Here's a report that is very concrete: "When his brother picked up one of his Lego characters, instead of grabbing it back, he picked up another character and said, 'Hey. I'm glad you are here. Do you want to help us out?'" The most useful reports create a mental image of exactly what happened.

If a parent or child gives a tutor a very abstract celebration, the first priority is to join in celebrating, and reinforce the report. We certainly don't want the parent or child to feel that the report has been rejected because of being too abstract. But then usually it's good to encourage the narrator to pinpoint some specific, concrete event. For example: "I'm really glad to hear that! By any chance, can you remember any specific thing that he said or did that was an example of that kindness?"

Tutors who create the positive example collection should note, for each, whether it was a real-life celebration, a skills story or fantasy rehearsal, or a celebration of someone else's choice. It's also good to classify each narrative according to which psychological skills it exemplifies.

Tutors can periodically share this document with the student and the parent(s), and supervisors. Tutor and student can read it together, and do lots of celebration about each of the entries. The document can grow larger and larger as tutoring continues.

Such a collection is valuable in many ways. The creation of it prompts everyone to be aware of positive examples. The positive examples get run through the neuronal circuitry more times – positive fantasy rehearsal is encouraged. Parents may have their attention turned toward noticing and reinforcing the child's positive examples. Children may have a new attitude toward reading and writing, when they see that the written word records their celebration-worthy acts. They may become more motivated to make the written collection larger. They get an intense message of being valued, to find that their tutors have taken the time to prepare such a document. They get a feeling of cumulative accomplishment in reporting their celebrations and skills stories and fantasy rehearsals, rather than having the feeling that they just have to do something over and over.

30: Promoting morale among tutors

In our organization, we hope that tutors can find it convenient to meet with each other regularly, face to face or through phone conferences. Since many of our tutors are college students, it make sense for tutors who go to the same college to get together face to face for discussion. We hope that the mutual support that tutors can offer one another can make their jobs even more fulfilling than it would be to labor in more isolated partnership with the child. We are very much open to input from creative tutors about how to increase the morale and team spirit among tutors.

Chapter 13: Psychoeducation for Parenting

Many books have been written to train parents to do their jobs well, including two that I've written: *The Competence Approach to Parenting* (Strayhorn, 2001) and *Reinforcement and Punishment* (Strayhorn, 2015). This chapter gives a very quick overview of some of the points to be gotten across in a psychoeducational program for parents.

On the goals of parenting

What outcomes is "good parenting" meant to achieve? Very important goals include meeting the child's basic physical and economic needs and keeping the child as safe and healthy as possible. Beyond these, however, the goals of a parent and the goals of a mental health professional or psychoeducator overlap nearly 100%: the goal is to impart to the child the competences that enable the child to be happy and to make others happy. Children who are good at productivity, joyousness, kindness, honesty, fortitude, and so forth lead people to infer that their parents have "raised them right," and conversely -- despite how unfair such inferences can sometimes be, given that genetics, peer culture, and lots of other factors beyond parents' control play a large role in skill development or the lack thereof.

How can parents influence their children to become psychologically healthy individuals? By using the same methods of influence available to psychoeducators: objective-formation, hierarchy, relationship, attribution, modeling, practice opportunities, reinforcement and punishment, instruction, stimulus control, and monitoring.

A generic skill-promotion program for use by parents

There are two cases for which I recommend the following skill-promotion program: 1) when the child has behavioral or emotional problems, and 2) when the child does not have behavioral or emotional problems! Even in the second situation, the child is in the process of psychological development and can use all the positive influence parents can muster.

The following are the steps:

1. If there are behavioral or emotional problems, the parent identifies the psychological skills that are the opposites of these problems. If the child has problems with aggression or being a bully, the skills of kindness, nonviolence, respectful talk, and likely fortitude, friendship-building, and joint decision-making may be targeted. It the child has problems with anxiety, courage and joyousness skills may head the list. For a child with attention and impulse control problems, skills of concentration and organization, which are subskills of productivity, may be priorities, as may self-discipline and good decisions. For the oppositional child, compliance skills may be top priority. If there are no behavioral or emotional problems at present, the parent may simply go on a gut feeling of which skills are of highest priority to promote, or may simply promote all of them.

2. The second step for the parent is to get in mind lots of specific, concrete examples of the high priority skills. An appendix to this book give a menu that is a sample of the concrete behaviors that parents might get in mind.

It's very important to make concrete examples, rather than to go by the more abstract labels, because this mental activity helps the parent in the crucial task of recognizing the child's positive examples when they occur.

3. The parent tries to model the high-priority skills for the child, through the parent's real-life behavior. Speaking one's self-talk aloud, occasionally, can allow children to get models of thoughts as well as behaviors.

4. The parent exposes the child to many positive examples of the high-priority skills through stories, songs, writings, recordings, etc.

5. The parent watches "like a hawk" for positive examples that the child carries out. The goal is to notice a very high fraction of these. The parent is particularly careful to catch the examples that are quiet and not attention-grabbing, such as when the child responds with silent equanimity to a situation that could have evoked a tantrum.

6. When the parent sees the child do a positive example, the parent tries to strongly reinforce that behavior. For many children, the tones of excitement and enthusiasm in the parent's voice will be the most important reinforcer. Sometimes just enthusiastically naming the skill that the behavior was an example of is very reinforcing to the child—e.g., "Hey! You just did an example of fortitude!"

7. Later, the parent recounts the positive example to someone else, preferably in the child's presence or earshot. This "someone else" can be the other parent, a friend, another relative, a telephone tutor, or even a pet. Recounting to the child's siblings may be tricky. It's important that the person the parent shares the joy with is happy to get a good report, and not jealous. Sometimes siblings can be taught to take on this role; most do not fall into it automatically.

8. At bedtime, the parent does a "nightly review" of the positive behaviors by recounting the positive examples one more time. The narrative should be very concrete, naming specific behaviors rather than general ways of being.

9. Parents who want to make the program more fun can act out the positive examples for the child with puppets or toy people at the time of the nightly review.

10. Parents who want to go the extra mile can write down the positive examples in an ever-growing "positive behavior diary," and can read this to/with the child periodically from then on. It makes the positive behavior diary even more fun if the parent and child illustrate the stories that these narrative constitute. They can do this very quickly, writing the story with one or two sentences per page, and going back with crayons to make illustrations. If the child feels too old for illustrated stories, an ever-growing file of positive examples, occasionally printed out, is still a wonderful resource.

11. A way of combining positive models and positive reinforcement is for the family to do the celebrations exercise together. Family members narrate their own positive examples, as well as those of any other family members, and congratulate each other for these.

You'll notice that this program does not address the question that is often the one parents most want answered: how do I most effectively punish the child's unwanted behavior. If parents can start early enough with encouraging the positive skills, the positive examples often tend to "crowd out" the negative examples. The need for punishment often, but not always, may be obviated.

The need to be a "reasonable" authority

Noncompliance is one of the most frequent problems that parents want help with. We consider the skill of compliance that of complying with "reasonable" authority. Thus part of the job of the parent in promoting compliance is making rules and requests and directives reasonable. This means that the directives to the child should be 1) ethical to carry out, and 2) not overly controlling and bossy. In other words, before giving a command, the parent should consider: "Is it right?" and "Is it necessary?" When the commands are rationed and given only when necessary, the parent will be much more likely to enforce a very high fraction of commands, and the child will be much more likely to comply.

Another part of maintaining authority involves clearly differentiating between commands and suggestions, and making good decisions about when to use each. If the child must leave the house to go to a doctor's appointment, the parent is better off saying, "Please come with me now," (a command) rather than "Would you like to go now?" (a suggestion). On the other hand, if the child has the freedom to judge how hot or cold she feels and act accordingly, it's better for the parent to say, "You may want to take your coat off," (a suggestion) than "Take your coat off," (a command).

Understanding differential reinforcement

Suppose a child has temper outbursts at school, turning over desks, throwing books, and screaming. When this occurs, the mom is called to the school; the parent holds the child, rubs his back, speaks lovingly to him, and sometimes takes him home early. She, and the school personnel, regard this intervention as very successful, because it almost always stops his temper outburst quickly. However, over time, the frequency of such outbursts goes up. Upon further investigation and experimentation, it becomes clear that the mom's behaviors were reinforcing the temper outbursts by helping them lead to a desirable outcome for the child, even though the mom's behaviors ended the temper outbursts in the short run. When the mom is asked to come and celebrate the child's stretches of positive behavior and stay away during the temper outbursts, the child's behavior steadily improves.

Many parents and many teachers are not accustomed to thinking in this way. It seems natural for people to define as what "works," the strategies that bring a quick end to a given episode of undesirable behavior. It is not so natural to define effective strategies as those which have the best effect on frequencies of behaviors days or weeks from now. The book *Reinforcement and Punishment* presents lots of vignettes, many of which illustrate the point just made.

I have often only half whimsically recommended that parents meditate, using the phrase *differential reinforcement* as a mantra. The phrase means that reinforcers, including attention, conversation, excitement, touch, and giving what is wanted, are systematically more likely to occur after some behaviors than others. If the reinforcers follow the positive examples of psychological skill and are withheld following the negative examples, differential reinforcement is exerting its effect in the "right direction." Parents who are courageous and honest may recognize that they are systematically using differential reinforcement in the wrong direction. This can be a very important step toward improving the lives of all family members!

Dependability and honesty

The ability to lie comfortably and easily is almost necessary for conduct problems of all sorts; conversely, the child who has a strong aversion to lying has a much better chance of avoiding such problems. One of the best ways for parents to promote the skill of honesty is not to lie to their children. We're all human, and lying and deception are part of life. It can be very tempting for parents to try to avoid children's resistance and protests and sadness by deception. But the long-term consequences are almost always negative. In giving medicine, for example, I recommend never telling a child that a medicine is a vitamin or anything other than what it is, and never slipping it into food or drink. If the child is adopted, it's good to let the child know this as early in life as possible. When unfortunate events occur that are central to the child's life, it's good to go ahead and face the truth from the beginning. I even recommend against deceiving children about Santa Claus and the tooth fairy etc. -- my experience with my own children was that associating the word "pretend" with such rituals seemed not to diminish the fun even a little bit.

Especially in divided families, showing up when promised is a crucial skill for parents; the saying that "Eighty percent of life consists of showing up" is worth considering.

Tones of voice, the approval to disapproval ratio, and positive emotional climate

Children's behavioral and emotional problems tend to be worsened by a "negative emotional climate" and improved by a "positive emotional climate." A positive emotional climate is one in which people approve of one another, enjoy one another, are very often kind and helpful to one another, and listen to one another. In a negative emotional climate, there are often expressions of hostility, disapproval, anger, resentment, sarcasm, threats of violence, or actual violence. Parents can improve the emotional climate simply by saying more approving and affirming things, both to children and to each other.

I have long recommended that parents try to maintain at least a 4 to 1 ratio of approving utterances to disapproving utterances, both toward each child and toward one's spouse. That is, one should shoot for at least 80% approval in the statements that contain any approval or disapproval. Many parents have been candid enough to say that the 4 to 1 ratio is in the direction of more disapproval, and some have candidly acknowledged that there is very little approval going on whatsoever in the family. The generic skill-promotion program described above, if implemented, should result in a steep increase in the amount of approval that is expressed. It is particularly gratifying for a parent when after a certain length of time, the child starts to imitate the approving words and tones of voice that the parents model.

For parents, as well as for telephone tutors and their students, thinking about tones of voice is very useful. If parents become aware of how much the musical tones of their voices convey small to moderate approval, large approval, small to moderate disapproval, large disapproval, or whether they are neutral, and try to use these tones wisely, much good can be done. For many parents it comes as a major revelation that excited tones are reinforcing, even if they are disapproving; this is particularly true for children high in a trait of stimulus-seeking. If parents can start speaking excitedly, with high inflection, about the positive behaviors and in somber monotones about the negative behaviors, they can often improve the behavior of children greatly by this change alone.

CCCT versus REFFF

Utterances that when overdone produce a negative emotional climate can be remembered by CCCT: commands, criticisms, contradictions, and threats. The utterances that produce a positive emotional climate can be remembered by REFFF: reflections, telling about you own experience, facilitations, follow-up questions, and positive feedback. If parents can shift the bar graph of their own utterances away from CCCT and toward more REFFF, the corresponding graph for the children also tends to shift, and the emotional climate of the family shifts toward much greater happiness and cooperation.

Mutually gratifying activities

When people want to cultivate a positive relationship with one another, they naturally seek to do things together that are fun for both of them. This is true for couples in courtship, for children playing with each other, for child psychotherapists seeking to build a relationship with children, and others. To help foster positive relationships, do fun things together. If those fun things can also be productive, or if they can promote growth in psychological skills, so much the better. I recommend that parents keep an eye on how often they do mutually gratifying activities with each child (and spouse). If the answer is "never" or "hardly ever," something should be changed.

The quintessential mutually gratifying activity is social conversation. If people can enjoy chatting with each other, it is much easier to have fun while doing almost anything else, including going for walks together, playing catch, eating meals together, playing games, singing, dancing, doing art work, doing chores together, having study parties, working on sports skills, watching entertainment, reading to each other, cooking, hiking, camping, and others.

I tend to favor cooperative games over competitive ones. For example, rather than adult and child playing chess against each other, in "cooperative chess," they take turns making moves when playing against a computer opponent of appropriate skill level. In tennis, volleyball, or beach ball volleying, they can see how many hits they can do without a miss. The skills of graciously winning and losing in competitions are important, but sometimes the world presents too high a ratio of competition to cooperation.

Avoiding negative models in entertainment media

I have many times worked help children with problems of aggression and violence; part of my strategy has been to use positive models and positive fantasy rehearsals of anger control and nonviolence and rational decision making and kindness, and the other skills that are the opposites of violence. But for some of those cases, I have found that for every positive model or fantasy rehearsal that the parents and I can present, the child is engaging in literally thousands more fantasy rehearsals of violence through videogames or movies or other entertainment media. The typical "shooter" game allows fantasy violent acts only seconds, or perhaps fractions of a second, apart.

Not only violence, but bratty, insolent, disrespectful talk is widely modeled in entertainment media. Models definitely have an influence, and part of parenting involves the use of parental authority to make the child's diet of models and fantasy rehearsals as positive as possible. Parents may benefit from reminding themselves that it is their own hard-earned money that usually buys violent or antisocial models that harm their children, and they do have the right not to buy them or to get rid of them. They also have the right to get rid of them when grandparents, friends, or others give them to their children.

Punishment

The expert use of differential reinforcement, the generic skill-promotion program, lots of utterances that promote a positive emotional climate, lots of tones of approval, many positive models, and the elimination of negative models, all starting early enough, should dramatically reduce the need for punishment as an influence method. However, sometimes a child engages in harmful or dangerous enough behavior that punishment must be used in an attempt to suppress it. Withdrawal of electronic screens has moved into first place as a popular punishment among today's parents, according to my informal observation (just as the use of such screens has moved into first place as a leisure time activity for children). Time out (or having to stay in a room by oneself for a short time), "physical guidance" in complying with a command, withdrawal of other privileges, and verbal reprimands are among parents' choices.

Physical violence by a child—hitting, kicking, scratching, throwing things at people -- is a situation where it is especially important that the consequences not only stop the episode, but be effective punishment: that is, that the consequences reduce the probability of the behavior's being repeated. Physical restraint and seclusion in a time out room for a brief time (two or three minutes) can be quite effective consequences for violent behavior. But these are very easily misused by adults who lose their own tempers and who give way to the revenge motive rather than the rational use of punishment. For this reason, professional stakeholders sometimes proscribe seclusion and restraint altogether. Sometimes such rules transfer too much power to the violent child. Handling violent behavior by a child is thus a complex problem, and it is probably a case in which a skilled clinician, who is able to assess the parent's degree of self-control, is called for, rather than blanket psychoeducational instructions.

When giving punishment, the following principles should be kept in mind:

1. Punishment does often tend to induce negative emotional side effects, e.g. anger, in the person being punished, especially if the punishment seems unfair. Punishment also models the use of punishing behaviors that sometimes children imitate – for example, punishment by physical violence may teach violence through the modeling. For these reasons it is good to think carefully before using punishment, taking the side effects into account.

2. If the person being punished can escape the punishment by lying or refusing to cooperate with the punishment or by sneaking to get what was withdrawn, then the punishment arrangement can result reinforcement of undesirable behavior. Careful planning to cut off these escape routes in advance should be carried out before punishing.

3. The punishment should be as mild as possible, with the test of whether it works being not whether the person seems to be made very unhappy, but whether the undesirable behavior drops in frequency.

4. The punishment should last as short a time as is necessary to work; overly long punishments can be self-defeating in that they leave the parent without anything more to take away when negative behavior is repeated.

5. If the punishment consists of verbal reprimands and angry tones of voice, the parent should keep in mind that children can get used to these over time, so that they have little or no effect on the frequency of behavior; children can also come to imitate such verbal behavior, in ways that are very unpleasant for other family members. For this reason, verbal reprimands work as punishment only when given rather infrequently.

6. For this reason and others, punishment is best given in a calm, rational way. But calm tones can be strongly disapproving, and there are times when disapproval is definitely called for.

Parent as Psychoeducator

There are parents out there who can do the parenting tasks I've mentioned already, do all the work associated with making a living and running a household, and still have time and energy left over. For these, doing the psychoeducational tutoring activities can be mutually gratifying as well as hugely beneficial for both.

You sit together on a couch and do alternate reading. You gradually learn to do the psychological skills exercises together, by reading the *Programmed Course in Psychological Skills Exercises*. You spend some time chatting. If you are away on a trip or working late, you call home and have the session by phone. If the parents are separated or divorced, the child can have a session with each parent daily, one in person and one by phone.

My track record so far does not contain much success in persuading parents to do these activities anywhere close to as regularly, faithfully, often, and long as telephone tutors can do them. But I hope strongly to improve this record!

Chapter 14: Telephone Tutoring for Psychoeducation

Why the telephone?

There are certainly benefits to in-person, face-to-face work with children. You can do physical activities together. You can pat the child on the back. You and the child can see each other smile. You can point to things. Acting out plays and singing together is much easier.

On the other hand, in many ways telephone interaction works even better than face to face interaction. Alternate reading for some reason feels more natural over the phone than in person. Children who would get attention from the tutor by physically distracting moves find that if they want the tutor's attention, they have to verbalize – and making such bids for attention in words strengthens the child's verbal ability.

But the main reason for the use of the telephone is that the hassle, labor, time, money, effort, and fossil fuel that would be spent on physically bringing the tutor and the student together are saved. Both tutor and student can take out from the daily schedule only the time for the tutoring itself, not the time for transportation and waiting for the other to show up. Tutors who are geographically distant can work together as well as those who are close, and thus matching tutors with students is vastly easier.

Spaced rather than massed practice

With telephone tutoring, it is possible, and usually the case, for the student and tutor to work together 5 or 6 days a week, for half-hour sessions. When the transaction cost of getting tutor and student together is higher, sessions tend to be less frequent and longer. There are benefits to having more frequent sessions; among them are that forgetting has less time to operate between sessions.

Time on task

A major finding from educational research is that when students spend more time working on a subject, they learn more (Huyvaert, 1998), This finding seems so consistent with common sense that one might question why researchers needed to investigate it. But as I have reviewed elsewhere in this book, many mental health interventions tend to ignore the fact that learning many complex skills can take a long time. A typical child attending a mental health clinic will invest less than 10 hours in the effort. A typical child who is tutored 6 times a week, half an hour per session, can accumulate close to 150 hours per year. And students have been known to continue telephone tutoring for three or years. The potential for meaningful change is dramatically higher with the increased time on task.

The two reasons school programs are hard

Why not simply do psychoeducation at school? During much of my career I negotiated for in-school psychoeducational programs, sometimes successfully. I believe that the model in which older children and youth are thoroughly trained to be tutors for younger peers, and wherein one-on-one tutoring is a prominent part of every school day, would work well if those in charge of schools could develop the will to implement it.

But in trying to implement such programs, school leaders continually return to two problems: lack of time, and lack of space. Whenever more time gets devoted to psychoeducation, less time has to be devoted to something else, and in current school climates, those other things have strong claims, particularly if they are meant to increase test scores. And even if the time is available, usually the space for one-on-one interaction is hard to come by on a large scale basis in schools. Telephone tutoring bypasses the need to convince many people in the power hierarchy of school systems to make the time and space necessary for psychoeducational tutoring.

Telephone tutoring as incremental change

If by waving a magic wand, it were possible to create a revolution in society wherein all parents were intent on providing psychoeducation for their children, where schools intensely trained older students to be very competent psychoeducational tutors for younger ones, and where individuals devoured psychoeducational curricular materials as voraciously as they read scary novels, telephone tutoring would not be as important as I believe it is now. But it presents a way for tutors and children to participate in large doses of psychoeducation, now, before any such revolutionary change takes place, and to see what results from such experiences. If we can demonstrate how helpful it is, it can perhaps move humanity a step closer to becoming a "psychoeducating society."

Chapter 15: College Students as Tutors

The extent of college students' mental health problems

Surveys of college students reveal reason for concern. The following are quotations from Henriques (2014): "According to the American College Health Association (ACHA) the suicide rate among young adults, ages 15-24, has tripled since the 1950s and suicide is currently the second most common cause of death among college students. That study also found 9.4% of students reported seriously considering attempted suicide at least once in a 12 month period, a marked increase from several decades ago." " A 2013 survey of college students found that 57% of women and 40% of men reported experiencing episodes of "overwhelming anxiety" in the past year, and 33% of women and 27% of men reported a period in the last year of feeling so depressed it was difficult to function. Studies suggest that between a quarter and a third of students meet criteria for an anxiety or depressive illness during their college experience." "Studies have found that over 30% of students met criteria for a diagnosis of alcohol abuse and 6 percent for alcohol dependence in the past 12 months." These statistics do not prove that college student life is more conducive to mental health problems than other stages of life, but they do suggest that if the culture of college student life plays a role in mental health, there is a good bit of room for improvement in that culture.

Problems with the college environment

What is wrong with studenthood? In human cultures of the past, as soon as human beings gained the strength conveyed by puberty, or even earlier in life, they contributed to the economic welfare of their families by working in the fields, taking care of younger children, hunting, foraging, helping to build shelter, helping to prepare food, and so forth. And many students do such "useful work" in today's culture – but many do not. Many students have their time so spoken for by academic demands and perhaps sports activities that useful work time has been almost totally eliminated from the schedule.

Asking children, adolescents, and young adults to do useful work has not had an unblemished record in human history. There has been much exploitation of children into slave-labor-like conditions, and such continues.

However, the child, adolescent, or young adult who carries out useful work for his or her family or tribe at least has reason not to feel "useless." When effort results in more food for the family, including for oneself, or more money, or protection from the elements, that effort produces a payoff. The feeling of an "effort-payoff connection" results – a belief, a feeling, that the choices one makes and the effort one exerts do have the capability of bringing about meaningful rewards.

A large literature suggests that the effort-payoff connection is central to happiness and avoiding depression and anxiety (Azrin and Besalel, 1981; Dimidjian et al., 2006; Hopko et al., 2006, Roberto and Santos, 2008).

The lives of many students are certainly not devoid of the effort-payoff connection. They study hard, and in return they get good grades. They earn acceptance to high quality institutions for more of the same. But many others study hard, earn mediocre or bad grades, and get fairly consistent messages of "You're not good enough." And even among the successful students, I hypothesize, there is a certain emptiness in the quest for good grades. Writing a paper for a course, for example, does not directly help anyone else, but allows oneself to be judged. Often the teacher is the only one who reads the student's writing; the grade is recorded; the writing then gets thrown away. If that grade is a C or D or F, or even sometimes when it is a B, the student often feels more punished for the effort of writing than rewarded, and the conditions for learned helplessness are pretty thoroughly set up.

Happiness is greatly facilitated by positive, long-lasting, social bonds. (Kawachi and Berkman, 2001, Ozbay et al., 2007). When students leave both the families and the communities in which they grew up, stress and anomie can come from the dissolution or weakening of social bonds. And as much as college alumni can keep in touch and have lasting friendships, the social relations of college are influenced by the knowledge that after college, people tend to scatter geographically and the relationships that they cultivated will be weakened if not broken.

Chapter 15: College Students as Tutors

"Work hard, play hard" is the proud watchword of many colleges. This sounds good, except that working hard often translates into solitary study or writing, and playing hard often translates into binge drinking with very loud ambient noise. Neither of these situations promote quality social bonds. The toxic effects of alcohol often then accentuate the mental health difficulties, the pain of which the alcohol was meant to assuage, in a vicious cycle.

Psychoeducational tutoring to enhance students' mental health?

The following are ways in which hiring college student tutors and fostering social bonds among them could possibly help tutors to be happier:
1. Useful work, that offers a sense of meaning and purpose not fulfilled by the quest for good grades.
2. A strong social bond with the student, where there is much positive exchange.
3. Social bonds with the supervisor of tutors, and other tutors.
4. A sense of effort-payoff connection when and if the student improves skills as a result of the tutoring.
5. Exposure to the body of written information on psychological skills, that is just as relevant to adults as to children.
6. Practice of psychological skills through psychological skills exercises, which provide practice for the trainer as well as the trainee.

Measuring, analyzing, and reporting the amount of good done for tutors, like all research endeavors, are cumbersome tasks, but they should be carried out soon.

Meanwhile: we are extremely grateful to the college students and others who have done very important and useful work as psychoeducational tutors for OPT, the Organization for Psychoeducational Tutoring.

Chapter 16: Psychoeducation and the Economy

The argument of this chapter

This chapter:

1. Will try to define what a "good" economy is, and will emphasize that a major criterion is that human effort is channeled into activities that are truly good for humanity.

2. Will make the point that agriculture and manufacturing require much less effort now than in any previous point in human history.

3. Will argue that much of human labor appears to be expended in ways that don't advance the human condition very much, or even harm it.

4. Will hypothesize that psychoeducational tutoring represents a way of harnessing human effort in ways that should truly advance the welfare of humanity, and that tutoring by telephone presents an opportunity to employ people and to serve people without regard to the obstacles of geography or physical distance.

The goals of the economic system

What are the goals of a well-functioning economy? An economic system works well if it does three things:

1. It provides enough jobs. It provides activities for people to put their effort into, and that provide a reasonable income as the effort-payoff connection for those efforts. (And "income" is defined as the wherewithal to access the goods and services provided by other people's jobs.)

2. The goods and services produced by those jobs are those that most enhance the welfare of people (and other sentient beings). As a corollary, the economy channels effort to producing the "necessities" of life with higher priority than the "luxuries."

To the extent that people recognize that their jobs really are making people better off, and to the extent that others recognize the value of their contributions, their jobs convey a feeling of "meaning" and "dignity" in life.

3. The activities preserve and enhance the environment for future generations, and do not pollute or destroy it.

Often public policy makers confront dilemmas in which these goals conflict with one another.

For example: a state government subsidizes the movie and television industry by tax breaks, to encourage companies to make their movies in that state. The argument is that this will create jobs for state residents. The counterargument is that the subsidies are thus supporting luxuries, when adequate education, health care, and bridge repair are more deserving of public funds. Public funding of football stadiums, gambling casinos, breweries, symphonies, and other entertainments brings up similar issues.

As another example, a state government has to decide whether to allow "fracking" methods that create jobs and provide energy, but do so at costs to the environment.

As another example, a government has evidence that economic growth, as measured by the increase in the total goods and services produced, will be higher if tax rates are lower. But higher tax rates, it is argued, funnel more of human effort into activities such as health care and education for low income people, repair of bridges, monitoring of neurotoxic pollutants, etc., that would not be affordable with lower tax rates.

As an example on an individual level, a recent college graduate finds that he can make a high income working for a public relations firm that helps other businesses, in his words, "take bad things that they've done and put positive spins on them." By contrast, if he were to work for an agency trying to provide quality preschool education to low-income children, he himself would qualify for food stamps.

Agriculture and manufacturing require less human effort

A New York Times economic writer (Porter, 2016) pointed out that in the 1960's, it took 45,000 workers to harvest 2.2 million tons of tomatoes grown in California. By the year 2000, 5000 workers could harvest 12 million tons of tomatoes. This represents about a 50-fold increase in output per worker, brought about by selective breeding of tomatoes and mechanization of the harvest. Agriculture, which for most of human history required a huge fraction of human labor, has become more automated and mechanized. To the pessimist, this means a loss of millions of jobs. To the optimist, this means that millions of hours of human effort are freed up for other activities that can better the human condition.

The same article pointed out that the reduction in jobs is occurring with manufacturing, world-wide. Joseph Stiglitz, Nobel-winning economist, was quoted: "Global employment in manufacturing is going down because productivity increases are exceeding increases in demand for manufactured products by a significant amount."

Thus, the human race has gotten much more efficient at growing food and making things. The bad effect is that jobs in agriculture and manufacturing have disappeared in huge numbers, globally, and protectionist strategies to keep those jobs within national borders are probably doomed for failure. The good effect is that because the human race can produce many of its major needs with much less labor, human effort is freed up for other purposes. That good news fails to lift the spirits of the people who because of joblessness, cannot partake of the bounty from the increased productivity of farm and factory.

People's buying choices don't always promote the greatest good

The more economies are driven by people's free choices on what goods and services to spend their money on, the more efficiently those goods and services are delivered. The problem is that individual buying choices do not necessarily reflect what is in the long-term best interest of the buyer, and even less necessarily the long-term benefit to humanity. When someone goes to a gambling casino, he is probably not thinking, "How can my dollars best harness someone's efforts to promote the welfare of humanity?" but rather something like, "How can I maximize my short-term pleasure?" Similarly, when a psychology major accepts a job as a bartender, the most salient issue is not "How can I contribute to the betterment of the human condition," but rather, "How can I maximize (or get) an income?" And so it is with countless other decisions to produce and consume – consumption for short-term pleasure and production for maximization of income, not necessarily leading to the long-term welfare of humanity.

One problem with trying to take the long-term benefit to humanity into account is that people disagree so much on what promotes it. For example, to one person, football brings out toughness, teamwork, the competitive spirit that brings out the best in people, and an endless source of joyousness in fans. To another, football represents barbaric violence, a source of aggressive models for impressionable children, brain damage to many of the participants, and a colossal waste of human energy on a fundamentally harmful activity.

Despite disagreement on values, societies can, and do, make value judgments about what governments should subsidize by tax breaks and what they should penalize by sin taxes. We allow an organization teaching job skills to low income kids to escape taxation as a nonprofit. My current home state (New York) levies much higher sales taxes on the sale of cigarettes than on the sale of candy, which is in turn taxed more than the zero sales tax on vegetable produce. The difference in tax rates spring from value judgments about how much the service or the product contributes to the good versus harm of the citizens.

There's another problem with our all-important second criterion, that economic activity should contribute to the good of humanity: it's very difficult to measure how much good is being rendered. The most frequent indicator of whether the economy is doing well is the GDP, the gross domestic product. This number is an attempt to sum the total dollar value of goods and services that are bought and sold in the country in a certain time period. The GDP per capita results from dividing this number by the population size. Rising GDP per capita is seen as good. GDP per capita that is falling or rising too slowly is seen as bad. Another indicator of economic soundness is the rate of employment and unemployment; higher employment is better. A third measure of economic success is the mean or median income per person or per family; higher income equals a better economy. And a fourth measure of soundness of the economy is the rate of inflation or deflation; when prices are fairly consistent, economic health is better.

It is quite understandable that such conceptions of soundness of an economy should be used, because they are much easier to measure than anything having to do with happiness or psychological health. It takes quite a bit of effort to collect the requisite numbers of dollars (or units of other currency), but once the amounts of money are known, the measures are achieved.

Traditional measures are easier because they present no need to differentiate between "good" and "bad" uses of time and effort by society as a whole. The GDP and the employment rate don't "care" whether the activities that raise them are helpful or harmful for people. We can increase GDP and employment rates by creating more breweries, and also by hiring more addiction counselors to deal with problem drinkers. We can increase GDP and employment rates by creating a legal system with maximal incentives for people to sue each other: we hire more lawyers for the plaintiffs, more lawyers for the defense, more risk managers, more people hired to train people how to survive a lawsuit, more judges, more mental health counselors to help people deal with the stress of being sued, and so forth. We can employ thousands in growing tobacco and producing and marketing cigarettes, and thousands more in taking care of the medical problems that the cigarettes directly result in. We can hire many bright and energetic marketers and advertisers to try to take market share from Budweiser and give it to Coors, and at the same time hire many more to try to take market share from Coors and give it to Budweiser. We hire millions to grow, create, market, and sell junk food; we also fund a huge weight loss industry to try to counteract the success of the junk food industry. Great minds create ballistic missiles, and more great minds create missile defense systems to try to undo what the other great minds have created. The more money is spent on these mutually-canceling activities, the higher GDP becomes.

Meanwhile: the effortful hours that parents spend playing with their children, teaching them (including teaching them psychological skills!), having conversations with them, and taking care of them, contribute nothing to GDP. The hours that people spend in: supportive conversations between friends and couples, contemplative or meditative thought, volunteer work for charitable causes, unofficial volunteer work in helping their friends and acquaintances, keeping their own living spaces cleaned up and organized, going for walks or runs, growing their own gardens, cooking their own food, and providing each other the social support that is vital to mental health – all these contribute nothing to GDP. The point is that GDP is far from perfectly correlated with the quality of the human condition.

Partly because people can't agree on what constitutes "good" use of labor and resources, the free market solution is for each person to decide how to spend disposable income in the ways that that person decides is "good" for him or her. And this solution is more democratic than allowing a small group of government officials to decide what goods and services are best for society and how much of each should be produced. But the results of free market choices can be unsettling. The following is a quotation from the web site of Worldwatch.org, using data reported in 1998:

* * *

Matters of Scale—Spending Priorities

Amount of money needed each year (in addition to current expenditures) to provide reproductive health care for all women in developing countries:$12 billion
Amount of money spent annually on perfumes in Europe and the United States: $12 billion

Amount of money needed each year (in addition to current expenditures) to provide water and sanitation for all people in developing nations: $9 billion
Amount of money spent annually on cosmetics in the United States: $8 billion

Amount of money needed each year (in addition to current expenditures) to provide basic health and nutrition needs universally in the developing world: $13 billion
Amount of money spent each year on pet food in Europe and the United States: $17 billion

Amount of money needed each year (in addition to current expenditures) to provide basic education for all people in developing nations: $6 billion
Amount of money spent each year on militaries worldwide: $780 billion

Combined wealth of the world's richest 225 people: $1 trillion
Combined annual income of the world's poorest 2.5 billion people: $1 trillion

* * *

      According to a Rand Corporation report summarized in the Huffington Post (Femer, 2014), the amount spent in the USA on illegal drugs between 2000 and 2010 remained steady at about 100 billion dollars per year. A UN publication (United Nations Technical Series, 1998) estimated about $400 billion per year spent worldwide on illegal drugs.

      According to the Guinness World Records (Lynch, 2013), the video game Grand Theft Auto V generated $2 billion in sales in the first three days after its release, setting a world record for speed of revenue-generating by any entertainment in human history. People in the USA spent about $17 billion total on videogames in 2011 (Reilly, 2012). The same source reports that $34.6 billion were spent in the USA in 2011 on gambling; $96 billion on beer, $65 billion on soft drinks; $25.4 billion on professional sports, and $40 billion on lawn care.

      In 2012, $6 billion were spent on guns and ammunition in the U.S., according to an article in Time Magazine (Sandbum, 2012).

      Meanwhile, worldwide: According to the World Bank (2016), "Over 2.1 billion people in the developing world lived on less than US $ 3.10 a day in 2012, compared with 2.9 billion in 1990- so even though the share of the population living under that threshold nearly halved, from 66 percent in 1990 to 35 percent in 2012, far too many people are living with far too little."

And the following numbers were obtained from UNICEF (2009).

2.5 billion people lack access to improved sanitation
1 billion children are deprived of one or more services essential to survival and development
148 million under 5 in developing regions are underweight for their age

101 million children are not attending primary school, with more girls than boys missing out
22 million infants are not protected from diseases by routine immunization
7.6 million children worldwide died before their 5th birthday in 2010
4 million newborns worldwide are dying in the first month of life
2 million children under 15 are living with HIV
>500,000 women die each year from causes related to pregnancy and childbirth

There is huge variation in what our society pays people for their labor, with remuneration not necessarily proportional to the amount of benefit to society. The CEO of the Lehman Brothers financial firm, from 2000 until the firm went bankrupt in 2008, received somewhere around $484 million in total compensation (Ross & Gomstyn 2008). If we assume that the CEO worked 80 hour weeks, 50 weeks a year, this wage comes out to a little over 15 thousand dollars per hour. A day care center worker, meanwhile, who may be a major influence in a child's psychological development during very important years of life, according to payscale.com (2016) got a median of around $9.12 per hour.

Some of the wealthiest people in the world have accumulated a net worth of billions of dollars through operating gambling casinos. Meanwhile, payscale.com (2016) reports average salaries of addictions counselors who might help people with gambling addictions: "Certified Addiction... Counselors aren't exactly in the most profitable line of business; these folks earn a belt-tightening average of $36K per year."

A newspaper cartoon (Scott & Kirkman, Baby Blues, 9/29/2015) has a father telling his son, "Hammie, as you grow up, you have to decide if you're going to be part of the problem, or part of the solution." The son replies, "Oh," and looks thoughtful. Then he asks, "Which one pays better?"

In 1958, John Kenneth Galbraith, in his book, *The Affluent Society,* made observations about the fact that the free market by itself does not necessarily direct people's labor to some pursuits that create great benefit for society as a whole. Galbraith called for taxes on consumption and more public funding of the things that really do make society better and happier. Of course, the catch to this proposal is that people tend not to agree on what endeavors really make the world a better place. Nonetheless, most fierce free market advocates would not seek to end all public funding of bridges and roads, medical research, and education. Governments have even used the power of taxation to boost the free market in such areas of public good as professional football and baseball stadiums; an estimated $12 billion of public money has been spent on stadiums in the USA in the first decade of the 21st century (Harrop, 2015). Often people attempt to justify such expenditures by pointing to increased employment, or job-creation, that results. By criterion #2 above, such expenditures are reasonable only if they maximize the betterment of the human condition, relative to other ways of spending public money.

Society invests huge amounts of labor and effort into violence against one another and defense against such violence. If somehow society were made up of nonviolent individuals and war were nonexistent, (and I realize that this is a goal that is impossible to achieve unilaterally through the action of any one group or nation) the amount of labor freed up from the defense industry, the terrorism and anti-terrorism industries, the criminal justice system, the prison industry, and so forth, would be immense. Global military spending stands at about 1.7 trillion dollars per year, with the U.S. being by far the leader in military spending levels (Shah, 2013).

Psychoeducational tutoring as a source of jobs and societal good

What does all this have to do with psychoeducational tutoring? I want to propose four economic-related hypotheses, as follows.

First, there are those who say that one-on-one tutoring is too expensive – that it will never be feasible to devote one teacher to only one student. If psychoeducational tutoring does indeed significantly increase the skills that it is meant to increase, then the previous sections should make the point that the labor, and the money, should be available to hire psychoeducational tutors in large numbers – if society comes to place a high enough priority upon the teaching of psychological skills.

Second: The Keynesian model proposes, with very good evidence, that in periods of economic downturn, governments can grow economic activity by "fiscal stimuli" consisting of spending money on almost anything, ranging from war efforts to conservation corps to "shovel ready" construction. One does not need to be a Keynesian to believe that in regions with high unemployment, directly hiring people can reduce unemployment. Telephone tutoring can be funded with low investment in infrastructure; nothing needs to be built. If governments at any time wish to increase GDP, and employment, they can do so by funding the training and hiring of many more people as psychoeducational tutors. If there is a certain region whose major industry has been set back, we can train and hire more tutors in that area. The fact that tutors do not need professional degrees and many years of schooling before being ready to be deployed is a major fact in favor of using it as a method of "job creation." A certain fraction of any population is already dependable, kind, enthusiastic, and competent enough to be telephone tutors with fairly little training. A much larger fraction requires much more extensive training; however, if many people are trained in the interpersonal skills of telephone tutoring, that in itself arguably makes society better off, before tutoring even begins. If there is a region where students seem to be performing poorly either academically or behaviorally or both, we can deploy more tutors to that region. For telephone tutoring, tutors and students need not be geographically close. Without needing to build any more buildings or lay any more infrastructure, governments can stimulate economic activity whenever they want.

The third hypothesis is about very long-term consequences. In a free market, people "vote" with their dollars for the types of activities that society devotes itself to, for the types of efforts people make. The quality of economic choices society makes is proportional to the psychological skill of its members. A more psychologically skilled society will use its dollars to harness human effort in ways that better the human condition more. For example: if every person in society were extremely skilled in self-care, the cigarette industry would cease to exist, leaving a large amount of labor to be devoted to other efforts (such as psychoeducational tutoring). If more people choose to buy healthy food, much of the labor involved in weight loss and in health care for conditions caused by obesity, as well as the labor devoted to the junk food industry, could be devoted to other efforts (e.g. psychoeducational tutoring). The biggest payoff to society would accrue if by some miracle and/or by world-wide intense training in nonviolence and joint decision-making skills, the huge amounts of labor devoted to the defense industry could be diverted to other pursuits. This was the sentiment expressed by general and president Dwight David Eisenhower (1953), when he said,

"Every gun that is made, every warship launched, every rocket fired, signifies in the final sense a theft from those who hunger and are not fed, those who are cold and are not clothed. This world in arms is not spending money alone. It is spending the sweat of its laborers, the genius of its scientists, the houses of its children.
"This is not a way of life.... Under the cloud of war, it is humanity hanging itself on a cross of iron."

I believe that much time could be well spent in visualizing a society in which people had the "conservation" and "good decision" skills to make much better choices on what to spend their money on, and devoted their resources to those things that really make life better. One consequence would be that when people looked for work, they would find jobs that really contribute to the welfare of society. When people came home from work, more of them could feel that they had done something meaningful. This is not a vision of a variation of socialism in which government officials decide what goods and services are most useful to humanity. Rather, it's a vision in which the free market directs human labor toward more honorable pursuits, because people have the psychological skills to vote with their dollars to create demand for them. Obviously this vision will not come to pass soon.

The fourth claim, I hope, is not overly complimentary to either the human race or to the makers of psychological skills curricula. People's jobs serve a goal beyond that of providing income: that goal is to provide a sense of meaning and purpose. People want to feel that they are contributing to a worthy effort. For many people, the effort to teach the next generation the most important skills of living may fulfill the human need to make an impact. "I am giving spoiled and entitled people what they demand with their dollars, but at least some of those dollars are coming to me," is the way many people think about their work. If more people are able to think, "I am creating an impact that makes someone better off and helps make the world a better place," I believe those people will be happier.

To recap: it is not the total amount of economic activity, not the gross domestic product, that promotes the good of humanity; the type of goods and services that economic activity motivates is crucial. A major economic task for the human race is somehow to increase the jobs that make the human condition better, and to reduce the jobs that waste our effort or even worsen the human condition.

The goal of increasing "right occupation" and decreasing frivolous, wasteful, or harmful work is not new. This idea was expressed eloquently by Henry David Thoreau, (1854/1863). (In the following quotation from Thoreau I have eliminated some of the wording that would now strike us as distractingly sexist.)

"Most … would feel insulted if it were proposed to employ them in throwing stones over a wall, and then in throwing them back, merely that they might earn their wages. But many are no more worthily employed now. For instance: just after sunrise, one summer morning, I noticed one of my neighbors walking beside his team, which was slowly drawing a heavy hewn stone swung under the axle, surrounded by an atmosphere of industry, — his day's work begun, — his brow commenced to sweat, — a reproach to all sluggards and idlers.... And I thought, Such is the labor which the American Congress exists to protect, — honest ... toil.... Indeed, I felt a slight reproach, because I observed this from a window, and was not abroad and stirring about a similar business. The day went by, and at evening I passed the yard of another neighbor, who keeps many servants, and spends much money foolishly, while he adds nothing to the common stock, and there I saw the stone of the morning lying beside a whimsical structure intended to adorn [the]... premises, and the dignity forthwith departed from the teamster's labor, in my eyes. In my opinion, the sun was made to light worthier toil than this. I may add that his employer has since run off, in debt to a good part of the town, and, after passing through Chancery, has settled somewhere else, there to become once more a patron of the arts....

"Government and legislation! these I thought were respectable professions....but think of legislating to regulate the breeding of slaves, or the exportation of tobacco! What have divine legislators to do with the exportation or the importation of tobacco? What humane ones with the breeding of slaves?

"... The chief want, in every State that I have been into, was a high and earnest purpose in its inhabitants.... When we want culture more than potatoes, and illumination more than sugar-plums, then the great resources of a world are taxed and drawn out, and the result, or staple production, is, not slaves, nor operatives, but [human beings],—those rare fruits called heroes, saints, poets, philosophers, and redeemers."

In other words: let's direct human effort less toward the production of junk, and more toward the "production" of high-quality human beings!

Thoreau's take on what society produces as contrasted to what it really needs is remarkably similar to that of Allison Arieff in a 2016 op-ed article in the New York Times. To quote:

"Every day, innovative companies promise to make the world a better place. Are they succeeding?

"Here is just a sampling of the products, apps and services that have come across my radar in the last few weeks:

A service that sends someone to fill your car with gas.

A service that sends a valet on a scooter to you, wherever you are, to park your car.

A service that will film anything you desire with a drone.

A service that will pack your suitcase — virtually.

A service that delivers a new toothbrush head to your mailbox every three months.

A service that delivers your beer right to your door....

"Products and services are designed to "disrupt" market sectors (a.k.a. bringing to market things no one really needs) more than to solve actual problems, especially those problems experienced by what the writer C. Z. Nnaemeka has described as "the unexotic underclass" — single mothers, the white rural poor, veterans, out-of-work Americans over 50 — who, she explains, have the 'misfortune of being insufficiently interesting.'

Chapter 16: Psychoeducation and the Economy

"Are we fixing the right things? … Empathy, humility, compassion, conscience: These are the key ingredients missing in the pursuit of innovation...."

* * *

Thoreau and Arieff agree that a major task is to divert human labor, effort, and creativity from relatively wasteful or harmful pursuits to those which will most improve the human condition the most. If psychoeducational tutoring can succeed in teaching qualities such as "empathy, humility, compassion, and conscience," it qualifies as a pursuit where much human labor could be well used.

Chapter 17: A Vision of a Psychoeducating Society

The story of "Each one teach one"

Moore (2016), among others, recounts the story of Frank Laubach's achievements in promoting literacy. In the early 20th century, Laubach was working in the Philippines with the Moro people. At the time, these people had no written alphabet; Laubach learned their language, associated alphabetic symbols with the sounds of the language, and with his staff, began to teach literacy. In keeping with the ethos of the times, the project initially followed the missionary model in which the "more enlightened" were to teach and help the "primitives" (and in the process convert them to the religion of the enlightened). The project was threatened when the great depression hit the United States and much of the funding for the missionary work dried up. When Laubach spoke with the chief of the group with whom he was working, the chief refused to drop the literacy project, saying something like, "I'll make everybody who knows how to read teach somebody else, or I'll kill him." Thus literacy instruction as taught only by the U.S. professionals came to an abrupt halt, and a massive "peer tutoring" project was born. Laubach wrote, "Everybody taught. Nobody died. Everybody liked it. I did not like the motto 'teach or die' and so changed it to 'Each One Teach One.'" (Quoted in Lawson, 1991, p. 9)" The Laubach literacy methods apparently resulted in literacy for millions, and they are still being widely used. A chief reason for success was the deprofessionalization of reading instruction – the realization that restricting instruction to certified teachers could not supply the enormous quantity of labor needed for the cause of literacy.

Vision for the nonprofessional model for psychological skills

What if each person who was willing and able to teach psychological skills, could be enlisted to the cause? What if the teaching force included not just licensed professionals, but anyone worthy and willing to take on a student? While not reaching the "Each one teach one" criterion, it is feasible that huge numbers of people could spend half an hour a day for two or more years teaching a younger person psychological skills. The massive person-power needs for the "moon shot" goal of vastly improving the psychological skills of society could be met.

In this vision, most tutors would require a good deal of training and supervision. Those tutors who showed the greatest skill and conscientiousness in tutoring could use their skills to be trainers and supervisors of more tutors.

In this vision, the creation and revision of the manuals and textbooks for the project would remain a job for highly trained people who keep a close eye to the accumulated knowledge about what patterns of thought, emotion, and behavior are most compatible with ethics and mental health, under what circumstances. Such professionals would also be closely attuned to how well the manuals appeared to work in their ongoing use with tutees.

Research on the best ways of responding to situations

In this vision, more psychological research is devoted to the question, what are the best ways of responding to situations? What sorts of responses tend to be most successful? What patterns of behavior should we teach people to carry out? For example: Our current data base supports us in not teaching people with anger control problems to seek a "catharsis" of anger, a way of "getting out" their negative feelings. We would not know this without research on the topic. There is room for lots more research on the question of what behavior patterns are more skillful than others, and how to achieve them.

Being tutored, and being a tutor, is close to a universal experience

In a society in the envisioned "age of psychoeducation," we would come as close as possible to hiring as tutors all those who are willing and able, and supplying tutoring to all those children who are willing and able to receive it. We would not need to restrict services to those who already have developed psychiatric disorders.

If the idea of universality could take hold, there would be no stigma attached to seeking psychoeducation.

The internalization of tones of approval is a result of both tutoring and being tutored

Psychoeducational tutoring is the occasion for much celebration, and much use of enthusiastic, reinforcing tones of voice. In our fantasied society, the use of approval and reinforcement between people, and the use of self-reinforcement within individual people, would be dramatically higher. It would be reasonable to hypothesize that the prevalence of depression would be correspondingly lower.

The content of psychoeducation is learned in tutoring and reviewed as a tutor

If an individual receives several years of psychoeducational tutoring, that person should need much less training to become a psychoeducational tutor. Those who have been tutored can pass their experience on to others.

Psychological skills exercises are a routine part of life, as is physical exercise

In current society the value of regular physical exercise is widely agreed upon. In the envisioned society, regular psychological skills exercises would be a part of life – the 12 thought exercise, the brainstorming options exercise, the pros and cons exercise, reflections, listening with four responses, fantasy rehearsals, social conversation role plays, Dr. L.W. Aap joint decisions, and so forth would take their place alongside running and weightlifting.

Families incorporate tutoring into their agendas

Psychoeducational tutors who have experienced the depth of relationship that comes from spending half an hour a day of one-on-one time with a child may wish to have such a rich experience with their own children. The vision of parents and children doing alternate reading, psychological skills exercises, and social conversation with each other regularly is one we should add to the wish-fulfillment fantasy of this chapter.

I was lucky enough to have homeschooled two daughters. Some of the happiest moments of my life were spent sitting on a couch, working and learning together, others were spent walking around, talking about ideas. In an ideal vision, more parents would be able to experience the pleasure and joy of being psychoeducators for their own children. (As I've mentioned before, some way of precluding the "battle royal" over homework for some families, as well as the drain on energy and time created by homework for many others, would need to be fashioned.)

The culture systematically produces and collects positive models of psychological skills

The psychoeducational culture would create and collect a huge bank of positive models, not for entertainment purposes, but for the sake of modeling the highest and best patterns that society can teach to succeeding generations. These models would be stored in a variety of formats: written stories, written fantasy rehearsals, songs, written plays, plays performed with toy people, animation, or actors and recorded in movies. Examples of all 62 skills would be organized and cataloged. Models would exist for the situations encountered at every age group and reading level, and in a wide variety of life circumstances. Psychological skill training would continually make use of the positive model data bank.

Along with the bank of positive models would be a bank of situations for practice. Provocations for anger control; choice points for individual decision-making; situations for conflict-resolution and joint decision-making training; ethical dilemmas for discussion; urges for UCAC fantasy rehearsals; social pressure situations for practice in resisting pressure toward unwise behavior; social situations for "what would you do or say" practice in social skills; and many others.

Psychological skills training as the frontier for humanity

The human race has made amazing progress in science and technology in a very short fraction of its total history. Along with such progress is the knowledge of how to bring about mass destruction and death, with unprecedented effectiveness. The threat of mass destruction from nuclear warfare has not gone away, although relative to past decades it appears to have become less frightening and the possibility is met with more denial.

The major piece of progress that humanity needs is the mass production of psychological skill in human beings. We have the technology with which to deliver this instruction in a nurturing, one-to-one interpersonal environment. We have huge amounts of human effort and labor that have been freed from agriculture and manufacturing by technological advances in mechanized productivity.

We can debate how much various technological advances have increased human happiness. Television, for example, has brought us greater connection with other human beings, but has also vastly increased the exposure to violent models. Computer chips allow vastly more efficient scholarly research; they also enable vastly more time spent in fantasy rehearsal of antisocial actions (see Grand Theft Auto).

But a revolution in the amount and quality of time that future generations spend in learning psychological skills would directly foster the behavior patterns that should result in a culture of happiness, nonviolence, creativity, productivity – the marks of an ethical, successful, well-functioning human culture.

Can we even imagine a world where almost all people have been very effectively trained for a full complement of psychological skills, starting with earliest life and into, perhaps throughout, adulthood? It is challenging enough to imagine a world where almost all have the self-care, self-discipline, and good decision-making skills to avoid substance abuse and addiction. Can we imagine a world in which almost all human beings were taught the skill of nonviolence well enough, not even to disavow all violence, but to use it only as a last resort? Can we envision what interpersonal relationships and families would be like in a world where all people were trained from birth to maximize the chances of good relationships?

In the current society in which the number of hours deliberately allocated to the psychoeducation of the average child is probably close to zero, this vision is totally unrealistic. How many hours of psychoeducation would produce what sorts of effects, on individuals and on society? Is it even possible to deliver very high quality psychoeducation on a large scale? These are questions that can, and should, be answered empirically. Humanity has the potential person-power available to devote to the cause. Can we enlist sufficient human labor and effort to find out how much good really can be produced by large scale psychoeducational tutoring? To do so could change the course of history for the better. To do so would be the most worthwhile of ventures.

Appendix 1: Example List for Psychological Skills

1. Productivity:

Doing useful work for one's family, for example cleaning up after a meal, helping put silverware back into a drawer; taking trash out; putting things away after using them; washing dishes; cleaning floors; helping with laundry or putting laundry away; cutting grass; taking care of a pet; organizing one's room; carrying groceries into the house, helping put groceries away; helping prepare meals; helping fix something that needs repair; raking leaves, shoveling snow, helping with any other chore.

Working on schoolwork, doing homework, doing extra drill on things to learn for school, taking turns reading aloud with someone, reading a book that wasn't assigned, learning something by reading books or magazines etc. or on the internet, solving puzzles or problems that exercise the brain. Working out, exercising. Creating a work of art or building something.

Especially for young children, Sustaining attention: Listening while someone reads to him or her, for a little longer than before; having a chat with one of his or her parents without having to run off to get into something else; playing with the same toys for a reasonably long time; paying attention to a play that someone puts on for him or her with toy people; telling a story, and staying on the topic for a reasonable time; working at a task longer than before. Especially for young children, Practicing Using Language: Listening while someone reads him or her a story, having a chat with someone; asking a good question about something he is curious about; telling about things he has seen and done; talking back and forth with someone; using a longer sentence than before; using some new words.

2. Joyousness:

Appendix 1: Example List for Psychological Skills

Smiling or laughing about anything other than someone else's bad fortune. Saying, "I like this," or "This is fun," or "I'm glad I get to do this," or "Yay!" or any other celebratory comment. Liking doing something well enough to want to keep doing it. Seeming to enjoy a conversation. Looking enthusiastic and animated. Speaking with an enthusiastic or animated voice. Feeling proud of an accomplishment. Feeling proud of an act of kindness. Being able to tell about something that he is glad to have done. Seeming to feel good when reminded of something good she has done.

Humor: Saying something funny, appreciating it and laughing when someone else says something funny; doing an imitation of something or someone that is funny but not derisive; imagining a silly situation and having fun with it; surprising someone with a trick that is not harmful.

3. Kindness

Helping someone do something, complimenting or congratulating someone, expressing thanks, being a good listener, teaching someone how to do something, forgiving someone who has harmed you, consoling someone who is sad, spending time with someone, keeping someone company; being cheerful or approving, being affectionate, giving or lending something, being assertive in a nice way, writing a nice note to someone.

Saying "Thanks for the supper" to his or her parent; picking up something his or her mother drops and giving it to her; saying "Good morning" in a cheerful tone to a family member; speaking gently to his or her pet and petting him nicely; saying "That's OK" in a gentle manner when a parent forgets to do something he wanted him or her to do; saying "That's interesting," when his or her sister mentions some of her thoughts; saying "Don't worry about it" in a gentle way when his or her brother seems to feel bad about a mistake he made in a game; giving his or her brother a piece of his or her dessert; saying "What have you been up to?" and listening nicely to his or her sister when she tells him about her day; offering to help a parent carry something; saying "You're welcome" in a gentle way when someone says "Thank you"; sharing a toy with another child; patting another child on the back, affectionately; offering to push someone in the swing; offering to take turns, and letting someone else take the first turn; going up to another child and socializing in a nice way; smiling at someone.

4. Honesty

Reporting a mistake or failure; taking responsibility for a bad outcome; answering correctly when asked if something she said was real-life or made up; answering correctly when asked about something he needs to improve in; telling about a personal experience; reporting some feelings about something in an honest way; when asked if she is sure about something, reporting honestly.

5. Fortitude

Saying "OK" in a nice way when he asks for some candy and is told he can't have any; keeping cheerful when the rain spoils his or her plans to play outside with his friend; handling it without yelling when his or her brother breaks one of the things he owns; looking calmly for something he can't find, without losing his temper; not yelling when he has to stop watching a television show to come to supper or to go out somewhere with his or her parent; being cool when his or her little brother grabs something out of his or her hand—getting it back, if he wants, but not yelling or hitting; being cheerful when he doesn't get a present that he has asked for; being cheerful when he has to come inside...

Enjoying Aloneness: Playing by himself when his or her parents pay attention to a sibling; paying attention to something else when a parent is on the phone; letting his or her parents talk to each other for a while without interrupting; watching what some peers are doing with each other, without butting in immediately; letting a sibling play with something, and get the parent's attention, without taking that thing away; drawing a parent's attention to a sibling in a favorable way; letting a parent read or write or lie down and rest without interrupting, being able to handle it if some peers do not want him or her participating with them in an activity.

Handling your own mistakes and failures: In a game, failing to make a goal or win a point etc. without getting too upset; losing a game without getting discouraged; failing to do something he tries, and then working harder rather than giving up; being corrected for something, and then making an effort to do better; remembering a previous time he made a mistake, and saying "This time I won't (or will) do X, because I learned from the last time"; talking out loud to himself when he has made a mistake or failure, and saying "What can I do about this? I could do this, or that...";

6a.   Good individual decisions:

Thinking before acting; saying out loud, "Let me think about this"; saying out loud, "What options do I have here?"; talking about a decision and listing options; talking about a decision and mentioning the pros and cons of an option; saying that she was glad to have chosen one action rather than another, for a good reason; looking up some information helpful in making a decision; saying "I'll have to think about that" rather than deciding right away with a difficult and important decision; making a random decision right away with a very unimportant decision; doing any action that is wiser than an alternative.

6b. Good joint decisions or conflict-resolution

Taking turns with someone; asking to use something when someone else is done with it; talking calmly with someone about what the two people should do; listening carefully to someone else's point of view about a problem the two people are trying to solve; doing a reflection of what the other person has said; stating clearly and calmly what she wants; refusing to go along with someone else when it is appropriate; deciding to go along with someone else when it's appropriate; thinking of a creative option for a joint decision; thinking of compromise options for resolving a conflict.

7. Nonviolence:

Not hitting back when a sibling pushes or hits; not hitting when someone does a provocation; not getting into a fight when the opportunity is there; going for x length of time without any violent act; making a comment in favor of nonviolence; choosing not to watch a violent movie or TV show or play a violent video game; reading about nonviolence; singing a nonviolence song.

8. Respectful Talk:

Using tones of approval; using approving facial expressions while talking. Saying "Good morning," or "Welcome home," or "I'm glad to see you," or "Hi" in an enthusiastic tone of voice. Saying "Please," "Thank you for doing that," "You're welcome!" or "Excuse me, please." Saying things like, "Could I ask you to move a little?" instead of "Get out of my way." Saying things like, "Would you mind not doing that?" instead of "Quit doing that!" Saying things like, "Here's another way of looking at it," rather than "You're totally wrong." Saying something like, "Here's another option," instead of "That's a stupid idea."

9. Friendship-Building

Social initiations: Watching some peers do whatever they're doing before joining in with them; paying attention to what peers are paying attention to rather than drawing attention to himself; starting to socialize in any way that does not irritate the peer; saying "Hi" to a peer he knows; introducing himself to a peer he doesn't know; asking if some peers would like another participant in an activity; finding someone who is lonely, and talking or playing with that person; offering to share something he has with a peer, as a way of getting interaction started; asking a question about something a peer is doing, as a way of getting interaction started; inviting people to do things with her.

Appendix 1: Example List for Psychological Skills

Social conversation: Figuring out how to find a topic to talk with someone about, that both can be interested in; talking with another person in an interesting way; telling about his own experience; following up on what someone else has said by asking a question; following up on what someone else has said by making a statement about it; doing reflections to confirm understanding of what the other person said; doing "facilitations" (like uh huh, yes... I see.... OK!) to demonstrate that she is listening and encourage the other to continue; giving positive feedback about what the other person has said or done; using enthusiastic and approving tones of voice during a conversation; seeming to enjoy a social conversation; talking about not-very-personal things when just getting to know a person; talking about more personal things with someone he knows really well and trusts; avoiding talking too long without stopping to give the other person a chance; having enough to say in a conversation; smiling or laughing or nodding or giving other clues of enjoying a conversation; choosing to spend time talking with someone rather than watching TV or playing video games.

Non-bossiness, Letting the other do what she wants: In playing, letting the other play with a toy without taking it away from her; responding to the other's suggestion of "Let's do this" by saying "OK!"; responding to the other's question of "May I do this?" by saying "Sure!"; responding to the other's looking over her shoulder at something she is doing by tolerating it, rather than asking the other to go away; responding to a younger sister's tapping lightly on her knee by tolerating it rather than bossing her to quit doing it; in dramatic play, letting the other person direct the course of the plot for a while; in dramatic play, when the other person says something like "Pretend this is a lake" or "Pretend that this is a goat," going along with the suggestion; letting sister show off without telling her not to be such a show-off; letting a friend play with something that she is not particularly interested in playing with, without telling the friend to put it down and play with something else.

10. Self-discipline

Doing chores, doing school work, starting work early; keeping concentrating on school work for a long time; participating in a tutoring session, exercising hard, spending time organizing and putting away your things; doing unpleasant but important work; going to bed early; getting up on time; leaving for school on time or early; avoiding high-calorie food if one is overweight; eating nutritious food such as vegetables and salad; resisting impulses to waste money; working on chores; resisting social pressure from peers to do unwise things; deciding not to waste time on TV or video games; deciding to read something educational; practicing a musical instrument; practicing a sports skill; practicing an academic skill; practicing handling a feared situation if one has unrealistic fears; talking about something unpleasant but useful to talk about; resisting pressure to drink alcohol, smoke cigarettes, or do drugs; remembering to do things like take care of teeth; keeping track of an appointment with someone; planning ahead so as to get to an appointment early or on time; writing down school assignments; organizing the papers needed for school; resisting the urge to be aggressive or yell at someone; resisting urges for sexual activity that could get one into trouble; staying cool when one is tempted to "freak out"; finishing a project even though it gets boring; handling waiting time well; choosing to do something unpleasant in order to achieve a goal; choosing to gradually make some activity more pleasant because it is necessary to achieve a goal.

11. Loyalty

Sticking up for a friend, not wanting to lose touch with someone, calling up an extended family member to say hi, looking out for the welfare of a sibling, disagreeing with people who put down a sibling or other family member, disagreeing with people who put down a good friend, inviting a friend to get together, writing a letter to a friend or family member; remembering someone's birthday; helping out a friend or family member when the going gets rough, for example when the person is sick or having trouble of some sort.

Appendix 1: Example List for Psychological Skills

12. Conservation:

Having the concept of using time well versus wasting time; choosing not to waste time. Choosing to spend waiting time doing something useful. Choosing to get some work done rather than playing video games. Choosing to think about something useful or interesting rather than wasting time being bored.
Turning lights out to save energy; turning other appliances off; not buying things that aren't necessary; saving money rather than wasting it; choosing not to spend money on junk food; being interested in having a bank or brokerage account; being interested in ending pollution; wanting to keep using an old thing instead of buying a new one;

13. Self-care:

Brushing teeth; washing hands before eating; exercising; eating nutritious food; for someone underweight, eating a big meal; for someone overweight, eating a small meal; not smoking; making a comment not in favor of smoking; not drinking alcohol; making a comment not in favor of drinking alcohol; not using recreational drugs; making a comment in favor of not using recreational drugs; buckling seat belt; putting helmet on before cycling, skating, etc.; not listening to loud music (to keep from damaging hearing); avoiding getting sunburned; going to bed at a regular time; getting up in the morning at a regular time; eating fruits and vegetables; riding a bike in a non-risky way; staying away from the edges of cliffs; taking vitamins or any medicines that have been prescribed by a doctor, in the right amounts.
Practicing relaxing the muscles, practicing meditation by observing what comes to mind, meditating on the word one, meditating on acts of kindness, doing the good will meditation, doing the psychological skills meditation, doing the pleasant dreams exercise, reading inspirational writings.

14. Compliance: Coming quickly in response to the command, "It's time to go; please come with me now"; saying "OK" without arguing when he's told it's bedtime; keeping his voice low when his mother asks; playing inside on a rainy day for an hour and following the "no throwing the football inside" rule; leaving something alone that his or her parent asks him or her not to touch; playing gently with his or her friend after his or her mother tells them to stop wrestling, coming when his or her mother says "Come with me"; getting dressed without problems when asked to do so; brushing teeth when asked to do so; following the rule of staying at the table during a meal; turning the television off, or not turning it back on once it is turned off, as requested; stopping doing something annoying when requested to.

15. Positive Fantasy Rehearsal:

Doing a fantasy rehearsal of one of his high priority skills; reading a fantasy rehearsal of a psychological skill; purposely reading about or watching a positive model; doing fantasy rehearsal to help with a performance such as music or public speaking or a sport.
Avoiding violent or rude models presented in movies or TV shows or video games.

16. Courage: Trying an activity he's never tried before; getting to know people she's never met before; venturing the answer to a question raised in a group, when she's not very sure of the answer; doing something in the dark; doing something that is not dangerous that she was inhibited about doing at some point in the past; doing something that he or she had an unrealistic fear of or aversion to or avoidance of; working on reducing unrealistic fears or aversions.

Appendix 2: The More Complete List of Psychological Skills

Group 1: Productivity
1. Purposefulness. Having a sense of purpose that drives activity
2. Persistence and concentration. Sustaining attention, concentrating, focusing, staying on task
3. Competence-development. Working toward competence in job, academics, recreation, life skills
4. Organization. Organizing goals, priorities, time, money, and physical objects; planfulness

Group 2. Joyousness
5. Enjoying aloneness. Having a good time by oneself, tolerating not getting someone's attention
6. Pleasure from approval. Enjoying approval, compliments, and positive attention from others
7. Pleasure from accomplishments. Self-reinforcement for successes.
8. Pleasure from your own kindness. Feeling pleasure from doing kind, loving acts for others
9. Pleasure from discovery. Enjoying exploration and satisfaction of curiosity
10. Pleasure from others' kindness. Feeling gratitude for what others have done
11. Pleasure from blessings. Celebrating and feeling the blessings of luck or fate
12. Pleasure from affection. Enjoying physical affection without various fears interfering
13. Favorable attractions. Having feelings of attraction aroused in ways consonant with happiness
14. Relaxation. Calming oneself, letting the mind drift pleasantly and the body be at ease

15. Gleefulness. Playing, becoming childlike, experiencing glee, being spontaneous

16. Humor. Enjoying funny things, finding and producing comedy in life

Group 3: Kindness

17. Kindness. Nurturing someone, being kind and helpful

18. Empathy. Recognizing other people's feelings, seeing things from the other's point of view

19. Conscience. Feeling appropriate guilt, avoiding harming others

Group 4: Honesty

20. Honesty. Being honest and dependable, especially when it is difficult to be so

21. Awareness of your abilities. Being honest and brave in assessing your strengths and weaknesses

Group 5: Fortitude

22. Frustration-tolerance. Handling frustration, tolerating adverse circumstances, fortitude

23. Handling separation. Tolerating separation from close others, or loss of a relationship

24. Handling rejection. Tolerating it when people don't like or accept you or want to be with you

25. Handling criticism. Dealing with disapproval and criticism and lack of respect from others

26. Handling mistakes and failures. Regretting mistakes without being overly self-punitive

27. Magnanimity, non-jealousy. Handling it when someone else gets what I want

28. Painful emotion-tolerance. Tolerating feeling bad without having that make you feel worse

29. Fantasy-tolerance. Tolerating unwanted mental images, confident that they will not be enacted

Group 6: Good decisions

6a: Individual decision-making
30. Positive aim. Aiming toward making things better. Seeking reward and not punishment
31. Reflectiveness. Thinking before acting, letting thoughts mediate between situation and action
32. Fluency. Using words to conceptualize the world: verbal skills
33. Awareness of your emotions. Recognizing, and being able to verbalize one's own feelings
34. Awareness of control. Accurately assessing the degree of control one has over specific events
35. Decision-making. Defining a problem, gathering information, generating options, predicting and evaluating consequences, making a choice
6b: Joint decision-making, including conflict resolution
36. Toleration. Non-bossiness. Tolerating a wide range of other people's behavior
37. Rational approach to joint decisions. Deciding rationally on stance and strategies
38. Option-generating. Generating creative options for solutions to problems
39. Option-evaluating. Justice skills: Recognizing just solutions to interpersonal problems
40. Assertion. Dominance, sticking up for oneself, taking charge, enjoying winning
41. Submission: Conciliation, giving in, conceding, admitting one was wrong, being led
42. Differential reinforcement. Reinforcing positive behavior and avoiding reinforcing the negative

Group 7: Nonviolence
43. Forgiveness and anger control. Forgiving, handling an insult or injury by another
44. Nonviolence. Being committed to the principle of nonviolence and working to foster it

Group 8: Not being rude (Respectful talk)

45. Not being rude, respectful talk. Being sensitive to words, vocal tones and facial expressions that are accusing, punishing or demeaning, and avoiding them unless there is a very good reason

Group 9: Friendship-Building
46. Discernment and Trusting. Accurately appraising others. Not distorting with prejudice, overgeneralization, wish-fulfilling fantasies. Deciding what someone can be trusted for and trusting when appropriate
47. Self-disclosure. Disclosing and revealing oneself to another when it is safe
48. Gratitude. Expressing gratitude, admiration, and other positive feelings toward others
49. Social initiations. Starting social interaction; getting social contact going.
50. Socializing. Engaging well in social conversation or play
51. Listening. Empathizing, encouraging another to talk about his own experience

Group 10: Self discipline
52. Self discipline Delay of gratification, self-control. Denying oneself pleasure for future gain

Group 11: Loyalty
53. Loyalty. Tolerating and enjoying sustained closeness, attachment, and commitment to another

Group 12: Conservation
54. Conservation and Thrift. Preserving resources for ourselves and future generations. Foregoing consumption on luxuries, but using resources more wisely. Financial delay of gratification skills

Group 13: Self-care
55. Self-nurture. Delivering assuring or care taking thoughts to oneself, feeling comforted thereby
56. Habits of self-care. Healthy habits regarding drinking, smoking, drug use, exercise and diet

57. Carefulness. Feeling appropriate fear and avoiding unwise risks

Group 14: Compliance
58. Compliance. Obeying, submitting to legitimate and reasonable authority

Group 15: Positive fantasy rehearsal
59. Imagination and positive fantasy rehearsal. Using fantasy as a tool in rehearsing or evaluating a plan, or adjusting to an event or situation

Group 16: Courage
60. Courage. Estimating danger, overcoming fear of non-dangerous situations, handling danger rationally
61. Independent thinking. Making decisions independently, carrying out actions independently
62. Depending. Accepting help, being dependent without shame, asking for help appropriately

References

Achenbach, T.M. (1978). The Child Behavior Profile: I. Boys aged 6–11. Journal of Consulting and Clinical Psychology, 46, 478-488. http://dx.doi.org/10.1037/0022-006X.46.3.478

Aizer, A., & Doyle, J.J. (2013). Juvenile incarceration, human capital and future crime: Evidence from randomly-assigned judges. NBER (National Bureau of Economic Research) Working Paper No. 19102 Issued in June 2013. Retrieved from http://nber.org/papers/w19102

American Psychiatric Association (2013). Diagnostic and statistical manual of mental disorders, fifth edition. Arlington, Virginia: American Psychiatric Association.

Anderson, C.A., & Bushman, B.J. (2001). Effects of violent video games on aggressive behavior, aggressive cognition, aggressive affect, physiological arousal, and prosocial behavior: A meta-analytic review of the scientific literature. Psychological Science, 12, 353-359.

Anthem Blue Cross Blue Shield (2015). Clinical UM guideline. Psychiatric disorder treatment. Retrieved from https://www.anthem.com/medicalpolicies/guidelines/gl_pw_c164429.htm

Arieff, A. (2016). Solving all the wrong problems. New York Times, July 9, 2016. Retrievable from http://www.nytimes.com/2016/07/10/opinion/sunday/solving-all-the-wrong-problems.html?_r=0

Avellar, S., Paulsell, D., Sama-Miller, E., Del Grosso, P., et al. (2014). Home visiting evidence of effectiveness review: Executive summary. Washington, D.C., Office of Planning, Research and Evaluation, Administration for Children and Families, U.S. Department of Health and Human Services.

References

Azrin, N.H., & Besalel, V.A. (1981). An operant reinforcement method of treating depresssion. J Behav Ther Exp Psychiatry, 12, 145-151.

Bandura, A. (1971). Social learning theory. New York: General Learning Press.

Bandura, A. (1973). Aggression: A social learning analysis. Englewood Cliffs, NJ, Prentice Hall.

BBC News (2013). David Cameron promises £1m 'Longitude Prize' for big ideas. Retrieved from http://www.bbc.com/news/uk-politics-22892443

Benson, H., & Klipper, M.Z. (1975). The relaxation response. New York: Harper Collins.

Birukov, P., & Tolstoy, L. (1911). Leo Tolstoy, his life and work: Autobiographical memoirs, letters, and biographical material, volume 1. New York: Charles Scribner's Sons.

Bloom, B.S. (1984). The two-sigma problem: The search for methods of group instruction as effective as one-to-one tutoring. Educational Researcher, 13, 4-16.

Bureau of Labor Statistics, U.S. Department of Labor (2016). Time adults spent caring for household children as a primary activity by sex, age, and day of week, average for the combined years 2011-2015. Retrieved from http://www.bls.gov/news.release/atus.t09.htm.

Burns, D. (1980). Feeling good: The new mood therapy. New York: Harper.

Bushman, B.J. (2002). Does venting anger feed or extinguish the flame? Catharsis, rumination, distraction, anger, and aggressive responding. Personality And Social Psychology Bulletin, 28, 724-731.

Bushman, B.J., & Anderson, C.A. (2001) Media violence and the American public: Scientific facts versus media misinformation. American Psychologist, 56, 477-489.

Bushman, B. J., Baumeister, R. F., & Stack, A. D. (1999). Catharsis, aggression, and persuasive influence: Self-fulfilling or self-defeating prophecies? Journal of Personality and Social Psychology, 76, 367-376.

Cautela, J., Flannery, R., & Hanley, E. (1974). Covert modeling: An experimental test. Behavior Therapy, 5, 494-502.

CDC (Center for Disease Control) (2016). The Tuskegee timeline. Retrieved from http://www.cdc.gov/tuskegee/timeline.htm.

Chang, E.C., D'Zurilla, T.J., & Sanna, L.J. (2004). Social problem solving: Theory, research, and training. Washington, D.C.: American Psychological Association.

Chapman S., Azizi L., Luo Q., & Sitas F. (2016). Has the incidence of brain cancer risen in Australia since the introduction of mobile phones 29 years ago? Cancer Epidemiol., pii: S1877-7821(16)30050-9. doi: 10.1016/j.canep.2016.04.010. [Epub ahead of print]
.

Clarey, C. (2014). Olympians use imagery as mental training. New York Times, February 22, 2014. Retrieved from http://www.nytimes.com/2014/02/23/sports/olympics/olympians-use-imagery-as-mental-training.html?_r=0.

Christensen H., Griffiths K.M., & Jorm A.F. (2004). Delivering interventions for depression by using the internet: randomised controlled trial. BMJ, 328; 265- published online January 2004, doi:10.1136/bmj.37945.566632.EE.

References

Coie, J. D., & Krehbiel, G. (1984). Effects of academic tutoring on the social status of low-achieving socially rejected children. Child Development, 55, 1465-1478.

Connolly, A. (2007). KeyMath-3 Diagnostic Assessment. New York: Pearson Education.

Constantino, J.N. (2016). Child maltreatment prevention and the scope of child and adolescent psychiatry. Child Adolesc Psychiatric Clin N Am, 25, 157–165. http://dx.doi.org/10.1016/j.chc.2015.11.003

Copeland W.E., Wolke D., Shanahan L., Costello E.J. (2015). Adult functional outcomes of common childhood psychiatric problems: a prospective, longitudinal study. JAMA Psychiatry, 72, 892-899. doi:10.1001/jamapsychiatry.2015.0730.

Csikszentmihalyi, M. (1990). Flow: The psychology of optimal experience. New York: Harper and Row.

de Bono E, & de Saint-Arnaud M (1982). Learn to think. Coursebook and instructor's manual. Santa Barbara, CA: Capra Press

de Bruin, E.J., Bögels, S.M., Oort, F.J., Meijer, A.M. (2015). Efficacy of cognitive behavioral therapy for insomnia in adolescents: A randomized controlled trial with internet therapy, group therapy and a waiting list condition. Sleep, 38, 191326. doi: 10.5665/sleep.5240.

Dèttore, D., Pozza, A., & Andersson, G. (2015). Efficacy of technology delivered cognitive behavioural therapy for OCD versus control conditions, and in comparison with therapist administered CBT: Metaanalysis of randomized controlled trials. Cogn Behav Ther, 44:190211. doi: 10.1080/16506073.2015.1005660. Epub 2015 Feb 23.

Dimidjian, S., Hollon, S.D., Dobson, K.S., Schmaling, K.B., et al. (2006). Randomized trial of behavioral activation, cognitive therapy, and antidepressant medication in the acute treatment of adults with major depression. J Consult Clin Psychol, 74, 658-670.

Donelan-McCall, N., Eckenrode, J., Olds, D.L. (2009). Home visiting for the prevention of child maltreatment: Lessons learned during the past 20 years. Pediatr Clin North Am, 56, 389–403.

Donker, T., Griffiths, K.M., Cuijpers, P., & Christensen, H. (2009). Psychoeducation for depression, anxiety and psychological distress: a meta-analysis. BMC Medicine, 7:79 doi:10.1186/1741-7015-7-79 Retrieved from: http://www.biomedcentral.com/1741-7015/7/79

Eisenberger, R. (1992). Learned industriousness. Psychological Review, 99, 248-267.

Eisenberger, R., and Cameron, J. (1996). Detrimental effects of reward: Reality or myth? American Psychologist, 51, 1153-1166.

Eisenberger, R., Pierce, W.D., & Cameron, J. (1999). Effects of reward on intrinsic reward – negative, neutral, and positive: Comment on Deci, Koestner, and Ryan (1999). Psychological Bulletin, 125, 677-691.

Eisenhower, D.D. (1953). The chance for peace speech. Speech to American Society of Newspaper Editors. Retrieved from http://www.edchange.org/multicultural/speeches/ike_chance_for_peace.html

Ericsson, K.A., Krampe, R.T., and Tesch-Romer, C. (1993). The role of deliberate practice in the acquisition of expert performance. Psychological Review, 100, 363-406.

Federal Communications Commission (2015). Wireless devices and health concerns. Retrieved from https://www.fcc.gov/consumers/guides/wireless-devices-and-health-concerns.

References

Femer, M. (2014). Americans spent about a trillion dollars on illegal drugs in the last decade. Huffington Post, 3/14/2014. Retrieved from http://www.huffingtonpost.com/2014/03/13/americans-trillion-dollars-drugs_n_4943601.html.

Finnerty M., Neese-Todd S., Pritam R., et al. (2016). Access to psychosocial services prior to starting antipsychotic treatment among Medicaid-insured youth. J Am Acad Child Adolesc Psychiatry, 55, 69-76.

Fleming, J. (2004). Erikson's psychosocial developmental stages. Chapter 9 in Fleming, J., Psychological perspectives on human development. Retrieved from http://swppr.org/textbook/ch%209%20erikson.pdf.

Floyd, M., Scogin, F., McKendree-Smith, N.L., Floyd, D.L., & Rokke, P.D. (2004). Cognitive therapy for depression: A comparison of individual psychotherapy and bibliotherapy for depressed older adults. Behav Modif, 28, 297-318.

Forehand R., Lafko N., Parent J., and Burt K., (2014). Is parenting the mediator of change in behavioral parent training for externalizing problems of youth? Clin Psychol Rev., 34, 608–619. doi:10.1016/j.cpr.2014.10.001.

Freud Museum (2016). Freud Museum London: Frequently asked questions. Retrieved from https://www.freud.org.uk/about/faq/.

Freud, S. (1930/2002). Civilization and it discontents. London: Penguin.

Galbraith, J. K. (1958). The affluent society. Fortieth anniversary edition. Houghton Mifflin Company: New York, 1998. (First edition was 1958)

Geen RG, Stonner D, & Shope GL.(1975). The facilitation of aggression by aggression: Evidence against the catharsis hypothesis. J Pers Soc Psychol, 31, 721-726.

Glaze, L.E., Herberman, E.J. (2013). Correctional populations in the United States, 2012. Bureau of Justice Statistics. Retrieved from http://www.bjs.gov/index.cfm?ty=pbdetail&iid=4843

Goldstein, A.P., and Glick, B. (1994). Aggression replacement training: Curriculum and evaluation. Simulation & Gaming, 25, 9-26.

Gopalan, G., Goldstein, L., Klingenstein, K., Sicher, C., et al. (2010). Engaging families into child mental health treatment: Updates and special considerations. J Can Acad Child Adolesc Psychiatry, 19, 182-196.

Greenwood, C.R., Dinwiddie G., Terry B., Wade L., et al. (1984). Teacher-versus peer-mediated instruction: An ecobehavioral analysis of achievement outcomes. Journal of Applied Behavior Analysis, 17, 521-538.

Greer, C., & Kohl, H. (1995). A call to character: A family treasury of stories, poems, plays, proverbs, and fables to guide the development of values for you and your children. New York: Harper Collins.

Halford WK , & Bodenmann G. (2013). Effects of relationship education on maintenance of couple relationship satisfaction. Clin Psychol Rev, 33:51225. doi: 10.1016/j.cpr.2013.02.001. Epub 2013 Feb 19.

Hardell L., Carlberg M., Soderqvist F., & Hansson K. (2013). Case-control study of the association between malignant brain tumours diagnosed between 2007 and 2009 and mobile and cordless phone use. International Journal of Oncology, 43, 1833-1845.

Harpaz-Rotem, I., Leslie, D., & Rosenheck, R. A. (2004). Treatment retention among children entering a new episode of mental health care. Psychiatric Services, 55, 1022–1028.

Harrop, K. (2015). 7 things we could have spent $12 billion on instead of new sports stadiums. Retrieved from

References

http://thinkprogress.org/sports/2015/07/14/3680065/7-things-spent-12-billion-instead-new-sports-stadiums/.

Henriques, G. (2014). The college student mental health crisis. Retrieved from https://www.psychologytoday.com/blog/theory-knowledge/201402/the-college-student-mental-health-crisis

Hodgins, D.C., Peden, N. (2008). Cognitive-behavioral treatment for impulse control disorders. Rev Bras Psiquiatr, 30(Supl I):S31-40.

Hopko, D.R., Robertson, S.M.C., and Lejuez, C.W. (2006). Behavioral activation for anxiety disorders. The Behavior Analyst Today, 7, 212-232.

Huyvaert, S.H. (1998). Time is of the essence: Learning in schools. Needham Heights, MA: Allyn & Bacon.

Jacobson, E. (1924). The technic of progressive relaxation. J. Nervous & Mental Disease, 60, 568-78.

Jacobson, E. (1976). You must relax. London: Unwin Paperbacks.

Jones D.J., Forehand R., Cuellar J., Kincaid C., et al. (2013). Harnessing innovative technologies to advance children's mental health: Behavioral parent training as an example. Clin Psychol Rev, 33, 241–252. doi:10.1016/j.cpr.2012.11.003.

Kalkowski, P. (1995). Peer and cross-age tutoring. School improvement research series. Retrieved from http://educationnorthwest.org/sites/default/files/peer-and-cross-age-tutoring.pdf.

Kaltenthaler, E., Brazier, J., De Nigris, E., Tumur, I., Ferriter, M., Beverley, C., et al. (2006). Computerised cognitive behaviour therapy for depression and anxiety update: a systematic review and economic evaluation. Health Technol Assess, 10(33).

Kato, N., Yanagawa, T., Fujiwara, T., & Morawska, A. (2015). Prevalence of children's mental health problems and the effectiveness of population-level family interventions. J Epidemiol, 25:507-516. doi:10.2188/jea.JE20140198507

Kazdin, A.E. (1974a). Comparative effects of some variations of covert modeling. Journal of Behavior Therapy and Experimental Psychiatry, 5, 225-231.

Kazdin, A.E. (1974b). Covert modeling, model similarity, and reduction of avoidance behavior. Behavior Therapy, 5, 325-340.

Kazdin, A.E. (1974c). Effects of covert modeling and model reinforcement on assertive behavior. Journal of Abnormal Psychology, 83, 240-252.

Kazdin, A.E. (1974d). The effects of model identity and fear-relevant similarity on covert modeling. Behavior Therapy, 5, 624-635.

Kazdin, A.E. (1976). Effects of covert modeling, multiple models, and model reinforcement on assertive behavior. Behavior Therapy, 7, 211-222.

Kazdin, A.E. & Blase, S.L. (2011). Rebooting psychotherapy research and practice to reduce the burden of mental illness. Perspectives on Psychological Science, 6, 21-37.

Kawachi, I., & Berkman, L.F. (2001). Social ties and mental health. Journal of Urban Health: Bulletin of the New York Academy of Medicine, 78, 458-467.

Kaye, P. (1987). Games for math: Playful ways to help your child learn math, from kindergarten to third grade. New York: Pantheon Books.

References

Kilpatrick, W., Wolfe, G., & Wolfe, S.M. (1994). Books that build character: A guide to teaching your child moral values through stories. New York: Touchstone.

Kohlberg, L. (1975). The cognitive-developmental approach to moral education. Phi Delta Kappan, 56, 670-677. Reprinted in Smith, P.K., & Pellegrini, A.D. (2000) Psychology of Education: Major Themes, Volume III: The School Curriculum. London and New York: Routledge Falmer. Re-published in Taylor and Francis e-library, 2004. Retrieved from http://perpus.stkipkusumanegara.ac.id/file_digital/Buku%20Digital %2048.pdf#page=608.

Kray J., Karbach J., Haenig S., & Freitag C. (2012). Can task-switching training enhance executive control functioning in children with attention deficit/hyperactivity disorder? Frontiers in Human Neuroscience, Volume 5, article 180. doi: 10.3389/fnhum.2011.00180

Lahkola A., Tokola K., Auvinen A. (2006). Meta-analysis of mobile phone use and intracranial tumors. Scand J Work Environ Health, 32, 171-177 doi:10.5271/sjweh.995

Larson, D. (1984). Teaching psychological skills: Models for giving psychology away. Monterey, CA: Brooks/Cole Publishing. Available in full text at https://books.google.com/books/about/Teaching_Psychological_Skills.html? id=UJE6NBaY64EC.

Lazarus, A. (1977). In the mind's eye: The power of imagery for personal enrichment. New York: Rawson Associates.

Lee, J. (1993). Facing the fire: Experiencing and expressing anger appropriately. New York: Bantam.

Lockee, B., Moore, D. M., & Burton, J. (2004). Foundations of programmed instruction. In Handbook of research on educational communications and technology, 2nd ed.,edited by D. H. Jonassen, 545–569. Mahwah, NJ: Lawrence Erlbaum Associates.

Lovaas, O.I. (1987). Behavioral treatment and normal educational and intellectual functioning in young autistic children. Journal of Consulting and Clinical Psychology, 55, 3-9.

Lovaas, O.I. (1993). The development of a treatment-research project for developmentally disabled and autistic children. Journal of Applied Behavior Analysis, 26, 617-630.

Luthar S. S., & Zigler E., (1991). Vulnerability and competence: a review of research on resilience in childhood. Am J Orthopsychiatry, 61, 6–22.

Lynam, D.R., & Henry, W. (2001).The role of neuropsychological deficits in conduct disorders. In: Hill J, Maughan B, eds. Conduct disorders in childhood and adolescence. Cambridge: Cambridge University Press.

Lynch, K. (2013). Confirmed: Grand Theft Auto 5 breaks 6 sales world records. Retrieved from http://www.guinnessworldrecords.com/news/2013/10/confirmed-grand-theft-auto-breaks-six-sales-world-records-51900/

Maltz, M. (1960). Psycho-cybernetics: A new way to get more living out of life. New York: Simon and Schuster.

Manber R., Bernert R.A., Suh S., Nowakowski S., et al. (2011). CBT for insomnia in patients with high and low depressive symptom severity: Adherence and clinical outcomes. Journal of Clinical Sleep Medicine, 7, 645-652.

Manzoni G.M., Pagnini F., Castelnuovo G., & Molinari E. (2008). Relaxation training for anxiety: a ten-years systematic review with meta-analysis. BMC Psychiatry, 2008, 8:41 doi:10.1186/1471-244X-8-41. Retrieved from http://www.biomedcentral.com/1471-244X/8/4

References

Markwardt, F.C. (1997) Peabody individual achievement test, revised, normative update. New York: Pearson.

Masten A.S., & Reed M.J. (2002). Resilience in development. In: Snyder CR, Lopez SJ, editors. Handbook of positive psychology. New York: Oxford University Press. pp. 74–88.

McKay, M.M., Harrison, M.E., Gonzales, J., Kim, L., & Quintana, E. (2002). Multiple-family groups for urban children with conduct difficulties and their families. Psychiatric Services, 53, 1467–1468.

Merikangas, K.R., He, J.P., Burstein, M., Swanson, S.A., Avenevoli, S., et al. (2010). Lifetime prevalence of mental disorders in U.S. adolescents: Results from the National Comorbidity Survey Replication--Adolescent Supplement (NCS-A). J Am Acad Child Adolesc Psychiatry, 49:980-9.

Merikangas, K.R., He, J., Burstein, M.E., Swendsen, J., et al. (2011). Service utilization for lifetime mental disorders in U.S. adolescents: Results from the National Comorbidity Survey Adolescent Supplement (NCS-A). Journal of the American Academy of Child and Adolescent Psychiatry, 50, 32-45.

Michelson, L. , Marchione, K., Greenwald, M., Glanz, L., et al. (1990). Panic disorder: cognitive behavioral treatment. Behav Res Ther, 28, 141-151.

Moffitt, T.E., Gabriellie, W.F., Mednick, S.A., & Schulsinger, F. (1981). Socioeconomic status, IQ, and delinquency. Journal of Abnormal Psychology, 90, 152-156

Mohr, D.C., Vella, L., Hart, S., Heckman, T., and Simon, G. (2008). The effect of telephone-administered psychotherapy on symptoms of depression and attrition: A meta-analysis. Clin Psychol (New York), 15, 243–253. doi:10.1111/j.1468-2850.2008.00134.x.

Moore, P. (2016). Teach or die. Retrieved from
http://www.literacyconnexus.org/2016/02/teach-or-die/

Morgan, L.L., Miller, A.B., Sasco, A., & Davis, D.L. (2015). Mobile phone
radiation causes brain tumors and should be classified as a probable human
carcinogen. International Journal of Oncology, retrieved from
https://www.spandidos-publications.com/ijo/46/5/1865.

National Cancer Institute (2016). Cell phones and cancer risk. Retrieved
from http://www.cancer.gov/about-cancer/causes-
prevention/risk/radiation/cell-phones-fact-sheet.

National collaborating centre for mental health and social care institute for
excellence (2013). Antisocial behaviour and conduct disorders in children
and young people: Recognition, intervention and management. National
Clinical Guideline Number 158. Leicester and London: The British
Psychological Society and The Royal College of Psychiatrists.

Naylor, E.V., Antonuccio, D.O., Litt, M., et al. (2010). Bibliotherapy as a
treatment for depression in primary care. J Clin Psychol Med Settings, 17,
258-271. doi: 10.1007/s10880-010-9207-2.

Ozbay, F., Johnson, D.C., Dimoulas, E., Morgan, C.A., et al. (2007). Social
support and resilience to stress: From neurobiology to clinical practice.
Psychiatry (Edgmont), 4, 35–40.

Pagnini F., Manzoni G. M., Castelnuovo G., & Molinari E. (2009).
The efficacy of relaxation training in treating anxiety. International Journal
Of Behavioral Consultation and Therapy, 5, 264-269.

Payscale.com (2016a). Child care / day care worker salary (United States).
Retrieved from http://www.payscale.com/research/US/Job=Child_Care_
%2F_Day_Care_Worker/Hourly_Rate.

References

Payscale.com (2016b). Substance abuse counselor salary (United States). Retrieved from http://www.payscale.com/research/US/Job=Substance_Abuse_Counselor/Salary.

Pierce, W. D., Cameron, J., Banko, K. M., & So, S. (2003). Positive effects of rewards and performance standards on intrinsic motivation. The Psychological Record, 53, 561-579.

Porter, E. (2016). Moving on from farm and factory: The presidential candidates' calls to revive industry are futile. New York Times, April 27, 2016, page B1.

Putallaz, M., and Gottman, J. (1983). Social relationship problems in children: An approach to intervention. In B.B. Lahey and A.E. Kazdin (eds.) Advances in Clinical Child Psychology, 6, 1-43. New York: Plenum Press.

Reichow, B., Steiner, A.M., &Volkmar, F. (2013). Cochrane review: social skills groups for people aged 6 to 21 with autism spectrum disorders (ASD). Evid Based Child Health, 8:266315. doi: 10.1002/ebch.1903.

Reilly, L. (2012). By the numbers: How Americans spend their money. Retrieved from http://mentalfloss.com/article/31222/numbers-how-americans-spend-their-money.

Roberto, P., & Santos, C.E. (2008). Behavioral models of depression: A critique of the emphasis on positive reinforcement. International Journal of Behavioral Consultation and Therapy, 4, 130-145.

Rodriguez, T. (2014). Mental Rehearsals Strengthen Neural Circuits. Scientific American Mind. Retrieved from http://www.scientificamerican.com/article/mental-rehearsals-strengthen-neural-circuits/.

Ross, B., & Gomstyn, A. (2008). Lehman Brothers boss defends $484 million in salary, bonus. ABC News. Retrieved from http://abcnews.go.com/Blotter/story?id=5965360.

Sandbum, J. (2012). America's gun economy, by the numbers. Retrieved from http://business.time.com/2012/12/18/americas-gun-economy-by-the-numbers/

Scogin, F., Jamison, C., & Gochneaur, K.,(1989) Comparative efficacy of cognitive and behavioral bibliotherapy for mildly and moderately depressed older adults. Journal of Consulting and Clinical Psychology, 57, 403-407.

Seda, G., Sanchez-Ortuno, M.M., Welsh, C.H., Halbower AC, et al. (2015). Comparative meta-analysis of prazosin and imagery rehearsal therapy for nightmare frequency, sleep quality, and posttraumatic stress. J Clin Sleep Med, 11, 11–22.

Seligman L.D., & Ollendick T.H. (2011). Cognitive behavioral therapy for anxiety disorders in youth. Child Adolesc Psychiatr Clin N Am, 20, 217–238. doi:10.1016/j.chc.2011.01.003

Shah, A. (2013). World military spending. Retrieved from http://www.globalissues.org/article/75/world-military-spending

Sharma, N., & Baron, J. (2013). Does motor imagery share neural networks with executed movement: A multivariate fMRI analysis. Frontiers in Human Neuroscience, Volume 7, article 564.

Shimodera, S., Furukawa, T.A., Mino, Y., Shimazu, K., et al. (2012). Cost-effectiveness of family psychoeducation to prevent relapse in major depression: Results from a randomized controlled trial. BMC Psychiatry, 12:40 http://www.biomedcentral.com/1471-244X/12/40

Singer, J.L.(1974). Imagery and daydream methods in psychotherapy and behavior modification. New York: Academic Press.

References

Skinner, B.F. (1958). Teaching machines. Science, 128, 969-977.

Skinner, B.F. (1986). Programmed instruction revisited. The Phi Delta Kappan, 68, 103-110.

Smith, J.M. (2013). U.S. Department of Education: Homeschooling continues to grow! Website of Homeschoolers' Legal Defense Association. Retrieved from https://www.hslda.org/docs/news/2013/201309030.asp.

Smith, M.J. (1975). When I say no, I feel guilty. New York: Dial Press, 1975.

Snider, V. (1993). The relationship between phonemic awareness and later reading achievement. The Journal of Educational Research, 90, 203-211.

Spivack, G., Platt, J.J., & Shure, M.B. (1976). The problem solving approach to adjustment: a cognitive approach to solving real-life problems. San Francisco: Jossey Bass.

Stallard, P., Skryabina, E., Taylor, G., Anderson, R., et al. (2015). A cluster randomised controlled trial comparing the effectiveness and cost-effectiveness of a school-based cognitive–behavioural therapy programme (FRIENDS) in the reduction of anxiety and improvement in mood in children aged 9/10 years. Public Health Res, 3(14).

Stanton, W.R. Feehan M., McGee R., & Silva, P.A. (1990). The relative value of reading ability and IQ as predictors of teacher-reported behavior problems. Journal of Learning Disabilities, 23, 514-517.

Strain, P.S. (1981). The utilization of classroom peers as behavior change agents. New York: Springer.

Strain, P. S., & Joseph, G. E. (2004). A not so good job with "Good Job": A response to Kohn. Journal of Positive Behavior Interventions, 6, 55-59.

Strayhorn, J.C. (2014). Three studies on measurement of psychological functioning in children. Undergraduate thesis, Cornell University Department of Psychology.

Strayhorn, J.M. (1983). A diagnostic axis relevant to psychotherapy and preventive mental health. *American Journal of Orthopsychiatry*, 53: 677-696.

Strayhorn, J.M. (1988). The competent child: an approach to psychotherapy and preventive mental health. New York: Guilford Press.

Strayhorn, J.M. (2001). Exercises for psychological skills. Wexford, PA: Psychological Skills Press.

Strayhorn, J.M. (2001). Programmed readings for psychological skills. Wexford, PA: Psychological Skills Press.

Strayhorn, J.M. (2001). The competence approach to parenting. Wexford, PA: Psychological Skills Press.

Strayhorn, J.M. (2001). What the letters say. CD. Also on the Internet at https://optskills.org/songs/.

Strayhorn, J.M. (2001). Spirit of nonviolence. CD. Also on the Internet at https://optskills.org/songs/.

Strayhorn, J.M., & Fischer, C. (2002). The letter stories. Wexford, PA, Psychological Skills Press.

Strayhorn, J.M. (2003). A programmed course in friendship-building and social skills. Wexford, PA: Psychological Skills Press.

Strayhorn, J.M. (2003). Illustrated stories that model psychological skills. Wexford, PA: Psychological Skills Press.

References

Strayhorn, J.M. (2003) Plays That Model Psychological Skills. Wexford, PA: Psychological Skills Press.

Strayhorn, J.M. (2009). Manual for tutors and teachers of reading. Second edition. Wexford, PA: Psychological Skills Press.

Strayhorn, J.M. (2012). A programmed course in anxiety-reduction and courage skills: Reducing obsessions, compulsions, aversions, and fears. Wexford, PA, Psychological Skills Press.

Strayhorn, J.M. (2012). Reading about math. Wexford, PA, Psychological Skills Press.

Strayhorn, J.M. (2013). A Programmed Course in Psychological Skills Exercises. Workouts to Build Psychological Strength. Wexford, PA: Psychological Skills Press.

Strayhorn, J.M. (2015). Reinforcement and punishment: Vignettes for practice in applied behavior analysis. Wexford, PA: Psychological Skills Press.

Strayhorn, J.M. (2016). Learning the math facts with the broken number line method. Wexford, PA: Psychological Skills Press.

Strayhorn, J.M. & Bickel, D.D. (2002). Reduction in children's symptoms of attention deficit hyperactivity disorder and oppositional defiant disorder during individual tutoring as compared with classroom instruction. *Psychological Reports* 91, 69-80.

Strayhorn, J.M., Strain, P.S., & Walker, H.M. (1993). The case for interaction skills training in the context of tutoring as a preventive mental health intervention in schools. Behavioral Disorders, 19, 11-26.

Strayhorn, J.M., & Strayhorn, J.C. (2010). Manual on task-switching or set-shifting. Wexford, PA: Psychological Skills Press.

Strayhorn, J.M., & Strayhorn, J.C. (2014). Psychological skills questions on novels. Wexford, PA: Psychological Skills Press.

Strayhorn, J.M., Weidman, C.S., & Majumder, A. (1990). Psychometric characteristics of a psychological skills inventory as applied to preschool children. *Journal of Psychoeducational Assessment*, 8, 467-477.

Sourander, A. , McGrath, P.J., Ristkari, T. , Cunningham, C., et al. (2016). Internet assisted parent training intervention for disruptive behavior in 4 year old children: A randomized clinical trial. JAMA Psychiatry, 73, 37887. doi: 10.1001/jamapsychiatry.2015.3411

Suinn, R.M. (1972). Behavior rehearsal training for ski racers. Behavior Therapy, 3, 519-520.

Tavris, C. (1989). Anger: The misunderstood emotion. Revised edition. New York: Touchstone Books. (Original edition published 1982.)

Thoreau, H.D. (1854/1863). Life without principle. ("This essay was derived from the lecture 'What Shall It Profit?', which Thoreau first delivered on 6 December 1854, at Railroad Hall in Providence Rhode Island. He delivered it several times over the next two years, and edited it for publication before he died in 1862. It was first published in the October 1863 issue of The Atlantic Monthly (Volume 12, Issue 71, pp. 484--495.) where it was given its modern title.") The previous annotation is quoted from the website https://en.wikisource.org/wiki/Life_Without_Principle, where the essay is also reprinted.

Torrey, E.F., Kennard, A.D., Eslinger, D., Lamb, R., & Pavle, J. (2010). More mentally ill persons are in jails and prisons than hospitals: A survey of the states. Retrieved from

References

http://www.treatmentadvocacycenter.org/storage/documents/final_jails_v_h
ospitals_study.pdf

Tse, J., Strulovitch, J., Tagalakis, V., Meng, L., & Fombonne, E. (2007).
Social skills training for adolescents with asperger syndrome and high-
functioning autism. J Autism Dev Disord, 37, 1960–1968. DOI
10.1007/s10803-006-0343-3

Tursi, M.F., Baes, C. V., Camacho, F.R., Tofoli, S.M., & Juruena M.F.
(2013). Effectiveness of psychoeducation for depression: a systematic
review. Aust N Z J Psychiatry, 47(11):101931. doi:
10.1177/0004867413491154.

Ungerleider, S., & Golding, J.M. (1991). Mental practice among olympic
athletes. Perceptual and Motor Skills, 72, 1007-1017.

Unicef (2009). The state of the world's children. Retrieved from
http://www.unicef.org/rightsite/sowc/pdfs/SOWC_Spec%20Ed_CRC_Main
%20Report_EN_090409.pdf.

United Nations Technical Series (1998). Economic and social consequences
of drug abuse and illicit trafficking. Retrieved from
http://www.unodc.org/pdf/technical_series_1998-01-01_1.pdf.

Vedantam, S. (2013). When crime pays: prison can teach some to be better
criminals. Retrieved from http://www.npr.org/2013/02/01/169732840/when-
crime-pays-prison-can-teach-some-to-be-better-criminals.

Wang, P.S., Lane, M., Olfson, M., Pincus, H.A., Wells, K.B., & Kessler,
R.C. (2005). Twelve-month use of mental health services in the United
States: results from the National Comorbidity Survey Replication.
Arch Gen Psychiatry, 62, 629-640.

Watanabe, N., Furukawa, T.A., Shimodera, S., Morokuma, I., et al. (2011).
Brief behavioral therapy for refractory insomnia in residual depression: An

assessor-blind, randomized controlled trial. J Clin Psychiatry, 72, 1651-1658. doi: 10.4088/JCP.10m06130gry. Epub 2011 Mar 8.

Wegner, D.M. (2011). Setting free the bears: Escape from thought suppression. Am Psychol. 66, 671-680. doi: 10.1037/a0024985.

Wolpe, J. (1958). Psychotherapy by reciprocal inhibition. Palo Alto, California: Stanford University Press, 1958.

Wolpe, J. (1969). The practice of behavior therapy. Pergamon Press, 1969.

World Bank, (2016). Poverty: Overview. Retrieved from http://www.worldbank.org/en/topic/poverty/overview

World Health Organisation. (1992). International statistical classification of diseases and related health problems, 10th revision (ICD-10). Geneva: WHO.

World Watch Magazine (1999). Data on expenditures. volume 12, No.1. Sources: U.N. Development Programme (UNDP), Human Development Report 1998 (New York: Oxford University Press, 1998), pages 30 through 37.

Xia, J., Merinder, L.B., and Belgamwar, M.R. (2013). Psychoeducation for schizophrenia. Cochrane Database Syst Rev, (6): CD002831. doi:10.1002/14651858.CD002831. pub2.

Index

academic skills training, 82

academic success, 159

adequate treatment, 22

ADHD symptoms and one-to-one instruction, 83

ADHD, parent training for, 78

adult relationship and child resilience, 57

adult-directed activity, 125

advanced self-discipline, 144

advantages and disadvantages, 110

advantages and disadvantages, in decision-making, 48

advertising as persuasive energy, 54

advice, 184

aggression replacement training, 79

agriculture and manufacturing, 231

alternate reading, 98, 103, 176

anger control, 39, 139

anger control, four thought exercise for, 113

anger control, inadequacy of treatment for, 22

anthologies for psychological skills, 65

anticipated life history, 57

antipsychotic drugs, 23

anxiety, 52

anxiety-reduction, 132

anxiety-reduction, 147

anxiety-reduction, four thought exercise for, 113

anxiety, cbt for, 75

applied behavior analysis, 59

appointment-keeping, 168

appointmentology, rules of, 168

approving tones as positive reinforcement, 59

assertion training, 135

assessment of dangerousness, 35

attribution and prophecy, 57

authority, 173
autism, social skills training for, 79
aversions, 147
aversions, conditioned to academic work, 197
avoidance versus mastery, 161
avoidance vs. mastery choice point, 52
away from the other as option, 142
Bandura, Albert, 58
behavior modification, 59
behavioral parent training, 77
behavioral problems, 14
bibliotherapy, 76
biofeedback, 153
blending and segmenting practice, 41
Bloom two sigma problem, 82
bond with adult, and resilience, 57
brainstorming options, 109
brainstorming options exercise, 59
breathing exercises to stop hyperventilation, 154
breathing exercises, for panic attacks, 37
broad spectrum skill training, 44
broken number line method, 90
Burns, David, 67, 76
Burt Reading Test, 87
carbon dioxide deficit, in hyperventilation, 37
catechism, as study technique, 160
catharsis hypothesis, 67
catharsis theory, 39, 140
CCCT, mnemonic for utterances for negative emotional climate, 219
celebrating luck, 112
celebrating my own choice, 112
celebrating others' choices exercise, 108
celebrations as fantasy rehearsals, 108
celebrations exercise, 107, 131
cell phones, possible hazards of, 194

character education, 68
child-directed activity, 125
choice points, 48
choice points, listing, 110
chronicity of mental problems, 23
classification of psychological skills, 43
clear speech, 201
coefficient alpha for skills ratings, 44
cognitive behavior therapy, 20
cognitive behavior therapy, for child anxiety, 75
cognitive therapy, 67
cognitive therapy, big idea of, 111
college students, mental health of, 227
commitment, required for tutors, 164
competence training methods, 19
compliance, 216
compliance skill, 136
compliance skills, 51
compulsions, 156
computer, for programmed instruction, 97
computerized cbt for anxiety, 76
concrete examples, for vocabulary acquisition, 129
conditioned aversions, 198
confidentiality, 31, 195
conflict-resolution, 135, 139
conflict-resolution role play, 115
conflict-resolution skills, 49
conservation skills, 51
conversation skills with preschoolers, 125
conversation, purpose of in psychoeducation, 34
conversations with students, 180
cooperative vs. competitive game, 43
coping and mastery rehearsals, 154
correctional facilities, negative effects of, 26
counseling, distinct from tutoring, 200

courage skills, 52, 132, 147
crime, guilt, evil language, 17
criticism, options for, 142
curriculum outline for psychological skills, 44
dangerousness, assessment of, 35
data bank of psychological skills models, 247
decision skills, joint, 49
decision-making training, 80
decision-making, soil addle steps, 155
decisions skills, individual, 48
delinquency and reading skill, 83
dependability, by parents, 218
diagnosis, time spent on, 35
Diagnostic and Statistical Manual, 16
diagnostic axis of psychological skills, 44
differential reinforcement, 60, 196, 217
differential reinforcement in dramatic play, 123
dilemmas, ethical, 134
disorder and disease language, 16
disruptive disorders, parent training for, 78
dissatisfaction with tutoring, dealing with, 204
divergent thinking exercise, 109
dominance, struggle for, 43
Dr. L.W. Aap (mnemonic, conflict-resolution), 115, 136
dramatic play, 121
drop in the bucket phenomenon, 21
drugs and psychotherapy, 21
drugs, dollars spent on illegal, 236
Each one teach one, 244
economics, 230
economy, goals of, 230
effort-payoff connection, 60, 84, 188
effort-payoff connection, and happiness, 228
eighty percent rule, approval, 219
eighty percent rule, for hierarchy-ology, 193

emotional associations with learning, 93
emotional climate, 155, 218
emotional climate, things to say for, 143
enabling of substance abusers, 50
encopresis, 38
entertainment media, models in, 64
entertainment models, 220
errorless instruction, 96
errorless learning, 85
ethical dilemmas, 134
evidence base for psychoeducation, 72
example list for psychological skills, 250
executive function, training of, 80
exercises for psychological skills, 107, 186
exercises to end hyperventilation, 38
externalizing and internalizing problems, 46
extrinsic rewards, 190
facilitations, 114
factor analyses of behavior ratings, 46
family psychoeducation for depression, 76
fantasy rehearsal, 51, 58
fantasy rehearsals, 116
fantasy rehearsals for courage skills, 154
fatigue, not reinforcing, 196
fear-reduction, 132
fecal incontinence, 39
Feeling Good, book on CBT, 67
follow-up questions, 114
forgetting curve, 162
fortitude skills, 48
four thought exercise, 112, 140
four ways of listening, 134
Freud, Sigmund, "love and work", 43
friendship-building skill, 137
friendship-building skills, 49

frugality, 51
frustrate the authority game, 83
Galbraith, John Kenneth, 237
Games for Math, 88
gangs, intervention with, 79
generic skill-promotion for parents, 214
goal-setting, 54, 111, 143
goals of academic training, 93
goals of parenting, 213
Goldstein, Arnold, 79
good decisions skills, 48
Grand Theft Auto, 236
gross domestic product, 233
guess the feelings exercise, 110
happiness of self and others, 43
hierarchy, 55
hierarchy-ology, 191
home visiting by nurses, 79
homeschooling, 64
honesty skills, 47
hours of training required for best results, 26
human nature, 16
hyperventilation, 37, 154
hypothetical situations, advantages of, 117
Ida Craft, mnemonic, responses to provocations, 141
imagery rehearsal for nightmares, 74
imaginal rehearsal, 51
imitation learning, 58
impulse control, cbt for, 79
inadequacy of treatment, 21
incarceration, prevalence of, 26
independent thinking skills, 52
insight, 31
insomnia, 73, 157
instruction as a method of influence, 60

Index

insurance system, depending on inadequate treatment, 22
insurance, no payment without disorder, 31
intercorrelation of skills ratings, 44
interference, minimizing in reading instruction, 86
intermittent explosive disorder, 22
internalizing and externalizing problems, 46
International Classification of Diseases, 16
Internet education for depression, 67
IQ and delinquency, 83
Jacobson, teacher of relaxation, 75
joint decision role-play, 115
joint decision skills, 49
joint decision-making, 135
Journey Story, 100
joyousness skills, 47
Kazdin and Blase, on rebooting, 27
KeyMath Test, 88
kindness skills, 47
Kohlberg on moral development, 134
Laubach, Frank, 244
law of club and fang, 51
learning from the experience, 112
linguistic relativity, 128
listening skills, 182
listening with four responses, 114
listening, four ways of, 134
listing choice points, 110
listing options and choosing, 112
Lovaas studies of autism, 23
loyalty skills, 50
manufacturing and agriculture, 231
marital satisfaction, psychoeducation for, 80
mastery and coping rehearsals, 154
mastery versus avoidance, 148
math facts fluency, 89

math, ideas for teaching, 88
mathematics, time on task for, 24
measurement of motivation toward a goal, 54
median hours of therapy, 23
medical insurance, 32
medical model, 16
meditation and relaxation, 75
meet the challenge game, 83
mental health goals, 43
Merikangas study on comorbidity, 45
methods of influence, 54
modeling, 58
modeling plays, 121
models, for preschoolers, 120
models, in entertainment, 220
modified programmed format, 99
monitoring, 61
morale among tutors, 213
motives conducive to violence and nonviolence, 141
musical skill, time on task for, 24
mutually gratifying activities, 220
National Comorbidity Study, 21
nightmares, 158
nightmares, imagery rehearsal for, 74
nonprofessional model for psychoeducation, 244
nonviolence skills, 49
not awfulizing, 111
novels, skill questions on, 65
nurse home visiting intervention, 79
objective-formation, 54
obsessions, 42, 157
obsessive-compulsive disorder, 156
OH RAM PRISM, mnemonic for methods of influence, 61, 148
one-to-one instruction, 12, 69, 82
option-generating, 109

option-generating practice, 59
option-generating skills, 48
Organization for Psychoeducational Tutoring, 69
outcome studies of psychoeducation, 72
overlap in psychiatric diagnoses, 45
panic attacks, 37, 154
PAPER, mnemonic for topics of conversation, 138
parent training, 77
parenting, psychoeducation for, 213
parents as psychoeducators, 63
PAST BAD, mnemonic regarding fear reduction, 150
Peabody Individual Achievement Test, 88
peer tutoring, 68, 82
performance measures, 118
personal problems, 14
phonemic awareness, 41, 85
placebo-controlled trials, 72
play, dramatic, 121
pleasure in achievement, 93
positive emotional climate, 172
positive example collection, 211
positive fantasy rehearsal skills, 51
positive feedback, 115
power, nonviolent means toward, 143
practice hours, 24
practice opportunities, 58
Premack Princlple, 84
preschool education for psychological skills, 69
preschoolers and toddlers, activities for, 120
prevalence of disorders in children, 21
prison as outcome for mental health problems, 26
prize for solving biggest problem, 12
problem-solving skills, 80
problems of society, 13
procrastination, 158

productivity as psychological skill, 46

professionalization, 16, 28

programmed instruction, 95

Programmed Readings, 100

prompts for reflections, 114

pros and cons exercise, 110

provocations, 140

psychoeducation contrasted with psychotherapy, 29

psychoeducation versus punishment, 18

psychoeducation, definition, 11

psychoeducation, efficacy of, 72

psychoeducational tutoring, definition, 11

psychological skills, 11

psychological skills axis, 43

psychological skills exercises, 107, 186

psychological skills exercises as performance measures, 118

psychological skills exercises as writing practice, 92

psychological skills exercises, for practice, 59

psychological skills list, more complete version, 259

psychotherapy and drugs, 21

psychotherapy as context for psychoeducation, 63

punishment, 221

punishment for crimes, 18

questions to student, avoiding too many, 180

random idea generator, 109

randomized experiments, 19

reading disorders, 41

reading skill and delinquency, 83

reading tests, 87

reading, hierarchy for, 127

reading, how to teach, 85

rebooting of mental health services, 27

record keeping in tutoring, 207

REFFF, mnemonic for positive utterances, 219

reflections exercise, 114, 160

reflections for practice of expression versus recognition, 104
reflections, prompts for, 104
reinforcement contingencies, 59
reinforcement for alternate reading, 98
relationship between teacher and learner, 56
relationship education, 80
relaxation and meditation, 75, 152
relaxation skills, 52
religious education, 66
repetition-tolerance, 121
research on psychoeducation, 72
research questions on living well, 21
research strategy for psychoeducation, 25
respectful talk skills, 49
review, frequency of, 162
rule of law, 51
rule-governed activity, 125
Sapir-Whorf hypothesis, 128
schizophrenia, psychoeducation for, 80
Schonell Reading Test, 87
scout rituals, 55
self-care skills, 51
self-discipline, 130, 143
self-discipline skills, 50
self-help books, 67
self-knowledge, 31
self-punishment, in work block, 40
self-reinforcement, 130
self-talk, 131
service delivery for psychoeducation, 63
service delivery through phone sessions, 11
shaping, 163
shooter videogames, 59
sin, crime language, 17
sixteen psychological skill groups, 46

skillization of novels, 65

skills axis diagnosis, 44

skills language, 18

skills list, 62 skill version, 259

skills stories, 108

Skinner, B.F., 95

sleep deprivation, 162

sleep hygiene, 73, 157

Slosson Oral Reading Test, 87

social and emotional learning, 68

social anxiety, 155

social bonds, and happiness, 228

social conversation role-play, 115

social conversation with preschoolers, 125

social problem solving, 80

social skills training, 79

social skills, improved by academic instruction, 83

social supports, 57

societal problems, 13

SOIL ADDLE, mnemonic for decision-making, 155

solution to societal and personal problems, 20

sounding and blending, 86

spaced versus massed practice, 224

spatial awareness, 41, 85

speech, clarity of, 201

spending priorities, 235

spontaneous dramatic play, 121

standardized test scores, 68

standards, as opposite of hierarchy-ology, 56

STEB, mnemonic for situation, thoughts, emotions, behaviors, 155

STEBC (mnemonic), 116

stebc fantasy rehearsals, 116

stigma of mental health treatment, 33

stimulus control, 61

stimulus-seeking children, 39

story reading, with preschoolers, 120

studenthood, success in, 159

SUD level (subjective units of distress), 149

suicide, and college students, 227

swimming, practice hours for, 24

T-PAARISEC, mnemonic for responding to criticism, 142

talent development, Bloom study of, 24

task-switching, 163

task-switching, training of, 80

teacher-learner relationships, 56

teaching methods for skills, 54

telephone tutoring, 69, 103, 224

telephone, in service delivery, 11

telephone, lower attrition with, 28

termination of tutoring, 167

Thoreau, Henry David, 241

thoughts, as influence on emotion and behavior, 131

three step process in psychoeducation, 129

time on task, 77, 81, 146, 225

time on task, 23

time spent by parents with children, 63

tones of approval, 172, 218

tones of approval as positive reinforcement, 59

tones of approval exercise, 113

treatment for disorders, not received, 21

treatment for mental disorders, 21

tutoring, 12

tutoring, academic, 82

tutors, guidelines for, 164

twelve thought classification, 133

twelve thought exercise, 100, 112

twelve-thought exercise, 111

two-choice comprehension questions, 106

two-sigma problem, 82

typing skill, 92

UCAC fantasy rehearsals, 116
violence, 13
violence, difficulty in treating, 22
violence, money spent on, 238
violent entertainment, 52
visits for treatment, few received, 21
vocabulary for expertise, 128
white bear problem, 42
work block, 40, 158
work capacity, 86
work therapy, 84
writer's block, 92
writing, ideas for teaching, 91
writing, stages of, 161

* 9 7 8 1 9 3 1 7 7 3 2 2 5 *